Really Sayin' Something

Memoirs of a Soul Survivor

Clive Richardson

First published in the United Kingdom in 2010 by
Bank House Books
PO Box 3
New Romney
TN29 9WJ UK
www.bankhousebooks.com

© Clive Richardson, 2010

The author hereby asserts his moral rights to be identified
as the author of this work.

All rights reserved. No part of this publication may be reproduced,
stored in a retrieval system, or transmitted in any form or by any means,
electronic, mechanical, photocopying or otherwise, without prior permission
of the publisher and copyright holder.

British Library Cataloguing in Publication Data
A catalogue record for this book is available from the British Library

ISBN 9781904408758

Typesetting and origination by Chandler Book Design

Really Sayin' Something

Memoirs of a Soul Survivor

CONTENTS

Acknowledgements vii

Forewords ix

Preface xi

Introduction xiii

1. Soul Beginnings 1
2. Fan Clubs and the Tamla Motown Appreciation Society 15
3. The Shows 21
4. Fanzines 43
5. Record Shops and Junk Shopping 71
6. Live Music 75
7. Funk 81
8. More Magazines 91
9. Sleevenotes and More 113
10. Record Collecting and Retailing 119
11. DJs and Gigs 127
12. Excursions to the Promised Land 133
13. Records and Collecting in the '80s 147
14. Gospel in London 151
15. Radio Days 155
16. Shout! Records 179
17. Into the New Century 195

Appendix: Where Are They Now? 205

Acknowledgements

That you are reading this is down to the labours and dedication of the Bank House Books team who have brought a dream to fruition on the printed page; so thanks to my friend of many years (probably more than we both care to enumerate) commissioning editor Sharon Davis, to publisher Dave Randle for agreeing to undertake the project, to Simon Fletcher, who has moulded my manuscript into an intelligible book, and to others at Bank House involved in getting the book to the reader.

Thanks to Tony Cummings for introducing me to the rigours of the fanzine writing/editing/publishing world with his pioneering journals *Soul* and *Soul Music Monthly*, which were forerunners of *Soul Music* and *Shout* magazines, and to Dave McAleer, Jon Philibert and Bill Millar for their immense contributions to the fledgling world of fanzines, not forgetting Ray Topping and Charlie Gillett, both now sadly departed, as is Dave Godin, who first opened the doors to the treasures of Motown for so many British soul fans.

Thanks to Alan Thompson, Paul Philips, Chris Gill and Debbie Kirby for allowing me so many column-inches in *Black Echoes* during the '70s and '80s in which to hone my journalistic abilities and reach a wider readership with the printed word.

Thanks to Brian Anthony for giving me my first opportunity in radio with London pirate station JFM in 1980, to Rodney Collins for my place on the schedule at RTM/Millennium Radio, my first encounter with ILR (Independent Local Radio), to Grant Goddard and Gordon Mac for including me on the launch schedule of Kiss 100FM in 1990, and to Tony Monson and Keith Renton for involving me in Solar Radio, first as a pirate in the '80s and with a growing reputation on Sky and the internet in the past decade.

Thanks to John Broven for helping me appreciate the pleasures of New Orleans music, to Lesley Stanford (via Stuart Colman) for giving me the first opportunity to visit the Crescent City, and to Nancy Covey and Louise Bailey for providing the means to make even more friends in Cajun Country during half a dozen more visits to my 'second home' during the mid-'80s, and the late Johnny Adams for sparing so much of his valuable time to talk to me at that time.

Thanks to Mark Stratford for giving me A&R freedom to create the Shout! Records catalogue, with seventy CD releases in the past decade, and to Adam Velasco for keeping faith in the label, Paul Robinson, Dave Timperley, Jon Roberts, Meg Greenhorn and all at Cherry Red Distributors for helping to put the CDs into the market.

Thanks to my brother Andrew and sisters-in-law Pauline and Margaret for being such a supportive family as I have battled to complete this venture, to my friends at Chislehurst Tennis Club, notably Diane, Diana and Bryan, for providing the chance to enjoy some healthy exercise when not putting pen to paper, to the RoDsters, pre-match drinking companions united in our support for Charlton Athletic Football Club, and – last but far from least – to my wife Barbara for her endless love and support (and for putting up with a house packed to the rafters with my forty-year collection of vinyl records and CDs!

Forewords

What can I say about Clive Richardson? We met thirty-five years ago when he interviewed us for *Shout* magazine. Clive is not just one heck of a nice guy but a real pioneer regarding the coverage of soul music. In this business you meet so many people but Clive is one person I'll never forget. He is just so genuine. If it were not for Clive so many artists would have been overlooked. What a blessing that the Persuasions and I intersected with such a dedicated soul music lover with such great taste and integrity.

>Jerry Lawson
>Original Lead Singer, arranger and
>producer of the Persuasions
>www.jerrylawson.biz

When Clive Richardson starts with *Really Sayin' Something*, there is only one thing to do: sit down and listen or, in this case, sit down and start reading. What better guide could take a passionate soul music fan along this journey? Only one who has been there himself, who knows every spot along the way, and now shares it with you.

I am privileged to have had a chance to collaborate with Clive in the making and release on his Shout! label of the album by my husband, Don Varner, *Finally Got Over*, in 2005. From the very beginning there was a connection, and yes, I will say a 'soul' connection that only the love of this music can create.

Clive is THE gentleman that we all, in the music industry, dream of working with, and when it happens, and it is all done, there he is, with his wonderful smile, his charming voice, all seasoned with a wonderful sense of humour and a friend forever.

Clive, on behalf of Donatienne and myself, thank you for this opportunity to tell the (very) few who might not know what a great ambassador of soul you are, to read this book and cherish it, because just like you, it will surely be a monument to soul music, a work of love, soul to soul and note for note.

Forever friends,
Francine Varner

Preface

It seems to be an ambition for many people to write a book, but it hadn't been on my list of things to do, despite my having spent a good deal of time in the years since the mid-1960s writing about soul music, either in magazines, weekly papers, glossy periodicals, modest contributions to encyclopaedias, LP sleeve notes and, more recently, CD booklets.

However, having been both impressed by and slightly envious of a fine book in which my old acquaintance Bill Millar gathered numerous articles and interviews that he had written over the years, I was prompted to suggest to my publisher that as I'd grown up with and lived through what is now thought of as the golden age of soul, perhaps there might be enough material for a book.

I prepared a synopsis and this project was born. In it I have tried to knit together numerous memories and anecdotes from my forty-something years as a soul fan, from the outside and from the inside.

The book has been written from twin perspectives. The first is that of '60s teenager. I developed my musical taste as we became aware of the 'Motown Sound' in London, when Atlantic and Stax gained their first autonomous identities in the UK, and Chess Records emerged as a major player in the increasingly sophisticated soul music – separate from R&B, which was seen as yesterday's era. I remember the era of distinctive colours for record labels, and Radio Luxembourg and AFN (American Forces Network) Europe being the only broadcast outlets for records that were gracing the near-mystical US R&B charts (before the pirate radio ships opened up a new world of awareness). I remember junk-shopping for old and sometimes rare records, and casting an enthusiastic eye over the weekly list of new 45s before taking a list to the nearest record shop.

The second viewpoint was gained by participating in the emergent specialist soul journalism in the fanzine era, and in the land-based pirate radio scene of the '80s. In recent years I've been involved with internet and Sky-based legal broadcasting on Solar Radio, and I've also been responsible for originating reissue CDs for Shout! Records. I have enough experience in the music business to be able to share some experiences and insights, but I've never relied on the business as my sole source of income: it's always been more of a paying hobby (with due deference to HM Inland Revenue!). I've generally been one step removed from an industry that tends to be a fairly volatile employer, but being on the fringe has been useful: I've learnt enough to know how things work, and have sometimes reaped reap some benefit from that, but I've not been close enough to the jaws of the alligator to be snared by its drawbacks.

I hope you enjoy this memoir about the golden era of soul.

Introduction

It all started for me with the Contours. I was drummer with a beat group, perhaps suitably named The Distortion, that was formed with three lads who lived on the housing estate in Chislehurst (then Kent, now suburban south-east London) where I grew up. During a practice session in Steve Rose's house we were talking about new hit records. Brian Poole & the Tremeloes were in the charts with 'Do You Love Me' – which dates the conversation to around autumn 1963 – and Tottenham's own Dave Clark Five had a rougher version, so I was very interested when Steve asked if I'd heard the original by The Contours. Steve was a man of good musical taste (among the LPs in his record rack was Gary US Bonds' 'Quarter to Three' on Top Rank), so I took a trip to nearby Bromley, and was in the record section of Debenhams just in time for a chance encounter with the Oriole Records rep. By good fortune he had with him a whole LP by The Contours, and my investment of 32*s* 6*d* has served me well during the ensuing forty-odd years!

There was no history of 'specialist' music in the family; I have no idea where my penchant for soul came from. My father, Bob, a bricklayer by trade and a Geordie by birth (he was invalided out of military service in the Second World War and came to London to do building repair work in 1941 in the aftermath of the Blitz), liked big band jazz and Al Bowlly – though he once surprised us all by bringing home a copy of Bill Haley & the Comets' 'Rock 'n' Roll Stage Show' (now part of my own vinyl collection). Mum, Gwen, a local government officer in the later decades of her life, liked musicals and show-tunes. I was even taken along to see the original stage version of *My Fair Lady* at London's Drury Lane as a schoolboy. The radio was often on, but this was the era of the BBC Light Programme, *Worker's Playtime*, *Henry Hall's Guest Night* et al, and no blues or R&B to whet my appetite. My younger brother, Andrew, was probably more musically aware than I was, being an early fan of Elvis Presley: the first single to arrive in the house was 'Too Much'/'Playing For Keeps' on the turquoise HMV label.

The first record I obtained was a 78rpm single by Lonnie Donegan, 'Jack O'Diamonds' on Pye Nixa. I say obtained rather than bought because I sent away for it as a reward for collecting soft-drink bottle tops in a promotion at a local sports event. I must have been impressed, as I then spent good pocket-money on follow-up 'Sally Don't You Grieve'. Now, in later years, as I've become more familiar with the blues and bluegrass roots of Donegan's records – the two I've mentioned as well as 'Rock Island Line', 'Bring A Little Water, Sylvie', 'Pick a Bale of Cotton' and 'Dixie Darling' – it has become evident whence this quirky musical taste came. Pushing it further, the gritty, frantic delivery of Donegan has a parallel in the Contours' rasping vocals in 'Do You Love Me', which, though somewhat atypical of the Motown Sound, triggered my interest in the soul genre.

I left school in May 1962 at the age of sixteen, clutching my five O-level certificates, and walked straight into the first job I applied for. I'd planned to go on to sixth form study and maybe university, but after I answered an ad in my local public library I became a junior assistant at Woolwich Library in south-east London. There were two immediate benefits: wages to spend and lots of shops! (A third benefit came later.) Radio Rentals had a small record department, where I was able to buy Little Stevie Wonder's 'Fingertips' single on Oriole American on the day of release (it's still in my collection in good condition), while, tucked away in a side street opposite Woolwich Arsenal railway station, there was Drysdale's, an old-fashioned music shop that sold instruments and all the new releases. It was there that I bought gems like Little Johnny Taylor's 'Part Time Love' and Bobby Bland's 'Yield Not To Temptation', both on Vocalion, and Don Covay's 'Mercy Mercy' on black-and-silver Atlantic, a record that was to influence the direction of my life.

The third benefit of library work was to be found in the music library. Along with shelves of biographies and sheet-music scores there was a small jazz section tucked in at the end of the classical records. This gave me an opportunity to borrow some great big band LPs by the likes of Duke Ellington and Cab Calloway, while also discovering the pleasures of the Blue Note catalogue (Jimmy Smith, Stanley Turrentine et al), as well as (thanks to the catholic taste of the music librarian, Audrey 'Bunty' Peacock) Bobby Bland's 'Two Steps From the Blues' and the cast recording of the *Black Nativity* gospel musical, with Alex Bradford and the Stars of Faith. The merit of being in the right place at the right time came when there was a record sale of old and worn stock, and I was able to buy the latter two albums for just a few pence.

It was the era of consumer music papers. These days the newsagents' shelves display an array of A4-size glossy magazines with photographic covers; back then, every Wednesday or Thursday (depending on whether you were in Central London or the suburbs) the news-stands were piled high with FOUR weekly tabloid music papers. *Melody Maker* had been running since the 1930s as the bible of the jazz world, occasionally nodding towards blues, but by the mid-'60s had realised that the British beat boom generated more readers than any feature by Max Jones on the jazz-greats. The authoritative *New Musical Express* had built its readership from the followers of Elvis Presley-driven rock'n'roll to the teenagers hooked on every syllable and semi-quaver emanating from Merseybeat. *Disc & Music Echo* gave the impression of being a kid-sister to the NME – and then there was *Record Mirror*.

Less 'grammar school' than *Melody Maker*, more erudite than *NME*, and certainly a mature cousin of *Disc*, *Record Mirror* found an audience with the growing minority of teenagers who were discovering the untold treasures and pleasures of Black American soul music, which had emerged from the sophistication of R&B. As the hard-edged black music that had grown from blues roots in cities like Detroit, Chicago and New York was blended with arrangements that boasted strings and plush brass sections, uptown soul began to make an impact on US radio stations and, consequently the Hot 100 charts – instead of being confined to regional R&B hit-lists. An occasional hit was released in the UK, perhaps on HMV, London or Vocalion before the emergence of Stateside and Pye International, and the only way anyone found out was by hearing them at London clubs or reading about them in *Record Mirror* reviews. These were often by one Norman Jopling, who was a notable (and under-recognised) pioneer of soul journalism. *Record Mirror* became essential for soul fans in the early 1960s, as awareness of our music began to grow.

It was the era of the fan club, and the pop press was heavy with small ads for singers who for many were just mysterious or exotic names in the R&B charts that were published in *Billboard*, the US trade weekly, and in *Record World*, both of which were becoming more readily available from newsagents in Charing Cross Road and Soho – though *Billboard* discontinued their R&B chart between November 1963 and January 1965. This was never fully explained, but two schools of thought have emerged over the years. One is that the method of counting sales was questionable, with four 'white pop records' reaching the no. 1 spot during 1963 – Paul & Paula's 'Hey Paula', Little Peggy March's 'I Will Follow Him', Lesley Gore's 'It's My Party' and Jimmy Gilmer & the Fireballs' 'Sugar Shack'. The second possible reason is that the increasing number of 'Black' R&B records reaching the Hot 100 was an indication that a separate R&B chart was deemed to be unnecessary. When the R&B chart resumed in January 1965 it was for a year dominated by Motown, who had six of the thirteen no. 1 hits (Temptations, Jr Walker & the All Stars, Marvin Gaye twice, the Supremes and the Four Tops), along with three for Atlantic (Solomon Burke, Wilson Pickett, Joe Tex), two for Chess (Little Milton, Fontella Bass) and two for James Brown (the landmark 'Papa's Got a Brand New Bag' and 'I Got You').

The soul era was truly established.

CHAPTER ONE

SOUL BEGINNINGS

In his biography of The Drifters published in 1971, my old friend Bill Millar coined the description 'Beat Concerto' for the group's 1959 recording session during which 'There Goes My Baby' was cut, with producers Jerry Leiber and Mike Stoller using strings on an R&B song. That wasn't the first time this had been done within the genre, but it served to break new ground for the group and for the music. Apart perhaps from Little Willie John material on King and Roy Hamilton on Epic, it was a lot easier to spot 'symphonic soul' after that session than before it. A glance at the list of *Billboard* R&B chart-toppers from 1960 onwards reflects the trend towards the relative sophistication of soul compared with the harder R&B sound that had previously been dominant. For example, 1960 gave us Jackie Wilson's bluesy ballad 'Doggin' Around' and dramatic 'Woman Lover Friend', along with Brook Benton's lilting 'Kiddio' and the Latin-tinged balladry of Jerry Butler's 'He Will Break Your Heart', all in stark contrast to Lloyd Price's 'Stagger Lee' and Ray Charles's 'What'd I Say' from the previous year. This serves to provide a reasonable boundary for the beginning of the soul era.

The arrival and emergence of soul music in England was initially a combination of accidental and incidental, mainly because of the licensing arrangements for US products that were in place at the turn of the decade. These were mainly a patchwork of deals involving UK major companies Decca and EMI and some independents, like Top Rank, Philips, Vocalion, Pye and Oriole. Decca used their London American logo as a generic label for all licensed product, while material from US Decca and Brunswick was issued on Coral, which metamorphosed into (UK) Brunswick. While UK Decca used a routine black and silver label design for their various outlets, things were rather more colourful with EMI. Early collectors gloried in an array of hues: Roulette material appeared on green-label Columbia, King tracks on bright red Parlophone, early Sam Cooke and pre-RCA Elvis Presley singles on mauve HMV, with light-green Verve and turquoise United Artists (Delacardos and Clovers) outshone by yellow MGM (Jimmy Jones, Impalas, Clyde McPhatter).

The colours spread to the independents, with Vee Jay (Jimmy Reed), Ember/Herald (Five Satins), Wand (Chuck Jackson) and Legrand (Gary US Bonds), US hits issued on Top Rank, either on the red and white or blue and silver labels, Vee Jay (Little Richard) and Motown (Marvelettes, Miracles) on blue and silver Fontana (from Philips), and the various label designs and colours of Pye International, from the dark blue with gold print (Marcels from Colpix, Clarence Henry from Chess) to the distinctive and classic halved red and yellow of the main Chess licence era and the pink and black of James Brown material from King. Vogue, with a distinctive blue and white label, released a hard-to-find catalogue of singles from Aladdin and Duke/Peacock before rebranding as Vocalion in routine black label/silver print as the continuing outlet for Duke/Peacock discs along with the Olympics material from ArVee, while Oriole launched an American line with white print (instead of its usual yellow) for its brief spell as Motown licensee.

As well as the label colours and designs, several companies also invested in distinctive designs for the paper sleeves of 7-inch 45s. In the USA, King, Motown, Atlantic and Cameo-Parkway all carried readily identifiable designs, Cameo going to an extreme in printing miniature LP covers from current releases on their singles sleeves. In the UK the coloured sleeves idea was used by EMI (mainly Columbia – pale green with white discs, and Parlophone – multi-colour horizontal stripes) and Decca (distinctive vertical blue stripes). For those of you old enough to remember buying

7-inch 45s, you will probably recall that most shops filed their stock upright, edge-on on their shelves, and to find a copy of a big seller you simply looked for an array of the right colour on the shelves! At a slight tangent, there was a similar trend in the USA for some companies (Columbia, Atlantic and Motown come to mind) to adorn the inner sleeve of LPs with miniature pictures (thumbnails in current parlance) of recent albums. This had – and has – some merit for fans and collectors, but was discontinued for the obvious reason that LPs thus advertised are only available as long as they remain in the catalogue, so the inner sleeves needed to be redesigned and reprinted regularly. A generic plain sleeve made more sense.

Stateside

It was labels, however, that played a key role in the development of the specialist soul market in the UK. In 1962 Stateside Records was launched by EMI, to bring all licensed product under a single logo. The early discs in the catalogue were by Chuck Jackson (Wand), Jimmy Soul (SPQR), Don Gardner & Dee Dee Ford (Fire) and Jerry Butler (Vee Jay), providing a solid foundation and a collectors' dream, and The Tams (ABC), The Chiffons (Laurie) and Five DuTones (One-Derful) provided further reassurance that pre-orders could be placed for new releases with the same confidence that had built the reputation of London-American during the same period, following the foundations laid for that label during the rocking '50s.

Sue

While Stateside was built on the solid corporate entity that was EMI Records, the next specialist label emerged from a financially more humble source. Island Records, owned by Chris Blackwell and with a catalogue of largely Caribbean music, launched the Sue label after doing a deal with Juggy Murray in New York, initially with the intention of giving UK release to American hits by Inez and Charlie Foxx, Baby Washington, and Ike and Tina Turner. Island Records began in Jamaica in the late '50s, with Blackwell initially releasing

American R&B records with a rock-steady beat (accentuating the second and fourth beat in a standard 4/4 time-signature), a good example being Rosco Gordon's 'No More Doggin'', and going on to produce records in similar style by local Jamaican singers – such as Laurel Aitken and Jackie Edwards. The operation moved to London in 1962 and found a home at 108 Cambridge Road, NW6 (Kilburn). An early catalogue lists the phone number as KIL 1921/22/23 – with apparently enough business to warrant three lines. There were early singles by the exotically named Lord Creator ('Independent Jamaica'/'Remember', WI-001), Owen Gray and Derrick Morgan.

The seeds for the UK Sue label were sewn when Chris Blackwell heard 'Mockingbird', a US 45 hit for Inez and Charlie Foxx on Juggy Murray's Sue label, during a visit to a US distributor's office in the summer of 1963. Murray already had a UK licence deal for his product with Decca Records, but despite his initial reservations at Blackwell's sales pitch, he eventually succumbed to vanity and the appeal of an overseas brand identity, resulting in the inception of the new label.

'Mockingbird' was issued on Sue WI-301 in December 1963, the yellow label carrying a distinctive logo comprising a central horizontal red bow-shape stretching across the full width, with 'Sue Records' in script in a yellow circle on the left of the bow and the catalogue number in a similar yellow circle on the right.

The first seventeen singles were all from the US Sue label, but thereafter things diversified somewhat. Blackwell appointed Guy Stevens as label manager, fresh from his trail-blazing role as DJ at the Scene Club, deep in London's Soho, and with a keen ear for the best in R&B and soul. He had previously advised EMI/Stateside and Pye/International on selection of licensed repertoire for their R&B releases. WI 324 brought us Patti LaBelle and the Blue-Belles' 'Down The Aisle' from Newtown, and subsequent singles were from diverse sources (including Sims, V-Tone, King and Instant) as Guy turned the label into a quintessential collectors' outlet for independent soul and blues gems. This gave us the chance to hear and buy discs by Willie Mabon, Louisiana Red, Chris Kenner, Freddie King and Bobby Parker, who had previously just been desirable names in blues discographies and on new release lists and regional charts in *Billboard*.

It was providential that Guy built this catalogue, as within a year of Sue's inception in the UK Juggy Murray took his product away to new deals with first Decca/London, and subsequently Liberty/United Artists, which meant that the initial strand of Sue-originated singles and LPs had to be deleted, leaving Stevens with his catalogue of more varied and often idiosyncratic tracks. This built over the following year or so into arguably the most collectable series of discs on a single label. He issued several discs from Vee Jay, then in Chicago, Duke in Houston and Modern in Los Angeles, along with some more obscure material from labels in the deep south (Sims – the Wallace Brothers) and on the west coast (Duo Disc – Effie Smith). The Sue UK catalogue grew to include a number of tracks that have since been accorded classic status – Elmore James's 'Dust My Broom', Bobby Parker's 'Watch Your Step', Freddie King's 'Hideaway', Chris Kenner's original version of 'Land of 1000 Dances', James Brown's seminal 'Night Train', Frankie Ford's 'Sea Cruise', and two discs which have reached legendary status in the annals of '60s soul: 'A Little Piece of Leather', the falsetto-voiced stomper by Donnie Elbert, and the relative sophistication (for 1963) of 'Harlem Shuffle' by Bob & Earl, issued originally on Marc Records from Hollywood, a few thousand miles from New York's Harlem. There was quite a lengthy saga-cum-debate at the time of the UK single release regarding the true identities of Bob and Earl, with Bobby Day and Bob Relf involved as possible 'Bob's and Ben E. King as a potential 'Earl', as his given name is Benjamin Earl Nelson. The debate was conducted mainly in the 'Disc Info USA' column in *Blues & Soul* magazine, in which discographer and Curtis Mayfield & the Impressions authority Roy Simonds fielded the enquiries and provided some answers, after consultation with fellow-discographers like Bill Millar and Ray Topping. The identity crisis was not helped by the fact that Day and Relf had also sung with the Hollywood Flames on Ebb and Class Records, and there were singles credited to 'Bob & Earl' on that label from 1960. The denouement came when it was discovered that 'Earl' was Earl Nelson, also singing as Jackie Lee, rather than Ben E. King, and that Bobby Relf had replaced Bobby Day as 'Bob' both on the Class singles and now on the Marc hit.

The original Sue series ran from WI-301 to WI-399 (Lee Dorsey's 'Messed Around' from Bobby Robinson's Fury label in New York) between December 1963 and January 1966, then added an extra '0' with WI-4001,(Little Richard's 'Without Love' from Vee Jay) in February 1966, through to WI- 4049 (Fascinations' 'Girls Are Out To Get You' from Mayfield) in June 1968. The 4000 series was drawn from an equally diverse range of US labels from all corners of that country, and gave us a similar helping of classics and great unknowns. The former included Phil Upchurch Combo's 'You Can't Sit Down' from Boyd, Richie Valens' 'La Bamba' from Del-Fi and Billy Preston's 'Billy's Bag' from Vee Jay, and the latter included Birdlegs & Pauline's 'Spring' from Cuca, Danny White's 'Keep My Woman Home' from White Cliffs and the Kelly Brothers' 'Falling In Love Again' from Excello.

If the singles catalogue was the soul fans' dream of the decade, Guy Stevens also put together several compilations of equally esoteric gems and three volumes of the Sue Story, each anthologising a dozen or so gems from the singles catalogue. It is notable that only the first two Sue LPs, by Inez & Charlie Foxx and the Soul Sisters, had photographs of the performer on the front sleeve. As much as I've read about Guy Stevens, his background, musical tastes and knowledge, and the legacy he has left for subsequent generations of soul fans, I've not seen any insight into his thoughts on LP sleeve design. A Huey Smith & the Clowns collection, *Rockin' Pneumonia* (ILP 914), featured a section of a painting of dancing peasants in the style of sixteenth-century Dutch artist Pieter Breughel, with design credited to Stevens himself. The next simply used *Elmore James* as the title in large font, and *Pure Blues* featured an African wooden sculpture. *50 Minutes 24 Seconds of Recorded Dynamite* showed a bundle of dynamite in the centre panel, flanked by lists of the tracks on the LP, and *We Sing the Blues* had a small photo of the right side of a black male head next to a large panel containing the title. *Lee Dorsey* used a list of song titles with tiny objects, while *Soul 66* had a photo of a black torso with a dark background, the title in white text on the torso. Billy Preston's *The Most Exciting Organ Ever* featured a small photo of Preston playing keyboards in the centre of a vast blue background. *Doctor Soul* (ILP 943 from 1967) had an African jug from which was pouring a list of artists' names, while LPs of Barbara Lynn, the Wallace Brothers and Bob & Earl continued Guy Stevens' policy of understating the featured artist.

1968 brought a change of style with the licensing of Duke/Peacock catalogue and three resultant LPs, Bobby Bland's *A Touch of The Blues* (ILP 974) and O.V. Wright's *8 Men 4 Women* (ILP 975) at least including a decent photograph of the singers, even if Wright's was almost lost amid origami cut-out shapes of the requisite jury members, while *The Duke and the Peacock* bore a glossy photo of ducal regalia and a peacock for its compilation of a dozen tracks. In closing this résumé of Sue, I will just mention that each of the four volumes of *The Sue Story*, which collated selections of singles releases, featured a picture of Guy Stevens himself in somewhat sombre pose, perhaps in the style of Alfred Hitchcock's cameo appearances in his own films! The singles, if not the LPs, were well advertised, through display ads in *Record Mirror* and *Melody Maker* (more likely to be read by R&B/soul music fans than the pop-focused *New Musical Express* and *Disc*) and on flyers and wallet-sized catalogues that were to be found on the counters of record shops. This was an era, remember, when the records were shelved on racks behind a counter, and the assistant selected them for you.

Just as London had a white sleeve with thin vertical blue pin-stripes, and Pye had its blue and white chequered edge, so Guy Stevens cleverly produced an eye-catching sleeve for Sue singles. There was a red border, and the body of the sleeve comprised a list of singers typed horizontally, split names wrapping onto the next line down, all done in bold lower-case font in the same red colour as the border. The Sue logo was in the top left and bottom right corners. This distinctive yellow and red logo on singles and LPs has become iconic, and the records themselves are very hard to find.

Pye International

As mentioned earlier, the Pye label was a steady source for R&B and soul music, with tracks from Colpix by Nina Simone and the Marcels, including their spring 1961 UK chart-topper 'Blue Moon' and less-successful follow-ups like 'Heartaches' and 'My Melancholy Baby' (cases in point of stretching a gimmick too far, with the manic burbling bass-voice intro), in the company of material from Arnold – Don Covay's ultra-rare 'Love Boat' on Hull, Shep & the Limelites' 'Daddy's Home' on Calico, and the Skyliners' 'I'll Close My Eyes' (follow-up to their hit 'Since I Don't Have You', issued in the UK on London), two doo-wop gems which had modest sales, and Chess, when it changed its UK-licensed outlet from Decca/London in 1960. Chess enjoyed Top 10 hits in summer 1961 by New Orleans pianist-singer Clarence 'Frogman' Henry with his rolling R&B-style 'But I Do' and a revival of the Mills Brothers' 1944 pop hit 'You Always Hurt the One You Love'. Henry's nickname was derived from his first hit 'Ain't Got No Home', in which he sang part-falsetto and part-throaty bass. The 1960 *Bo Diddley's a Gunslinger* LP was issued on Pye Jazz, before his *Rides Again* set was more fittingly issued on Pye International's R&B Series in 1961.

The yellow and red label continued to release a series of blues 45s by Howlin' Wolf, Sonny Boy Williamson, Muddy Waters and Little Walter during the early '60s, along with four-track extended-play 45s of material from the various blues tours. In 1964 Pye decided to re-launch the label as Tommy Tucker made the US Hot 100 and R&B charts with 'Hi-Heel Sneakers', and promoted a series of singles and LPs that included soul hits by Etta James, Jackie Ross and Tony Clarke, boosted by a licensing deal with Florence Greenberg's New York-based Scepter/Wand Records, previously released in the UK on EMI's Stateside label. This brought early success with Dionne Warwick's May 1964 Top 10 hit 'Walk On By' and the Kingsmen's memorable 'Louie Louie', which created immense interest among R&B fans without reaching the UK charts. The success of the Chess discs led to that label gaining its own identity, the distinctive yellow and red image being replaced by a black label with 'Chess' in gold lettering.

While the distinctive yellow and red Pye International label rightly gained respect and status among us soul fans, and has become legendary with the passage of decades, its more general impact should be put in perspective: few singles sold enough to break into the pop charts. My reference sources are limited to listing Top 20 hits, and only Chuck Berry ('Memphis Tennessee', October 1963, 'No Particular Place To Go', April 1964) and Dionne Warwick ('Walk On By', May 1964) registered. Dionne's impact in the UK had suffered when she lost out to a local cover version of 'Anyone Who Had A Heart' in February that year. The catalogue was rich in what are now soul classics, including US hits by Tommy Tucker, as mentioned above, Fontella Bass's 'Rescue Me', the Dixie Cups' 'Chapel of Love', Sugar Pie Desanto's 'Soulful Dress' and Chuck Jackson's 'Any Day Now', but while these discs were played in clubs and eagerly bought by collectors, they didn't reach a wider market.

There was one R&B breakthrough, when the weekly *Juke Box Jury* TV show, which played new releases to a panel of DJs and 'personalities' to be rated as hit or miss, featured Howlin' Wolf's 'Smokestack Lightnin', with Wolf hidden behind a screen while the verdicts were given. After the 'miss' vote he walked out to shake the hands of the panel and answered a short question from chairman David Jacobs, then disappeared off-screen, maybe the only bluesman to appear on prime-time UK television!

Some releases on the label were mysterious in origin and somewhat optimistic in their appearance on vinyl in the UK. Little Luther's 'Eenie Meenie Minie Mo', Tony Clarke's roaring, ostensibly live 'Ain't Love Good Ain't Love Proud', Nella Dodds's toe-tapping, Motownesque 'Come See About Me' and the Larks' ethereal floater 'The Jerk' occasionally found their way into collections at the time, but are rarely seen on auction lists these days. Neither are Alvin Robinson's gritty blues reading of 'Something You Got' or Sam & Bill's deep-soul ballad duet 'Fly Me To the Moon', though Dobie Gray's 'See You At The Go Go' remains a lasting favourite on the Northern Soul scene.

Motown

This was certainly the golden era of soul in the UK, as March 1965 saw the move of Motown discs from the Stateside label. This had also brought us a splendid series of four EPs entitled *R&B Chartmakers* and featuring some lesser-known hits from Berry Gordy's empire (including the Darnells, Eddie Holland, Kim Weston and Brenda Holloway). The first single after the launch of a dedicated Tamla-Motown logo by EMI was the Supremes' 'Stop In The Name Of Love' (a Top 10 UK hit in April), and it was followed by Martha & the Vandellas' 'Nowhere To Run' and the Miracles' ballad gem 'Ooh Baby Baby'.

Issued with a catalogue prefix of TMG, the singles released during the first couple of months reflected an optimistic view that the UK was ready to accept a range of styles. The next releases were from the Temptations ('It's Growing') and Stevie Wonder ('Kiss Me Baby'). Stevie shed his 'Little' tag between Stateside label releases 'Castles In the Sand' (April 1964) and 'Hey Harmonica Man' (August 1964): his fourteenth birthday was on 13 May. The Four Tops followed ('Ask The Lonely'), along with the then lesser-known Earl Van Dyke ('All For You') and Brenda Holloway ('When I'm Gone'). The limited exposure and sales of the latter two explains their rarity in recent years. US R&B chart-toppers in Junior Walker's 'Shotgun' and Marvin Gaye's 'I'll Be Doggone' were released in April 1965, but although popular in clubs and finding airplay on pirate radio (in this golden era of radio ships London and Caroline), neither reached the UK Top 40, so there was little hope for more obscure releases by Shorty Long ('Out To Get You') and the Hit Pack ('Never Say No To Your Baby'). It was the Four Tops ('I Can't Help Myself') and the Supremes ('Back In My Arms Again') who made more impact.

By the end of 1965 the catalogue largely comprised items by major names, those mentioned above together with The Contours, Kim Weston and the Marvelettes, and occasional surprise inclusions like Billy Eckstine, Dorsey Burnette and Tony Martin. By the end of 1966 the Temptations and the Four Tops had joined the Supremes as UK Top 20 regulars, though the great Marvin Gaye didn't manage a solo chart hit until 'Grapevine' in January 1969, despite a string of US successes and UK hits in duet with Kim Weston ('It Takes Two', 1967) and Tammi Terrell ('You're All I Need to Get By', November 1968, and 'The Onion Song' a year later).

Atlantic

Atlantic and Stax were also given brand identities for the UK market. Decca released the former on a black label graced with Atlantic in bold silver font and the fan logo, a relatively incidental feature of the US Atlantic label design enlarged into a key element. With the move to Polydor, 'Atlantic' was in capitals in smaller but bold black font and the fan logo reverted to a small black style, both elements contrasting well with the bright red background. At least the colours were consistent with the US parent. Polydor introduced Stax to the UK, using the US black on pale blue colour scheme and also incorporating the pile of discs logo from the parent label.

It's odd perhaps that none of the classic US soul label designs of that era were ever used 'as is' for their UK equivalents: maybe there were restrictions in registering the designs, or similar legal hurdles. The nearest we came was with a somewhat shambolic (it looks even worse now) 'Atlantic Masters' re-packaging of a series of Atlantic and Stax tracks issued in the early '70s when Warner (WEA) had assumed UK independence. The US Atlantic label design was used, but in black and silver and missing the fan design. A series of ten four-track extended-play 45s appeared, with much of the material in stereo-enhanced mono, each disc including tracks by two or three artists or groups. For example, ATM 1 was Don Covay's 'See Saw' and 'Mercy Mercy', Markeys' 'Last Night' and Barkays' 'Soul Finger'. Such a collection defied any obvious logic, and a similar crass contrast was evident on ATM 8: Carla Thomas's 'Gee Whiz' and 'BABY' with Arthur Conley's 'Funky Street' and 'Sweet Soul Music' – as if there were not four tracks by each artist strong enough to stand alone!

* * *

While the launch of these specialist labels was a landmark in the recognition of soul music in the UK, and each disc was eagerly sought by fans who had previously had to search hard among general catalogue items in order to satisfy their appetite for these transatlantic treasures, with a few notable exceptions sales were to the committed: few singles broke into the Top 20. It's perhaps ironic that the first major and sustained success was achieved by an act whose music is largely beyond the intended boundaries of this book, though there may be some mitigation in the involvement of Sonny Bono in the production of some R&B artists at Specialty Records. Sonny & Cher reached no. 1 in the UK Top 20 with 'I Got You Babe' on Atlantic in September 1965, following with another two Top 20 hits in September and November, and two more in March and September 1966. That year also yielded success for Atlantic with Otis Redding's 'My Girl' in January, stealing the thunder of the Temptations' UK release, and Percy Sledge, whose now-classic ballad 'When A Man Loves A Woman' was pushed to the no. 4 spot in the Top 20, courtesy of blanket air-play on pirate stations London and Caroline.

The impact and success of Otis Redding was sustained over the following two years, past his tragic death in December 1967, in hits with 'Tramp', in duet with Carla Thomas and issued on the Stax label, and the posthumous 'Dock of the Bay' in July 1968; 'Hard To Handle' charted on the Atlantic logo a month later. Atlantic also had a Top 10 hit in 1967 with Redding's protégé Arthur Conley in 'Sweet Soul Music', the frantic-tempo tribute to the soul stars of the day, cleverly adapted from Sam Cooke's 1964 hit 'Yeah Man', with Cooke's references to dances and sporting terms replaced with a chronicle of accolade to his peers. Also reaching the UK Top 20 in 1967 were Vanilla Fudge (psychedelic rock, I think, from the little I've encountered) with a version of the Supremes' hit (US and UK) from the previous year. The commercial reality was that pop hits such as this and those of Sonny & Cher served to subsidise the flow of soul gems by such as The Astors ('Candy'), Paul Kelly ('Chills and Fever') and Don Covay ('Take This Hurt Off Me'), which probably sold by the dozen rather than the thousand, though discs like Doris Troy's 'Just One Look', the Markeys' 'Philly Dog' and Rufus Thomas's 'Jump Back' have remained club favourites through the decades.

Matters were thus simplified for the growing band of soul fans in terms of avenues for buying UK releases, though imports were still something of a treasure hunt in the early 1960s. As I've said, the main source of information was *Billboard* or *Record World*, which had a greater focus on black music, and a few of us invested in *Cash Box*, which ran a Hot 100 chart but focused on the juke-box industry. One man who had access to all of these resources was John Abbey, and he had the vehicle with which to share the wealth of information he gathered with the growing number of soul fans. This was his magazine *Blues & Soul*, which grew from *Home of the Blues*. He upgraded to glossy litho printing in spring 1967, and retitled the magazine in October that year. John had published basic charts in *Home of the Blues*, and these continued in *Blues & Soul*.

CHAPTER TWO

FAN CLUBS AND THE TAMLA MOTOWN APPRECIATION SOCIETY

As the appreciation of soul music grew, fan clubs began to be organised. There were clubs for Irma Thomas, Nina Simone, Barbara Lynn, Otis Redding (pre-dating Polydor's 'Uptight 'n' Outasight' club for the whole catalogue of Atlantic and Stax artists by a couple of years!), James Brown and the Shirelles, as well as for Dionne Warwick, Maxine Brown, Chuck Jackson, Dee Dee Warwick and almost anyone on the Scepter/Wand labels (as organised by the industrious and dedicated but sadly now deceased Gloria Marcantonio), and also for Don Covay.

Conspicuous by its absence from this list is the succinctly named Mary Wells Fan Club and Tamla Motown Appreciation Society, which reached out to interested souls (pardon the accidental pun!) from the small ads of *Record Mirror*. The 'Hitsville' fanzines, published monthly by TMAS (which quickly became the society's accepted acronym), included copious display ads for the paper, which suggests that publishing costs may have been shared between Motown, EMI and *Record Mirror*. Although it was thought at the time that the cost of producing the Hitsville magazines was more than the revenue generated from TMAS membership, I'm not sure that many knew the extent to which Berry Gordy Jr had bankrolled Dave Godin's Motown fan club activities until the information came to light in obituaries after Dave's tragic death in October 2004.

It was late in 1963 when ads for the Mary Wells Fan Club first appeared, but as my initial appreciation of the Motown Sound was for the harder edge of the Contours, the subtleties of Ms Wells passed me by. The club was soon expanded to include all Motown artists, and I joined as soon as the postman could carry my letter and postal order those few miles across north-west Kent from my home in Chislehurst to Dave's address in nearby Bexleyheath. A membership card arrived (later to be signed by Berry Gordy Jr (and sadly stolen, along with other fan-club cards, when my wallet was snatched at the Flamingo Club in Wardour Street), followed later by the first issues of the *Hitsville* fanzine (named after the Motown studio on Detroit's West Grand Boulevard), which appeared monthly. Vol. 1 no. 1 was dated January 1965, and featured a report by Clive Stone on Christmas at Hitsville (his name never appeared again!). It also usefully included a list of Motown people who had visited the UK during 1964 – the first year of existence for TMAS, in which membership apparently reached the notable figure of one thousand – and brought back memories of the fan receptions held in a basement theatre at EMI Records' Manchester Square headquarters just north of Oxford Street. The list of Motown notables who attended these included Martha & the Vandellas, the Supremes, Marvin Gaye, Harvey Fuqua, Berry Gordy Jr, the Miracles and Earl Van Dyke.

This coincided nicely with a series of EPs issued on Stateside Records entitled *R&B Chartmakers*. It is worth noting that the title was *R&B* and not *Soul*, an indicator that the soul era was still gestating, and didn't come into common usage until after Berry Gordy Jr had launched the Soul label in March 1964, with Shorty Long's 'Devil With the Blue Dress', coinciding with the breakthrough of a new style of artists like Don Covay on Atlantic ('Mercy Mercy' in September 1964) and Otis Redding on Stax subsidiary Volt ('Come To Me' in March 1964). The chart in question was a generic reference to the US charts, with the tracks having reached the R&B listing in *Billboard*, and in some cases, the Hot 100.

The tracks included on those 45rpm extended-play discs were early hits by these new stars, which had not been available as singles in the UK. My treasured copy of no. 2 includes the Supremes' 'Breathtaking Guy' along with the signatures of Diana (Ross), Mary (Wilson) and Florence (Ballard), and that of Berry Gordy himself. No. 3 included Martha & the Vandellas' 'Quicksand' plus autographs of Martha, Betty (Kelly) and Rosalind (Ashford), while no. 4 has the Supremes' 'Run Run Run' and is also signed by the group, together with Motown PR person Margaret Phelps. No. 1 is somewhere in my archives, signed by Marvin Gaye and Harvey Fuqua. We were indeed privileged to meet our heroes, as well as to hear them sing their latest hit 'live' over a band track, and as I recall this was also stretched to include Harvey's tremulous baritone lead on the Moonglows' 'Ten Commandments of Love'!

Hitsville vol. 1. no. 2, dated February 1965, heralds 'See You In March', alluding to the upcoming UK tour by the Motown Revue, with Stevie Wonder, due to arrive in London on 12 March, followed by the Supremes, Martha & the Vandellas, Smokey Robinson & the Miracles and the Earl Van Dyke Sextet on 15 March. The tour was booked to open at Finsbury Park Astoria on the 20th and Hammersmith Odeon the next night, co-promoted by Harold Davison and Arthur Howes, with Georgie Fame (for some reason) added to the line-up.

Another treasured aspect of TMAS membership was a 45 rpm single that arrived in the post during 1965. Bearing a white label headed 'Hitsville USA', and housed in a simple blue paper sleeve, the disc was called 'Greetings to Members of the Tamla Motown Appreciation Society', and comprised personalised messages from PR girl Margaret Phelps and Berry Gordy Jr, Smokey Robinson, Stevie Wonder, Marvin Gaye, Wanda of the Marvelettes and the tremulous bass voice of Melvin Franklin from the Temptations on side one, and Martha Reeves of the Vandellas, Billy Gordon of the Contours, Eddie Holland, Kim Weston and Diana Ross of the Supremes on side two, each speaking their greeting over a clip of their respective hit single of the time. A 2009 television documentary, *Motown – The British Invasion*, revealed that just 300 copies of this disc were pressed, so the copy filed in my own racks is a true collector's item!

* * *

As the following for soul music grew, Dave had the wisdom to broaden the appeal of his fanzine as *Hitsville* metamorphosed into *Rhythm & Soul USA*, which ran for four issues and included features on Irma Thomas, Tammi Terrell, Wilson Pickett and Solomon Burke in issue 1 (April 1966), Bessie Banks, Sam & Bill, Dee Dee Warwick and Sam & Dave in issue 2 (May), James Brown, the Vibrations, Martha & the Vandellas and Gloria Gaynor ('People to Watch', a decade before she became a global star!) in issue 3 (June), and finally, 'new series' issue 1 featured Aretha Franklin, Solomon Burke and Darrell Banks, each issue also including half a dozen pages of album and singles reviews.

The geographic proximity of Chislehurst and Bexleyheath made it fairly easy to establish more personal contact with Dave Godin, and while there was no easy route by public transport my trusty Lambretta motor-scooter made the journey quite easy. For two or three years in the mid-'60s I visited Dave probably once a month and spent evenings in his room, effectively a bed-sit within his parents' house, discussing not only soul music but also philosophy and film censorship, which were Dave's other major crusades in life. He was always keen to share knowledge and lend books, and it is to my lasting shame that it took me about a decade to return his copy of *Worlds in Collision* by Immanuel Velikowski – not a science-fiction novel but a philosophy tome!

Our journalistic paths diverged later, as did our musical tastes, with Dave joining forces with John E. Abbey when *Blues & Soul* began to shape up as the bastion of specialist soul periodicals, while I was immersed in label lists, matrix numbers and session discographies with *Shout*. Dave's crusade for Northern Soul took us further apart in musical philosophy, with some of my critical and dismissive reviews of Northern favourites causing a rift in our friendship that was not resolved until the mid-'90s. Dave was living in Sheffield by then, handling film and censorship matters for the local authority, and I had the pleasure of conducting a live telephone interview with him on musical matters for RTM Radio in south-east London, which served to restore the burned bridges. We remained on good terms until his tragic and untimely death in October 2004.

Worthy of mention at this point is another fan club for Motown Records, Motown Ad Astra, which was launched in the early 1970s and run from a bedsit in west London by two enthusiastic and knowledgeable fans Jackie Lee and Sharon Davis. They produced a fanzine called *Motown Tracking* and continued the dedicated crusade for the promotion of Motown music that had been started by Dave Godin a decade earlier. There were mini soul-summit meetings in the mid-'70s when Roy Stanton, then publishing *Black Wax* magazine, and I (still publishing *Shout*) trekked across London from south to west to be wined and dined – well, coffeed and biscuited – by these 'sisters in soul'.

Sharon went on to become press officer for Motown Records UK and then for Fantasy Records, responsible for the UK success of Sylvester and Loleatta Holloway during the disco era, and did her reputation as an authority on Motown music no harm with her comprehensive tome *Motown – The History*, a coffee-table epic of almost 400 pages which was published in 1988 by Guinness Books; she has also published monographs on Marvin Gaye, Diana Ross and Stevie Wonder. As a contributing journalist with *Blues & Soul*, Sharon also interviewed numerous soul singers during the '70s and '80s, and a collection of her work can be found in the 2006 anthology *Chinwaggin'*, published by Bank House Books.

CHAPTER THREE

THE SHOWS

Package Shows

I was in the right place at the right time, to paraphrase Dr John's song title. I started work in Woolwich (south-east London) in August 1962, and soon wandered along the main shopping street (Powis Street) to find the Odeon and Granada cinemas facing each other adjacent to the ferry terminus. In later decades I went to the Odeon to see concerts by Frankie Vaughan (with my family) and Dizzy Gillespie (to rectify the street cred), but the bill-posters of the early '60s were all for stage shows at the Granada. My first show was on 8 February 1963, with Bryan Hyland and the more soulful Little Eva topping the bill. While I remember seeing the show, the detail and date are recorded by courtesy of a splendid book in the Music Mentor catalogue by Ian Wallis, entitled *American Rock 'n' Roll – the UK Tours 1956 – 72*, which chronicles full details of all dates and venues of package tours during the golden age of rock 'n' roll and into the early '60s, with the landmark debut UK tours by such as Chuck Berry, Carl Perkins and Fats Domino.

Package shows were just that – a package of performers whose music came under the broad definition of pop. Many showcased a couple of headline American stars and also included local groups and singers who happened to be on the agent's books. Elkie Brooks was one who did the rounds singing pop and soul songs, already showing her talent, but many were nebulous guitar/bass/drums combos enjoying their short period of fame in backing the stars. As time passed and the British beat boom took a hold, so the greats of American rock 'n' roll shared the bill with some incongruous locals. This meant having to endure sets by the likes of the Swinging Blue Jeans and Gerry & the Pacemakers in order to take in the musical magic of Dionne Warwick and Bo Diddley! As my musical tastes embrace vintage rock 'n' roll as well as soul/blues/R&B/gospel, I went to shows featuring Carl Perkins, Del Shannon and Little Richard, and witnessed the no-nonsense reactions of the Teddy Boy/rocker audiences when they were asked to sit through a set of lightweight pop before the headliner appeared. Some of the Brit groups attempted to appease us by peppering their repertoire with rock 'n' roll classics, but the theatre lobbies were sometimes packed solid with grumbling 'Teds' while the support acts soldiered bravely on!

This actually went a stage further on one occasion, when a lauded hero was drowned in a sea of booing. Little Richard has always been a rather enigmatic character, and his musical career has undergone numerous stylistic changes. In the mid-'60s, during a label-hopping era which included Vee Jay, Modern and OKeh, he was intent on establishing himself as a soul singer, trying to move away from a '50s rock 'n' roll persona. While the intent was good, and his voice was easily able to accommodate the change of style, his UK fans (a dedicated and vocal bunch) had other ideas. Always the extrovert, Richard took to wearing a waistcoat made of small square mirrors on stage. I recall one London concert at which he climbed onto a large monitor speaker-column while his band was vamping a lengthy instrumental break, took off his waistcoat in provocative striptease manner and proceeded to tear it up and toss it into the audience. This was not appreciated, and he left the stage amid a furious chorus of boos. Despite his subsequent acclaim on the UK Northern Soul scene, resulting from his brassy, up-tempo outings on OKeh, and some fine soul sides for Vee Jay and Modern, Little Richard never reached the soul audience here as a live performer. In fact his recording career from the '70s onwards comprised attempts to adapt his dynamic rock 'n' roll style to a new era with contemporary musicians and arrangements. Reprise LPs *This Is* (1970) produced by Richard at Muscle Shoals, *The King of Rock 'n' Roll* (1971), produced by H.B. Barnum, and *The Second Coming* (1972), under the auspices of his Specialty mentor Robert 'Bumps' Blackwell, all attempted to integrate R&B and rock musicians into Richard's by now stylised performing, but sadly none achieved any great success and now make somewhat painful listening, certainly holding no appeal for soul fans.

Perhaps I should move swiftly back to 1963. Woolwich was just a short bus-ride from Lewisham, where the capacious Odeon doubled as cinema and theatre venue for these package shows. The soul years had yet to arrive, so the billed attractions were drawn from the wide roster of rock 'n' roll, with the result that an October outing to Lewisham brought the chance to see the rhythmic R&B of Bo Diddley (with Jerome Green and 'The Duchess') together with the pop/bluegrass harmonies of the Everly Brothers and the torrid rock 'n' roll of Little Richard, with a first-half support set by emergent R&B group the Rolling Stones, who included local lads Mick Jagger and Keith Richard (both from Dartford) and Bill Wyman (from nearby Penge) plus Charlie Watts (Neasden) and Brian Jones (Cheltenham). During the same month came a visit to Woolwich by my then rock favourite Del Shannon, followed in November by another concert of varied interest in which the Shirelles opened and Little Richard closed the show. Sandwiched between them was guitar great Duane Eddy and his band the Rebels in their first and only UK appearance. Duane and the guys played a short and rocking set, but before their next date the Musicians' Union stepped in to block them, as no 'exchange' had been arranged to play the USA. This was a relic of an era in which touring American musicians were required to be balanced by British musicians playing the States, so as not to deprive our lads of income. I'll talk more about this later.

At that time Little Richard (or more likely his management) realised that there was probably more mileage in satisfying the demands of a European audience than in trying to regenerate his fading career in his homeland, and so between rounds of concerts in the UK and continental Europe he went to Manchester to record a television special for Granada TV in which he was supported by English instrumental combo Sounds Incorporated. *It's Little Richard* was screened on 8 January 1964, and some forty-five minutes of hyper-energetic rock 'n' roll was screened on national TV. I recall it as captivating viewing. It appears never to have been screened again – though a brief scrutiny of ITV network film archives reveals that a print is still available!

Back to the live concerts, and to Woolwich in January 1964 for 'Group Scene '64'. The headline groups were the Ronettes and the now established Rolling Stones, with support from the pop/rock 'n' roll era in the Swinging Blue Jeans, Marty Wilde & the Wildcats and Johnny Kidd & the Pirates. March brought a visit from the Ronettes' Philles label-mates, the Crystals, with another chance to see Johnny Kidd, and a more significant event – with all due deference to Mr Spector's protégés – the first visit to the UK by Chuck Berry. I saw the show at Woolwich Granada on the 25th. Promoter Don Arden's programme notes heralded the 'First appearance in England of the dynamic Rhythm and Blues King'. Chuck Berry had been released from Leavenworth Federal Prison in Kansas on his birthday, 18 October 1963, and his parole officer in Chicago allowed him to tour Europe as part of his rehabilitation, though he was not yet permitted to resume his recording career. Chuck recounted fond memories of the tour in his autobiography, including mention of sexual activities between the two girl dancers on the tour bus in overnight drives between towns!

Arden had assembled quite a roster of talent for this tour, with the Nashville Teens opening a first half which also included forgotten femme duo The Other Two, the now English-based Gene Vincent, the Animals from Newcastle-upon-Tyne, who used the Woolwich gig to give their new recording a live debut: Eric Burdon's soulful rendition of 'House of the Rising Sun', with Alan Price's stunning organ solo, was greeted with a rapturous ovation before going on to become a global million seller. The first half was closed by rockabilly star Carl Perkins, also on his first UK tour, and the second half began with romping R&B from King Size Taylor & the Dominoes, who had spent the preceding years developing and refining their huge talent in the clubs and bars of Hamburg, and together with Tony Sheridan had helped the Beatles put a first foot on the ladder of stardom. The Dominoes remained onstage as the backing band for the rocking, duck-walking, beaming Charles Edward Berry. As I recall (so clearly some forty years later) Chuck had the audience in raptures from his first note, and did all he had to do to confirm his status as star and legend. His solid, rocking set included so many of the hits we'd all gone to hear. While not wishing to diminish Chuck's talent, it's worth noting that Carl Perkins perhaps had the edge in guitar-playing technique. I managed to get my programme signed by Messrs Perkins, Vincent and Taylor, but somehow missed out on Mr Berry.

There were more notable first-timers to see when the autumn touring season got underway. A Tito Burns presentation bundled together a bewildering array of 'undercard' support for the UK debuts of the Isley Brothers and Dionne Warwick. Erstwhile trad-jazzman Alan Elsdon & the Voodoos opened ('You Can't Sit Down'/'Smokestack Lightnin'), followed by pop nobody Tony Sheveton ('Ooh Poo Pa Doo'/'My Prayer'), comedian/compères Syd & Eddie – later to feature on TV schedules as Little & Large, the Undertakers (with their name coyly truncated to the 'Takers) in place of the billed Zombies, and the Searchers playing up to the interval with an array of their pop hits. The Voodoos returned to handle backing duties for Dionne Warwick, more accustomed to Bacharach orchestrations than to horns and rhythm, who gave us the delightful 'You'll Never Get To Heaven', recent hit 'Walk On By', 'Reach Out For Me' and a rousing 'What'd I Say' to close. My notes list just three songs for the Isley Brothers, but what a trio – both of singers and of songs. They opened with their recent hit, the readily recognisable 'Twist & Shout', followed by 'Talk To Me', a fine version of Little Willie John's hit ballad to display their vocal versatility and gospel phrasing, and closed with an epic-length performance of 'Shout', building from brisk to frantic and using a full array of on-stage theatrics to simmer then boil the atmosphere in the 'Just a little bit softer now/Just a little bit LOUDER now' section of the song, rocking the Granada to its rafters.

In October came the return of Carl Perkins, this time in a Don Arden promotion labelled 'R'n'B '64'. This time Lewisham Odeon was the venue, and the programme reveals a line-up of the Animals, Nashville Teens, Quotations, the aptly named Plebs, the youthful (eighteen-year old) Elkie Brooks, a sub-Lulu girl pop singer named Barry St John, and Tommy Tucker, the 'Hi-Heel Sneakers' man, whom I didn't remember having seen live until I looked at the programme. There was quite a bit of shuffling involved with the published running order of this and several other package shows, either to accommodate reactions to some of the filler acts, to respond to a hit record breaking during the tour or, more usually, the realisation that some acts were more natural showstoppers and some were better on disc than in person, despite their respective chart status. With these factors also came a change, perhaps a refinement, in musical taste, certainly with the London audiences, and this was taken by the promoters as an indication that the times they were a-changing.

Motown Revue

I saw the Motown Revue on the opening night, 20 March 1965, at Finsbury Park, an easy tube journey on the Piccadilly Line from Leicester Square in the West End – a short walk from Charing Cross station for the journey home. The show programme pronounces 'The Tamla Motown Show' on a rather bland front cover that features an etching of a vintage car with 'Motor Town Revue' inscribed on its roof. Page 2 is an ad for Guy Stevens' Sue Records with a full catalogue listing, and opposite is a full-page photo of the Supremes, clad in city business suits, clutching rolled umbrellas and perched on a metal fence outside EMI's Manchester Square offices. On the next page is a biography of the Supremes, faced by a half-page photo of Martha & the Vandellas plus their short biography, then overleaf is a half-page photo of the Miracles, including Claudette Robinson, plus a short biography. Opposite the Miracles is the running order for the show, which opened with the Earl Van Dyke Six, followed by Martha & the Vandellas and a pause with compère

Tony Marsh, whose photo also appeared here. Georgie Fame and his Blues Flames preceded the intermission, then the Van Dyke combo launched part two, featuring the Miracles, Stevie Wonder, more of Mr Marsh, then finally the Supremes. The centre-page spread was a marvellous collage of live performance portraits, with the caption 'Some of the artists who have appeared in the Motor-Town Revue', including great shots of some recognisable stars and some whose identity escapes me some forty years later! Over the page is another collage, this time of press cuttings from UK national and music papers, a page for Stevie Wonder with thumbnail photos and short biography (in those days known as a pen-picture), a page of Georgie Fame with, opposite, a half-page ad for his latest LP and EP topped with a half-page for the Tamla-Motown Appreciation Society. The last two pages feature a photo of Earl Van Dyke with a few sentences of biography, and an ad from EMI featuring six LPs and six EPs issued on the new Tamla Motown label. The back cover is another EMI ad for four more LPs on the new label, by Mary Wells, the Supremes, 'The Marvellous Marvelettes' and 'Recorded Live – The Motortown Revue'.

Of such things were dreams made, but although I was there I would be lying if I pretended to remember anything about it, other than marvelling at seeing and hearing my heroes on a London stage and puzzling then as now about why there was a need for the inclusion of Mr Fame other than for political reasons.

The concert tour visited twenty-one venues over three weeks in March and April 1965, from the opening dates at Finsbury Park and Hammersmith to the last night at Portsmouth, via Bristol and Birmingham, Leicester, Leeds and Liverpool, Wigan and Wolverhampton, not forgetting Manchester, Newcastle, Sheffield and Glasgow. From comments in subsequent issues of *Hitsville* magazine, it seems that these were not well advertised and consequently not well attended, apart from the London shows – which sold on the basis of fans' networked knowledge rather than any paid promotion.

Those who missed out on the live shows had a chance to see *The Sound of Motown* TV special, filmed and screened by London ITV. The bonus for those of us with the treasured TMAS membership cards was an invitation to the Rediffusion TV studios at Wembley to witness the filming of this spectacular, produced by Vicki Wickham, which took place on 18 March 1965, two days before the tour hit the road, and was screened on 28 April 1965. It was hosted by Dusty Springfield who, despite her folk music background, was a huge fan of Motown and soul music, and would later (1969) record the highly rated 'blue-eyed soul' LP *Dusty in Memphis*. Again I can't remember any detail of the evening's events, other than being amazed at the sheer size of the studio – it was like an aircraft hangar – and observing proceedings from a remote gallery, but I don't think there was much time wasted, nor re-takes required. Some footage of the show was preserved long enough to be issued on video-tape as *Ready Steady Go – Special Edition: The Sounds of Motown* by Dave Clark (yes, the pop star/drummer) International through EMI Picture Music in 1985.

As mentioned earlier, the soul scene *per se* was beginning to create and establish its own identity, rather than being just an element of pop music (though London radio stations then – as now – failed lamentably to recognise this), and by coincidence of circumstance (and geography) identities tended to be polarised in specific locations. This resulted in the rise of Motown from Detroit, Stax from Memphis, Atlantic from New York – and, a decade later, the Philadelphia International phenomenon. The style of musical tours hinged on these, to the benefit of the fans and (possibly) to the reward of the record companies. The result was a number of solo tours, with the spotlight on stars like Aretha Franklin, the Four Tops, the Supremes and R&B veteran Fats Domino – though a quick scan through the programmes for these concerts reveals that among the local support acts on the under-card for Aretha was Robert Knight, though I fear the 'Everlasting Love' originator made little impact, and only warranted a token back-cover photo devoid of any biographical notes.

One key tour of this era took place in spring 1966 – the London debut of James Brown.

James Brown

My awareness of 'Mr Brown' (as he was generally known to all who came within speaking distance) began with purchase of the *Pure Dynamite* LP (HA 8177) and the *Live at The Apollo* LP on UK London American in 1964 (HA 8184), though the sleeve of this was hardly illuminating for the new fan, comprising an inferior impressionist watercolour on the front, presumably intended to depict a Harlem street scene, and a back cover with minimalist notes by King Records executive Hal Neely, a track listing (which failed to note that 'I Lost Someone', closing side one, also occupies much of side two, and the remaining ten tracks are squeezed into a medley) and a postcard-sized head and shoulders photo of James. Then along came Sue Records with a 45 coupling 'Night Train' and the contrasting blues ballad 'Why Does Everything Happen to Me', a London EP with 'Prisoner of Love', 'These Foolish Things', 'Choo Choo' and 'Feel It' (four less-representative examples of typical JB it would be hard to find!), and the London 45 of 'Papa's Got A Brand New Bag'. It was the last of these that helped to ignite wider interest in James Brown, and those few of us who were members of the first fan club, run by Alan Curtis from his Brixton home, made our circuitous way to Heathrow Airport (by airport bus from Victoria bus station) to meet our hero. Half a dozen young soul fans gathered around the Customs exit door, anxiously awaiting the door to open, and when the stocky, white-haired figure that was James's agent Ben Bart finally emerged he was closely followed by the diminutive but distinctive Mr Brown. We shuffled forward to greet our hero and to have our LP sleeves signed, but were almost crowded out when a throng of press photographers scurried towards us from all directions. The air was full of demands: 'Over here, Jimmy', 'This way, Jimmy!' The Famous Flames had also made the trip, and my LP sleeves were also adorned with the signatures of Bobby Byrd and Lloyd 'Baby Lloyd' Stallworth.

    I had tickets for the opening night at Walthamstow, which was Saturday 12 March 1966, and the second night at Brixton, which the handbill tells me was Sunday 13 March, at 6pm and 8.30. Barbara Lewis was billed as support at Brixton, while the programme for

Walthamstow has Doris Troy closing the first half. Quite how I travelled to Walthamstow from south-east London I cannot recall – I think it was a very long walk from the nearest tube station in an era pre-dating the Victoria Line – and how I got back at a very late hour is even more of a mystery. I don't remember anything about the show either, apart from a reviewer's phrase that James had 'swung the Granada clean out of Walthamstow', but it must have had an impact, as I fell ill the next day and was unable to attend the Brixton show. While in London, James was also booked to appear on ITV's Friday night pop show *Ready Steady Go* by producer Vicki Wickham, though his appearance' on 11 March turned into a one-hour spectacular which was in essence a potted version of the James Brown Revue and managed to grab headlines in the Saturday morning press. The *Daily Mirror* of 12 March carried the headline 'Pop Singer's Mock "Fits" Shock Viewers', reporting that 'scores of viewers phoned in to complain about his "disgusting behaviour"'. All who are familiar with Mr Brown's stage show know of the gospel-influenced fervour of his delivery, the near-manic repetition of the 'Please Please Please' finale, and the renowned cape routine with MC Danny Ray, with James hurling off the cape and stomping back to the microphone. The great British public and press were ignorant of this, and the cape routine was compared to mimicry of epileptic seizures: another front page proclaimed 'Soul singer Brown has fits on TV'. The old PR adage is that any publicity is good publicity (as long as they spell your name right), and certainly awareness of James Brown, soul singer, was increased significantly by this incident.

London Club Shows
A browse through issues of John Abbey's *Home of the Blues* reveals that other soul artists crossed the Atlantic during 1966 and 1967. They included Alvin Robinson, the gravel-voiced singer from New Orleans who gave us the original version of 'Something You Got' and played Tiles (Oxford Street's basement club) on 22 April 1966, fellow New Orleans-domiciled Lee Dorsey, promoting 'Do Re Mi', 'Ya Ya' and 'Ride Your Pony', who played there on 25 April,

the diminutive but belting Sugar Pie DeSanto from San Francisco, who spent as much time sprawled on the stage displaying her colourful knickers as singing about her 'Soulful Dress', this on 28 April, blues legend John Lee Hooker on 5 May, and the Original Drifters the next day, the group comprising Gerhard Thrasher, Bill Pinkney, Bobby Hollis and Bobby Hendricks. On 9 May there was an appearance by Patti LaBelle & the Blue Belles, including Cindy Birdsong, Sarah Dash and Nona Hendrix.

Tiles continued to deliver its banquet of soul, with Ben E. King on 23 May, then Roy C. (Hammond) on 9 June, promoting 'Shotgun Wedding' with an act that also included 'Bring It On Home To Me', 'Frankie and Johnnie' and 'It's Got the Whole World Shakin'' from the Sam Cooke songbook. The review closes with the prophetic statement that Roy 'could well have trouble finding a follow-up' to 'Shotgun Wedding'.

The June issue of *Home of the Blues* published a schedule of American acts booked into Tiles during June and July, which included Billy Stewart, the Orlons, Rufus Thomas, Joe Tex and Solomon Burke. The August issue duly carried reviews of the Orlons, then a trio comprising Audrey and Shirley Brickley and Rosetta Hightower, from 1 July, Rufus Thomas from 8 July and Billy Stewart from 20 June. Billy's act combined popular music hits like 'Moon River' and 'People' and his own soul gems 'Sittin' In The Park' and 'I Do Love You'. Joe Tex, scheduled for 22 July, didn't actually set foot in the UK until some five years later, when in January 1970 he was on the 'Soul Together' tour with Sam & Dave, Arthur Conley and Clarence Carter – though the latter withdrew from the show after the opening night at the Royal Albert Hall on 22 January 1970.

Tiles saw the return of Ben E. King on 11 November, then an appearance by Edwin Starr and Bobby Hebb on 2 December, during a visit to London to promote 'Sunny' on the weekly *Top of the Pops* chart show, while 1966 was brought to a rousing conclusion by the Soul Sisters, Theresa Cleveland and Anne Gissendanner, playing the All Star Club in Paddington on New Year's Eve and Liverpool's renowned Cavern Club on 1 January 1967. Alvin Cash & the Crawlers opened the new year at Tiles on Friday 6 January.

In his review John Abbey clarified the fact that the Crawlers were Alvin's brothers, George, David and Arthur Welch. They were just dancers, while the Registers were the band on Alvin's hits on Mar-v-Lus Records in Chicago.

Stax in London

Stax came to London in March 1967. The label's image was rather fragmented in the UK, partly because the music was so different from other uptown soul, almost too black with its funky sound despite many of the musicians being white, and partly because of the change in UK licensing rights from Decca to Polydor. In January 1966 Decca had scored a Top 20 hit for Otis Redding, lifting his cover of the Temptations' 'My Girl' ballad from the *Otis Blue* LP for release on the now-legendary black and silver Atlantic label, having assessed that his current US hits 'Respect' and 'I Can't Turn You Loose' weren't right for the British market.

Redding made his first trip to the UK and Europe in September 1966, promoting his hit cover-version of the Rolling Stones' 'Satisfaction' and his own epic ballad 'My Lovers Prayer'. The English schedule, as published in *Home of the Blues* in September 1966, included a contrast in venues – Bristol Colston Hall (12th), Manchester Odeon (15th), Tiles Club (16th), Boston Gliderdrome (17th) and Brixton's 'compact' Ram Jam Club in south-west London (18th), as well as featuring in a *Ready Steady Go* TV showcase appearance on Friday 16 September. The Tiles gig, reviewed by David Ryan in *Home of the Blues* in November 1966, described Otis as 'Tall, with a great big smile on his face', opening with a medley of 'Barefootin'', 'Land of 1000 Dances' and 'Satisfaction', followed by 'Hold On I'm Coming', 'My Girl' and his own ballad hits 'Pain In My Heart' and 'I've Been Loving You Too Long', and closing with a reprise of 'Barefootin'' and 'Satisfaction'. The reviewer ended with a prophetic pronouncement: 'Anyone who saw him will agree – he'll be back.'

Polydor acquired the UK rights to Atlantic on 1 April 1966. Dave Godin announced in a new item in *Rhythm & Soul USA* magazine dated June 1966 that Decca had a six-month sell-off period for their Atlantic issues before deletion, and the following spring established a separate identity for the Stax label. The March 1967 issue of *Gramophone Popular Record Catalogue* lists three Otis Redding LPs (including a prompt reissue of *Otis Blue*) as new releases, and the April 1967 issue of the newly glossy *Home of the Blues* included John Abbey's reviews of the first batch of five LPs on the new UK Stax label. 589001 to 589005 comprised *Memphis Gold* and *Hit The Road Stax* compilations and solo sets by Booker T & the MGs, Sam & Dave and Carla Thomas plus, rather strangely, a Markeys LP, *The Great Memphis Sound*, bearing an Atlantic logo and catalogue number.

Nipping off briefly at a semi-relevant tangent, it's worth mentioning that coincident with the Polydor UK launch of the Stax catalogue, Pye took the timely opportunity to promote their R&B licensed catalogue with a blues and soul marketing push in March 1967, including half a dozen albums from Chess on the budget-priced (12*s* 6*d*) Marble Arch label (the London landmark was just a stone's throw from Pye's Stanhope Place offices). These were Howlin' Wolf, John Lee Hooker, a Chuck Berry ten-track *Greatest Hits*, the classic *Muddy Waters At Newport* and Sonny Boy Williamson's *Down and Out Blues*, plus the oddly titled *Blues & Soul* compilation which was all great soul and absolutely no blues! There were also full price LPs by John Lee Hooker, Etta James (*At Last*), Muddy Waters and Bo Diddley (*The Originator*) on Chess and Chuck Jackson, James Brown (*Mighty Instrumentals*), Dionne Warwick, Chuck Jackson & Maxine Brown and a *Greatest Sing Their Soul Favourites* compilation of girl singers on Pye International, all from the Scepter/Wand catalogue, and Jimmy Rushing's Five Feet of Soul (good jazzy blues and anything but soul!) on the almost extinct Golden Guinea label, originally from Colpix.

The major result of the Polydor/Atlantic deal was to bring the Stax/Volt Revue to Europe, opening on 17 March at Finsbury Park Astoria, and running through to 9 April, with several nights in Europe squeezed into the schedule: Paris at the Olympia Theatre on Tuesday 21 March, then Oslo, Stockholm, Copenhagen and The

Hague before returning to London. Actually there was no Stax/Volt Revue in the USA – the idea was concocted by Otis's manager Phil Walden, British booker Arthur Howes and Polydor executive Frank Fenter; and the Markeys had to hurriedly learn the charts for the hits by Redding, Carla Thomas, Eddie Floyd, Sam & Dave and Arthur Conley. While they had played on the original records by these acts, none were memorised, and each had their own working road band. The Europe trip was quite an adventure for the Stax musicians, who had not travelled widely in their homeland, and the water was muddied slightly for some as the tour hit the road initially billed as The Otis Redding Revue.

I saw the Revue on its opening night, in an audience of enthusiastic soul fans who awaited the appearance of their new heroes with good-natured impatience, and the atmosphere was electric with anticipation. Booker T & the MGs opened, soul radio DJ Emperor Rosco handled MC duties, the Memphis Horns augmented the MGs to complete the Markeys, and Arthur Conley closed the first half – a non-Stax singer on the show as a protégé of Redding and managed by Walden. Eddie Floyd started the second half with timely promotion of his new single 'Knock On Wood', followed by more Rosco and then by Sam & Dave, whose double-dynamite stage act matched the energy and fervour of James Brown, whipping the audience into such an ecstatic frenzy that headliner Otis had to hit the ground at full gallop. I don't think my seat was used much that night, and certainly Redding's appearance prompted a rush towards the stage as the band vamped the intro to his first song at breakneck tempo. The tempo barely dropped for the entire set, which was good and bad – good in that the atmosphere was maintained at frenzy level, but bad in that Otis's vocal range was quite limited, despite the soulful intensity of his delivery, and the frenetic pace distorted the appeal of 'Day Tripper' and 'Try a Little Tenderness' to the point that they became 'over-souled' and lost the interest of this writer.

Such was the impact and appeal of the Stax Revue that Arthur Howes and Phil Walden worked together again later in 1967. This was with the Soul Explosion package, which brought Sam & Dave and Arthur Conley back to these shores along with Percy Sledge, hot with his Atlantic chart hits ('When A Man Loves a Woman' and 'Warm & Tender Love' if you really didn't know!), and further support from Southern Soul artists Sam Baker and Linda Carr, both of whom remain great unknowns outside the soul cognoscenti to this day. As a small-time journalist, I noted the songs on my show programme, which tells me that the Sam & Dave Band opened with 'Mercy Mercy Mercy', Sam Baker sang 'Cold Sweat', 'Sunny' and 'Number One in My Heart', Linda Carr featured 'You Can't Hurry Love', 'You Send Me' and 'Boy From Ipanema', and Percy Sledge closed the first half with 'Warm & Tender Love', 'It Tears Me Up' and 'When a Man Loves a Woman'. After the interval came Arthur Conley with 'Shake Rattle & Roll', 'A Change is Gonna Come', 'Whole Lotta Woman (Can Satisfy My Soul)' and 'Sweet Soul Music'; then Sam & Dave roared in with 'You Don't Know Like I Know', 'Soul Man', 'Hold On I'm Coming' and 'Soothe Me'. I also noted that the band comprised three tenor saxes, alto, soprano, trumpet, trombone, guitar, bass and drums.

Sunday at the Saville

Before I leave the realms of package shows two other major ventures come to mind, one of which served to widen my appreciation of black music into the realm of blues, and the other an oddity which may be seen either as bandwagon-jumping or a philanthropic gesture. Taking the latter first, a feature of 1967 was Sundays at the Saville, promoted by Beatles' manager Brian Epstein through his NEMS Enterprises, with bookers including Tony Bramwell and Vicki Wickham. London theatres traditionally don't – or didn't then – open on Sundays for their normal daily fare of plays and musicals, and thus the Saville Theatre on Shaftesbury Avenue proved to be a handy central London focal point for music one-nighters. I saw the 19 February show headlined by Chuck Berry and supported by Del Shannon (the programme had an eye-catching art-nouveau cover depicting Apollo and the Nine Muses), and the following week Chuck was back again with Herbie Goins and the Night Timers as main support. Subsequent Sundays showcased Fats Domino, Junior Walker, Ben E. King & Bo Diddley, Little Richard (18 December 1966 – in a show with support from the Alan Price Set and the Bluesology combo featuring Reg Dwight, later to become Elton John, on keyboards) and Gladys Knight & the Pips. On 26 November – after Epstein's death in August – there was a soul spectacular that included blue-eyed Motown lady Chris Clark, Barry White's west coast protégé Felice Taylor, and headlining Stax man Eddie Floyd, who spent most of his act encouraging the audience to clap their hands and say 'yeah'! The back page of the programme features an ad for Joe Tex and his Band, but I'm not sure that show ever took place, as I only saw Joe in the UK in an Atlantic Records revue at Croydon Fairfield Hall.

As a postscript, I was amazed to discover recently that programmes for Sunday at the Saville concerts by rock acts Cream and Jimi Hendrix are priced at around £400 on some auction sites!

American Folk Blues Festival

The final element of package shows was the American Folk Blues Festival, an annual aggregation of the finest traditional bluesmen and women, representing Chicago, Texas, Mississippi and West Coast styles, which was organised by German promoters Horst Lippmann and Fritz Rau from 1962 through to the early 1970s. As I had spent the early '60s developing an interest in soul, I had missed the chance to see Willie Dixon, Sonny Boy Williamson and Otis Spann, Sugar Pie DeSanto, Howlin' Wolf and Big Mama Thornton, and it wasn't until 1968 and 1969 that I went along to see such greats as T-Bone Walker, John Lee Hooker and an inebriated Jimmy Reed at Hammersmith Odeon, then Earl Hooker, Big Joe Williams and Magic Sam at the Royal Albert Hall. This interest coincided with my increased involvement in R&B journalism, of which more shortly, and also widened to encompass two years of London Jazz Expo tours, also in 1968 and 1969, co-promoted by Harold Davison, George Wein and Jack Higgins, and intended to replicate a scaled-down version of Wein's Newport Jazz Festival in the USA. The souvenir brochure (which cost 5*s*) covered the entire Expo, listing concerts by Dave Brubeck and Gerry Mulligan, the Dizzy Gillespie Big Band Reunion, a Drum Workshop with Art Blakey, Elvin Jones and Max Roach, an 'ancient and modern' mix with Gary Burton, Red Norvo and London's Ronnie Scott Band, further extravaganzas headlining the Earl Hines All Stars and Newport All Stars and the Count Basie Band. Tucked into the middle of the Expo, on Tuesday 22 October 1968, was the somewhat eclectic and patchwork 'Story of Soul', in which the Horace Silver Quintet (keyboard modern jazz) opened for the Muddy Waters Band, featuring Otis Spann's strikingly different keyboard, Luther Johnson's youthful guitar, Pee Wee Madison (drums) and Paul Osher (harp), the gospel of the Stars of Faith (who had previously toured the UK with Alex Bradford's Black Nativity show) and the UK debut of mellow Southern Soul balladeer Joe Simon. While it was great to have the chance to see and hear Joe, his musical style was mildly incongruous in such a vibrant setting, and years later his producer/mentor John Richbourg voiced the opinion that this showcase did Joe no favours. The audience was largely comprised of 'jazzers', who grudgingly accepted Muddy Waters because blues was considered to be on the periphery of jazz, but as soul wasn't part of this scene Joe stood out like the proverbial sore thumb when he delivered his sonorous balladry. The programme reveals, however, that the Folk Blues Festival was integrated into the Jazz Expo that year, with the Reed/Hooker/Walker show at Hammersmith just two days after the soul show. An enduring memory is that of the huge, rotund figure of Big Joe Williams (not the Basie jazz singer!) sitting on a wooden kitchen chair to play a captivating set of acoustic nine-string guitar blues.

A second Expo followed in the autumn of 1969, with a veritable galaxy of stars. It included concerts with Sarah Vaughan and Maynard Ferguson, Gary Burton, Kenny Clarke and Charlie Shavers, a guitar workshop with Barney Kessell, Tal Farlow and Kenny Burrell, two nights of swing era stars culminating with Lionel Hampton's Band, an evening of eclectic, introspective piano with Thelonious Monk and Cecil Taylor, and that master of introversion and originator of cool trumpet Miles Davis. That year the blues night was extended to include gospel, with the Robert Patterson Singers and the return of the Stars of Faith, along with Otis Spann's Chicago piano, John Lee Hooker's Detroit boogie, Jack Dupree's barrel-house piano and the St Louis blues of Albert King.

Live Shows: the Clubs

As a result of the Brit invasion of the US charts, a number of the R&B and soul acts thus displaced from regular work in their homeland found a ready market in the UK on the club circuit. Numerous artists came to England and *Blues & Soul*, *Record Mirror*, *New Musical Express* and the weekly local press, both in London and the provinces, began carrying small display ads for touring soul acts booked for one-nighters at local venues. They played our version of the 'chittlin' circuit', which included central London venues like the Flamingo (downstairs) and Whisky a-Go-Go (upstairs) in Wardour Street and Tiles in Oxford Street (the 100 Club was a jazz bastion and didn't feature blues and soul acts until years later). The Cue Club in Paddington was not far away, and various clubs were scattered around the London suburbs, including several just a few miles from my home – the Black Prince at Bexley, the Black Cat at Woolwich, the Bromel Club at Bromley and the Eden Park Hotel, Beckenham. My files and recollections tell me that I also made the odd visit to the Ram Jam Club at Brixton (Oscar Toney Jr), and on Friday 12 May 1967 saw Garnet Mimms at the Flamingo Club, promoted by *Home of the Blues* – soon to become *Blues & Soul*. There were also a number of clubs and music venues in the Midlands and North-West which had a full diary of touring soul artists. These are well chronicled elsewhere, being part of the much-documented Northern Soul scene, though the focus on the collectors in that fraternity didn't arise until the '70s.

For the suburban South Londoner there was a chance to see the likes of Inez & Charlie Foxx, Oscar Toney Jr, Ben E. King, Bo Diddley, Solomon Burke and even Screamin' Jay Hawkins at the Bromley, Bexley and Woolwich venues, as well as Jerry Lee Lewis at

Eltham Baths in a memorable gig in November 1964, supported by Screaming Lord Sutch and the Savages. This included on bass guitar one John Baldwin, then-recent organist at St Aidan's Church, New Eltham (the church I attended at the time), soon to become John Paul Jones with Led Zeppelin. (In a further pedantic detail, John was christened at the same service as me at St Andrew's Church, Mottingham, London SE9 in January 1946!)

The Black Prince Club was a regular Sunday night out. The venue was a dance hall with a small stage, an integral part of the pub/hotel which still gives its name to a major intersection on the M2 motorway but has long been supplanted by a corporate motel chain. The staple diet for the bookers was a rotation of blues/soul combos of the time, including the Graham Bond Organisation, Bond on Hammond organ, Dick Heckstall-Smith (sax), Jack Bruce (bass) and Ginger Baker (drums), playing small-combo blues, jump R&B and some jazzy pieces, with the spotlight on Dick and Graham. This helped me to get further into the Blue Note style of jazz and to appreciate the Hammond organ of Jimmy Smith, Jack McDuff and Jimmy McGriff, plus the tenor artistry of Stanley Turrentine a decade before he edged into the jazz-funk charts in his Warner days. There were also the Zoot Money Big Roll Band, the Peddlars (a moody jazz/blues piano/bass/drums trio who had a couple of 45s on Philips) and other local combos of similar style. From time to time came a major treat with the appearance of a touring American act: Inez & Charlie Foxx came to Bexley, as did the Showstoppers and, in the era of 'fake' groups booked by promoter Roy Tempest, the Fabulous Platters (actually US soul group the Steinways) and the Fantastic Temptations (new York doo-wop group the Velours, later to crack the UK charts in their own right renamed the Fantastics). The Black Prince also played host to a remarkable event on 11 June 1965 – its very own jazz festival! The hotel had quite extensive grounds, and enough room for a couple of stages for groups and bands of various styles. These included the self-explanatory Dutch Swing College Band and pop/R&B group Unit 4 Plus 2, who charted with their cover of Eddie Rambeau's 'Concrete & Clay' and who won a place in my affections by continuing to sing their set a cappella when a power failure in mid-afternoon deprived them of sound from their instruments. The festival closed with a romping set by Zoot Money and his Big Roll Band, playing a mixture of R&B and soul classics like 'Walking The Dog', 'Monkey Time' and 'Night Time is the Right Time', with Zoot leaving his seat to climb onto the PA speakers and then the scaffold framework of the bandstand, hollering the chorus of 'Night Time' while his brass section manfully continued with their twelve-bar vamp. But the major attraction was a set by the self-styled 'King of Rock 'n' Soul', Solomon Burke. I can't remember what he sang, but I still have a treasured photo of the man taken during a grey afternoon.

The Black Cat Club was in a basement behind a modest doorway opposite Woolwich Arsenal railway station, and was my destination on Friday nights in the mid-'60s. It had a similar roster of London-based R&B combos, to which can be added Bluesology and an occasional American visitor, the most famous and notable being Screamin' Jay Hawkins, who brought his full US stage act including coffin and skull-on-a-cane named Henry. That was a night to remember, though Jay's repertoire is lost to the mists of time. Also local were the Bromel Club, based in the ballroom of the plush Bromley Court Hotel, where Ben E. King and Bo Diddley were among touring American attractions, and just a couple of miles along the road was Chislehurst Caves – an unlikely venue for a music event, perhaps. I'm not sure if he was subject to Musicians' Union exchange regulations, but on Friday 16 December 1966 I was among a couple of hundred people who crammed into the subterranean labyrinth when Jimi Hendrix played a concert there. It was an unforgettable experience, though I can't remember (and wasn't bothered) what songs he played (apart from buying the 45 of 'Hey Joe' and keeping the odd promo LP of his bluesier material and pre-Experience doo-wop items I had little interest in his music), but I do recall my ears ringing for hours after the gig because of the loud volume and enclosed arena. Like most of the audience, my clothes were drenched in perspiration from the heat of the show.

Later came trips to London Airport to greet Ike and Tina Turner in January 1971, before their concerts at Hammersmith

Odeon, and Fats Domino and his band. We took the airport bus from Victoria Coach Station, often in the early hours in order to meet breakfast-time incoming flights, and stationed ourselves by the custom hall's exit doors: we were as keen to meet band-members as stars. Tina was clad in a huge leopard-skin fur coat and Ike in a dark leather jacket, and both were happy to sign autographs and pose for snapshots. I must have been sitting somewhere near the front to be able to comment on the Ikettes' knickers in my review! Four of these photos graced the cover of issue 64 of *Shout* magazine in March 1971. We also met Fats Domino, together with members of his band, when they arrived for a concert on 8 April 1973. Again photos were published on the cover of *Shout* (issue 86 in June that year). After that it became harder to find details of incoming flight times unless one paid to subscribe to industry press information lists.

We also had an invitation to meet Ember Records' chairman, Jeffrey Kruger, to discuss promoting soul nights at the Flamingo Club in Wardour Street, but that's part of another chapter in the annals of soul music in London.

The club circuit was active and thriving through the mid-'60s, and perhaps faded along with the recording careers of the artists concerned. Certainly by the turn of the decade such one-nighters were infrequent, and the focus changed back to concert package tours or one-off shows at major venues with a smaller name artist in a supporting role. As new names appeared in the charts, both as soul hits and occasionally as crossovers, so the pedigree of the supporting acts reaped reward for us veteran soul fans. A quick scan of my memory recalls Creedence Clearwater Revival at the Royal Albert Hall with Wilbert Harrison as support, the Stylistics at the London Palladium with Candi Staton supporting, Gladys Knight & the Pips also at the Palladium with Major Lance and Ben E. King supporting, and John Abbey's Contempo promoting shows at Finsbury Park Astoria starring Al Green and with support by Margie Joseph and Oscar Toney Jr. It was at the same venue, also in support of Al Green, that UK soul fans had their first chance to witness the sweet-soul harmony group Bloodstone. Unable to get a deal in their native LA, their landmark first LP was produced by

Mike Vernon and released on UK Decca. As befitted the status and history of the label, Atlantic provided the most high-profile concerts, which showcased the stars of the new decade in Sister Sledge, the Jimmy Castor Bunch and the Spinners (still billed as 'Detroit' for UK consumption), while Motown was represented by the Supremes – Ronnie Dyson in support – and Stevie Wonder, plus their label-mates now billed as Martha Reeves & the Vandellas.

Back-tracking slightly, there was another (very limited) option for seeing a few soul and R&B artists early in the '60s for those who had contacts or friends at US forces bases in England. These sites were, of course, effectively US territory and thus beyond the bounds of the Musicians' Union exchange arrangements, so they could book US stars as if they were at home. The London-based Douglas House featured artists including the Drifters and Bobby Lewis, both acts interviewed by Bill Millar, then of *Soul Music Monthly* magazine, while a number of artists including the Dells came to the UK to perform at the US Air Force base at Chicksands, near Bedford, where lived some-time *Shout* magazine contributor and Black Wax co-owner Roy Stanton.

CHAPTER FOUR

FANZINES

It all started for me with Don Covay: my first steps in journalism were taken when writing *DC1*, the inaugural magazine of the Don Covay Fan Club, early in 1967. I had received newsletters from other fan clubs that I'd joined, but had been particularly impressed with the small-format stapled magazines produced by The Organisation – a fan club devoted to jazz and soul organ-based music and run by Jon Philibert from Crystal Palace in south-east London. His neighbour Dave McAleer, in nearby Thornton Heath, produced a similar small booklet for members of his Fame & Goldwax Followers Club. Thus *DC1* comprised six pages of quarto paper (in the era before A4 became the standard size), and included news on Don Covay from Polydor label manager Frank Fenter, short lists of new and future releases on Ember and Island Records, a page of reviews of old Covay 45s, two pages of reviews of recent soul singles, both UK releases and some US imports, and a track-by-track review of Don's *See Saw* LP.

DC2 followed in May, the front cover being a photocopy of a signed portrait of Don obtained during his recent UK tour. Despite Covay's prolific activities as songwriter and recording artist in the USA, Polydor either had little news or information on his recent work, or couldn't be bothered to keep me informed, which resulted in the fan club magazine comprising some guesswork, a list of recent and forthcoming releases, reviews of recent LPs and, perhaps most significant, reviews of recent live shows, namely the Stax (Otis Redding) Show at Hammersmith Odeon on 8 April 1967 and the UK debut of Fats Domino and his Band at the Saville Theatre (mentioned in the Package Shows chapter), datelined 27 March 1967.

The roots of the soul fanzine era pre-date my own modest efforts by a year or so, with pioneering work by Tony Cummings in Plymouth. Tony's long history in music journalism began late in 1965 with *SOUL*, subtitled 'The Magazine for the R&B Collector'. The second issue, dated February 1966, provided some idea of both the range of music to be covered and of other magazines in the same field. It included Johnny Ace and T-Bone Walker, the Impressions and the Tams, Fontella Bass and Tammy Montgomery (Terrell to be), plus pre-war blues, gospel and lots of news snippets, while 'friends in the field' that were advertised were Mick (Mike) Vernon's (later of Blue Horizon fame) *R&B Monthly*, Bob Groom's quite eclectic *Blues World* and the archetypal/formative *Blues Unlimited*, edited by Mike Leadbitter from Bexhill-on-Sea. Within the year these had been joined by *Home of the Blues*, printed in duplicated (wax stencil and rotary printing machine) quarto format with glossy litho photographic cover, and published from his north London flat by John E. Abbey, whose equal appreciation of country music was occasionally reflected in the contents.

Home of the Blues (presumably named after the small Memphis record label, though I never got to ask John about this) first appeared in February 1966, running in 'fanzine' format up to issue 7, dated December 1966. Issue 8 followed in March 1967, by which time there had been an injection of capital and a major upgrade in physical appearance. The masthead credits were to Contempo Publications – though the editorial address remained the same – and the twenty-four pages were set in letterpress, printed on glossy paper throughout and wire-bound with a colour cover. There was advertising support from the Soul City record shop (probably a contra deal, as the magazine published the shop's LP and singles charts), *Record Mirror* and, significantly, a full page from EMI promoting the 'Soul Supply' series of albums. In October that year the magazine metamorphosed into *Blues & Soul*. The editorial explained the restrictions of the previous title without really explaining that there would henceforth be but lip service paid to the blues element of the title, but that hardly mattered as John built the magazine into the major-league bible of the soul world. Early advertising support came from President, Island, Atlantic, Ember, and EMI Records on the back page. While references remained to the magazine's *Home of the Blues* heritage, distribution was now through newsagents as well as mail-order subscription: it had left the realms of fanzines.

Back to the roots, however, and tracking the path of the early journalistic career of Tony Cummings. Tony (TC to friends and colleagues) progressed from the rotary-duplicated *Soul* issue 2 to the brave and costly litho-printed issues 3 and 4, followed by a title-change to *Soul Music Monthly*, issues 1, 2 and 3. The range of contributors was impressive, including Bill Millar, Trevor Churchill, Peter Gibbon, Roger St Pierre, John Abbey and Paris-based Swiss-born discographer Kurt Mohr. The range of live reviews reveals the period of 1966–67 to be a golden age for touring soul stars: Irma Thomas at the Flamingo, Don Covay at Blaizes, Patti LaBelle & the Blue-Belles at Tiles, all reviewed in *Soul*. In January 1967 *Soul Music Monthly* led with Alvin Robinson, Robert Parker at Woolwich, Roy C at Tiles, and also featured the Drifters and Bobby Lewis, who had performed for US servicemen in London at Douglas House. *SMM* 2 included Solomon Burke at the Marquee, the Dixie Cups in Southampton, the Coasters at the Whisky-a-Go-Go and Edwin Starr at Tiles, while no. 3 (the final issue under this title, in March 1967) featured Little Richard at the Saville, the Mad Lads (no less!) at Tiles, the basement club in Oxford Street, the Spellbinders, and Alvin Cash & the Crawlers at Streatham Locarno. The latter venue is significant: though the editorial address of the magazine was still in Plymouth (although Tony had moved from St Judes to Peverell), a major move took place in the Cummings household when Tony and his then wife Hilary moved to London to be at the hub of the music world, taking up residence in a bedsit in Kirkstall Road in suburban Streatham, south-west London.

Streatham was to become the centre of the soul fanzine world for about a year. Bill Millar lived there, and fellow journalist-fans Dave McAleer, Jon Philibert and Mick Brown lived just a mile or so away. Then I was invited to join the gathering, making the weekly journey of a few miles from Chislehurst by public transport to get involved in some deep discussions on soul music, enhanced by the almost competitive use of cringe-worthy puns by the gathered throng. The focal point of our discussions, however, was the plan to combine our journalistic and fanzine forces in a single market-leading soul music magazine, intended to reach the academic end of the market in the same way that the new, glossy *Blues & Soul* targeted the more popular-oriented soul fans. Another major name to be involved was Charlie Gillett, who had recently graduated from Columbia University in New York.

An impressive first issue of *Soul Music* appeared in July 1967, wire bound and litho printed, though neither issue number nor date appeared on either the front cover or the editorial page – in fact, with personal memory dimmed by the mists of time, I had to cross-check some discs listed in the 'new releases' section against their *Billboard* chart entry date to discover when the magazine was actually published! While it was litho printed, the pages were actually run from quarto-sized typed copy rather than being set by letterpress, and the contents combined the various elements of the contributors' previous magazines. A review of Sam & Bill live at Streatham Locarno, a backstage interview by Bill Millar and Tony Cummings, and a session discography from Kurt Mohr's files opened proceedings, setting the tone not only of this first issue but also for the 112 that followed over the next seven years. Bill Millar's contacts with the Ad Libs' manager Bill Downs was the source of his short biography of them, while 'Maximilion's Hunk of Funk' was a characteristic page of bullet-point news items gleaned from all parts of *Billboard* magazine by Dave McAleer. Bill and TC combined again for a feature on assorted fragments of the Drifters, derived from conversations with original Drifter Bill Pinckney, and Mick Brown contributed a vintage oldie record review headed 'Dustie Musties', the first and only appearance of this column!

The recent tour by Garnet Mimms provided more material for Bill, with a live review and artist interview, while Dave McAleer added a short article on Muscle Shoals music headlined 'Piney Woods Sound', which would have been quite at home in his *Fame/Goldwax Followers* fanzine, and Jon Philibert's track by track review of the first and short-lived debut LP on Smash Records by James Brown, titled after his 'Out of Sight' hit 45. Given the situation regarding Brown's attempted move from King to Smash and the lawsuits that followed, the LP was and is a collectors' item – though some tracks later appeared on the *Cold Sweat* LP which marked James' return to King. It was quite a scoop for Jon to include his review.

Next came a landmark feature *of Soul Music* magazine, the first instalment of the serialisation of 'Sound of the City'. In the preface, Tony Cummings explained that author 'Charles' Gillett was a graduate of Teacher's College at New York's Columbia University, and this work was part of his master's thesis. As Charles (or Charlie, as he became globally known) later explained, having Tony publish his thesis meant that he could submit it to a major publisher, and it was accepted by Outerbridge & Dienstfrey in New York. First published in paperback format in 1970, it has been revised and updated in hardback and paperback in the US and UK over the years, and has become a standard school textbook in the fields of music and sociology.

Another landmark came in the first proper attempt to create a session discography of the Drifters. It is worth explaining that the word discography has served to describe various styles of record listings. One is a basic listing of label, date of issue, catalogue number and titles for any given artist/group/band; another is a chronological listing of all recordings issued on a particular label; and a third is the more detailed session discography, which lists not only catalogue numbers and titles but also the probable recording date, location and musicians involved, plus the master/matrix number assigned to the recording. In recent years the trend for layered, over-dubbed and multi-tracked recording has tended to dilute the value of session information: if the vocals were recorded in New York, the background singers in LA, the rhythm section in New Orleans and the horns in Memphis, session information is rendered irrelevant. In previous decades, though, such information was of immense interest and value to music fans, and provided an important insight into musical history, style and tradition. As we met and interviewed visiting American singers and musicians during the '60s, we found that many had good memories and could recall plentiful information about their sessions – which were, of course, mainly live. Hence 'The Drifters – part one', which filled two pages of *Soul Music* 1 with session details from the combined research of Kurt Mohr, discographer supreme with files extending into the realms of jazz and blues, Peter Gibbon, a big fan of and expert on the group, and Bill Millar and Tony Cummings, who had recently interviewed Bill Pinckney and gleaned some useful personnel details.

A profile on Gladys Knight & the Pips was contributed by Jon Philibert, written shortly after the group had signed with Motown and giving a good perspective on their rise from church origins in Atlanta, Georgia, to the Hot 100 via New York productions by Bobby Robinson (Fury) and Larry Maxwell (Maxx). A full-page photo of Aaron Neville was 'dressed' to look like a paid ad from Parlo Records, and was followed by three pages listing new US single releases. TC provided a short biographic feature on Date femme trio the Glories, complete with a full-page photo, while the doo-wop heritage of soul vocal groups was acknowledged with a cameo profile of the Cardinals, prolific on Atlantic in the early '50s, which included an outline discography but no personnel information, this from Art Ardolino in New York and headlined 'From The Top Shelf'. The feature was significant as most of us on the editorial team were doo-wop fans but at that time there was no written coverage of the music: epic vocal-group fanzines like *Record Exchanger*, *Bim Bam Boom* and *Yesterday's Memories* were still a couple of years away. A page of gospel singles reviews on Jewel Records indicated that someone (there was no by-line credit) had bought some discs by mail-order from Stan Lewis's record store in Shreveport, Louisiana.

This first issue drew to a close with an interesting two-page essay backgrounding the history of the renowned Apollo Theatre in Harlem, a track-by-track review of James Carr's Goldwax LP

You Got My Mind Messed Up, presumably by house Goldwax expert Dave McAleer, then five pages of reviews of US and UK soul singles – including the sole contribution in the mag by yours truly, the UK issue of Homer Banks's 'Hooked By Love'/'Lady of Stone' – interspersed with photos of James Carr and Chris Bartley completing the thirty-six pages.

With a cover price of *2s 6d*, the idea of *Soul Music* was not to compete with *Blues & Soul* as such, but to provide a more erudite, scholarly and detailed alternative, the contents being derived from the co-operative of committed soul fans. Unfortunately, however, as is often the case, there was a disparity between economics and ideology, and in the short term economics won. There were also, it seems, some credibility gaps in our sales expectations, in that the subscription list for the new magazine was thought to need a print-run of 2,000 copies, but it was actually far less than that. Despite a promotion campaign, which included ads in *Billboard*, the magazine didn't sell enough copies to cover the printing costs, and under other circumstances that would have been that.

Tony Cummings was (and is) a man of immense principle, and the next step in his crusade was a phone call to me, in which he asked if I would be interested in becoming more actively involved in the fanzine world. I was positive, so we got together and worked out a plan to continue publishing *Soul Music*, even if it meant taking a massive reality check and a couple of steps back – reverting to typing copy onto wax stencils, buying numerous reams of suitable paper and begging the use of a rotary duplicating machine. As luck would have it, Jon Philibert's father ran a small business from the family home, a terraced house in Crystal Palace, and we were able to use his duplicator to print off the stencils, which were then carried back to my house in Chislehurst – the new editorial address – in an executive carrier-bag, ready for the laborious task of collating and stapling.

Thus, after a gap of some six months, issue two *of Soul Music* appeared, in a format which doubtless came as a surprise to subscribers. TC's editorial explained in detail the problems of economics, which had led to a thirty-six-page litho magazine metamorphosing into twenty-two pages of fairly primitive fare. Disenchanted with the modest response to and sales of the first issue, three of the original editorial quartet decided to look for a more viable approach and planned a new alternative venture to be called *Soul Express*, while Tony continued to fly the specialist flag, with my assistance. *Soul Music* now carried a qualifying strapline on the front cover: 'A comprehensive journal covering the vast field of Negro rhythm and blues music'. The cover date was January 1968, and the contents were listed as 'Documentation on' Otis Redding, Clyde McPhatter, the Velours, Cash McCall, Drifters, Cadets and Invitations. One key element in the editorial was the target to produce the magazine on a weekly basis!

I won't go into page-by-page detail of the contents of *Soul Music* 2, but the material published leaned heavily on the contributions of Bill Millar, with a four-page critical biography of Clyde McPhatter, ditto on the Velours and the Invitations. The serialisation of Charlie Gillett's thesis continued on three pages, another three contained an appraisal of the recordings of Otis Redding (tragically killed in a plane crash in the preceding month), put in perspective by Tony, who was not blind (deaf?) to the drop in quality of Redding's later material, and not afraid to publish such sacrilegious opinion. Kurt Mohr's invaluable contributions continued with session discographies of the Drifters (part two) and the Cadets/Jacks as a supplement to a short biography by Art Ardolino. My first editorial contribution was a biography of Chicago soul man Cash (Maurice Dollison) McCall, along with the majority of the record reviews, but a notable inclusion was a Velours interview. I made reference earlier to the 'fake groups' scenario that was alleged to have been perpetrated by promoter Roy Tempest, and the Velours were a major factor in this. We (the *Soul Music* editorial team) went to see the 'Fabulous Temptations', as they were billed, and in a journalistic style befitting tabloid reporters decades later followed the group back to their dressing room and asked if we could have a quick chat about their music as we'd enjoyed their act. The group members had nothing to hide, and were candid and informative about their personal backgrounds and musical careers. The Fabulous

Temptations, far from being any fraudulent Motown outfit, actually turned out to be classic doo-wop group the Velours, enjoying an expenses-paid trip to England. We interviewed the guys at some length – the first music journalists to do so, before the emergence of the American doo-wop specialist fanzines mentioned earlier – and noted their names as Don Heywood, John Cheatom, Jerome 'Romeo' Ramos and Richard Pitts (later to record solo as Ritchie Pitts and most recently touring as a member of the Invitations). They were making the most of their journey, so much so that they soon signed a UK record deal, with a new identity as the Fantastics (borrowing a Tempest prefix) and going on to score several chart hits. This was the first of several such groups to be seen and interviewed by us as soul fans/fanzine journalists, and future issues of the magazine revealed some very interesting backgrounds.

The next few issues of this adventurous and pathfinding magazine appeared on a (roughly) weekly basis, as promised, and gathered together a succession of session discographies on fairly obscure soul artists and doo-wop groups, biographical critiques on some major figures in the world of R&B and soul (the Platters, Freddie King and Lloyd Price were past their record-selling prime, but still worthy of enthusiastic appraisals of their careers), regular lists of new US soul 45s gleaned from the columns of *Billboard* and bullet-point news jottings from the same source, equally regular extracts from Charlie Gillett's thesis, and record reviews of singles either bought from under-counter boxes at the few London shops brave enough to deal in imports or blagged from label managers at sympathetic London record companies (Alan Warner and Trevor Churchill, both at EMI and both enthusiastic soul fans, to name just two). This was way before the magazine had achieved enough recognition or respectability to be serviced by any press offices. Pleas for physical help in producing the magazine were frequent but fell on deaf ears, so we soldiered on.

By the sixth issue TC had found the key to the photocopier room at Chappell's, the Bond Street music publisher where he worked in the copyright department, which resulted in a photo on the cover and a slight production problem: the smooth copier paper slipped in the duplicator and page two printed at an odd angle! As a mark of progress, however, it was easier to type text in odd positions on plain paper, mounted around the chosen illustration, resulting in adventurous vertical captions which had been impossible on the wax stencils. Another new skill was developed because we had to select a good half-tone (black and white) photo for the cover. Given the limitations of '60s photocopiers, it was vital to have plenty of black-white contrast to avoid the photocopy becoming a washed-out mass of grey.

Issue six contained news that the *Soul Express* project had been aborted, and our fellow soul fans returned to the editorial meetings at Tony's bedsit. Around this time we pooled our finances and sent an order to a New York warehouse, Apex Rendezvous, for a box of '1000 soul oldies', and eagerly awaited the arrival of the shipment. There was excitement and anticipation as we opened the carton and sorted the discs, and some disappointment as we unpacked multiple copies of obscure flops. There was one treasure to emerge, however, in thirty-five copies of 'Black Widow Spider' by Damon Fox on Crimson Records from Philadelphia, arranged by Thom Bell and produced by Billy Jackson. This doomy, intense soul-blues wailer grabbed our communal ear such that we all kept a copy, then decided to ask Soul City Records to take the remaining thirty copies to sell as a new import, which they did – helping us to recover some of our outlay!

But I digress. Other news in the editorial of this issue was the release of *Bell's Cellar of Soul* from EMI on their new launch of the renowned US logo, co-ordinated by label manager and soul fan Trevor Churchill. It was handy having an acquaintance and kindred spirit on the inside at a major label, and Trevor proved to be an invaluable source of review records and publicity photos. This and the next few issues continued to publish a mixture of session discographies, extensive news jottings, artist appraisals and record reviews, until issue 8 arrived on 9 March 1968 with a notable addition to the roster of contributors. Dave Godin was already a regular columnist for *Blues & Soul*, but editor John Abbey declined to publish his contribution 'R&B and The Long Hot Summer' on the basis that it might cause offence to readers of the large-circulation journal. Tony, however, saw it as a reasonable item of free speech with which to balance the soul music staple diet of rather dry discographies and in-depth interviews. In the two-thousand word piece Dave questioned the sociological aspect of collecting black music, and whether those of us who bought soul records gave any thought to the prejudices endured by the performers in their homeland and to aspects of integration and emancipation in America. I'm not sure that many of us saw ourselves as politically liberal in this respect, but just enjoyed great music. Dave Godin wanted us to be more aware, and *Soul Music* magazine was the vehicle that published his thoughts.

The touring season was upon us, and the editorial team was gainfully employed in tracking down and doing dressing-room interviews with the Showstoppers, a young trio from Philadelphia who were in the pop charts with a fairly primitive but energetic number 'Ain't Nothing But a Houseparty' on Beacon Records, a small London-based independent label for which soul journalist Roger St Pierre handled publicity, and the Fabulous Platters, a fake group which turned out to have recorded as the Steinways in their homeland. With Roger as PR man, I arranged to interview the Showstoppers through official channels, and talked to the guys backstage at the Black Prince in Bexley – but they were as inexperienced at answering questions as I was in asking them. The result was rather minimalist, but managed to capture all salient points! A week later came further revelations, and a significant factor in the magazine's role in investigative soul journalism, when we interviewed the group touring as the Fabulous Platters but with a fine pedigree back in the States as the Laddins and sometimes the Steinways, led by one Mickey Goody, whose vocal group history rivalled that of some Drifters (he'd grown up with the guys who formed the Five Crowns), and including James (Jimmy) Cherry, who went on to a UK solo career.

Following an interesting doo-wop group masquerading as megastars came an encounter with major talent when the 18 May 1968 issue was billed as a 'Bumper Ike & Tina Issue'. While it was not possible to make contact with the stars themselves (that would come in later years), Bill Millar did some sterling work in not only reviewing the Turners' gig at Streatham Locarno but also grabbing running interviews with Jimmy Thomas, singer with the Revue, and six members of the band. The rest of the magazine was devoted to a full session discography of Ike Turner's Band from the combined files of Kurt Mohr and Ray Topping. No rest for the wicked – and the next weekly issue of *Soul Music* included reviews of yet more touring soul stars, Aretha Franklin and J.J. Jackson. While Aretha was beyond the reach of fanzines at that time, TC completed a fine biographic interview with the rotund Jackson in a tiny room backstage at the Brixton Ram Jam Club. Robert Knight, touring with Aretha, was then given the Millar interview/interrogation treatment. Lou Rawls performed at the Royal Albert Hall with Ted Heath's Band, and his interview was published the following week!

Into June, and tours by Bell label-mates James and Bobby Purify and Oscar Toney Jr yielded further extensive interviews, while the tragic death of the great Little Willie John was chronicled: he had died in prison at Washington State Penitentiary on 26 June 1968. Pens, notepads and portable cassette recorders were kept busy with tours and interviews of Ruby & the Romantics and the Diplomats, though the latter were 'uncovered' during a now-routine *Soul Music* interview with the group being billed as 'the Fabulous Isley Brothers'. In a now legendary tale, the guys revealed that when they saw posters advertising the Isley Brothers at a venue in Nottingham they scoured the building searching for Ronald, Rudolph and O'Kelly before being made aware of the reality of their situation. The Topics were next on the list of 'discoveries', following Bill Millar's interview with three guys touring as the 'Fabulous Impressions'. Then we had the pleasure of seeing Garnet Mimms on stage as a very able substitute for the Crystals.

Cover photos for the magazine were a good reflection of which companies were helping us with records to review: Don Covay (Atlantic, through my connections in running his UK fan club), the Kelly Brothers (Excello via President) and Sari & the Shalamars (United Artists) graced consecutive issues, while the contents included the continued serialisation of Charlie Gillett's thesis, discographies of the famous and obscure, labels lists running to just a few lines or several pages, some 'borrowed' feature articles and various biographic appraisals of doo-wop groups. Sadly there were also more obituaries, with the sad death of Joe Hinton on 13 August 1968 duly noted. By the end of September it had become apparent that the weekly schedule was a bit ambitious, so amid reviews of William Bell, Ray Charles and Billy Preston came the announcement of fortnightly publication with issue 33, followed by even more dramatic changes from issue 34.

As I recall, one major factor in the magazine changing title from *Soul Music* to *Shout* was an article in *Record Mirror* about pop singer Cliff Richard. It was headlined 'My Kind of Soul' – this at a time when so many beat groups were spending hours of studio time recording cover versions of US R&B and soul hits.

Songs like 'Go Now', 'One Way Love', 'Sweets for my Sweet', 'Twist and Shout' and 'Come On' were to be heard frequently on the radio, but only thirty years later was it likely to be Bessie Banks, the Drifters, the Isley Brothers or Chuck Berry singing: in the mid-'60s cover-versions ruled. For all his merits in the field of entertainment, it was not our wish to be associated with Cliff Richard, so an editorial meeting was convened and the decision was taken to use a title that identified with the style and passion of soul music rather than sticking with the misused genre name. Legend has it that we were all asked to name our all-time favourite R&B track, and Tony's choice of the Isleys' 'Shout' won the election by a distance. Along with the change of title came a change of front cover quality, now litho-printed on glossy paper; Joe Simon graced issue 34. We actually printed covers for eight issues in the first batch, omitting credit captions, dates and issue-numbers so we could decide later on which cover to use with which issue, simply adding necessary details to the editorial page. It made the magazine look better, but proved to be confusing when filing them!

The Joe Simon cover was in honour of his UK appearance, and courtesy of his road manager (Willie Leiser) we had a short interview to run in issue 35. Chris Bartley did a short tour with manager Bill Downs, to be interviewed by Bill Millar in issue 36, and Inez & Charlie Foxx featured strongly in issue 37 with live show reviews, biography and full session discography.

Subsequent issues featured Bobby Parker, Bobby Byrd, William Bell and mention of a tie-in with the Flamingo Club in Wardour Street. Also mentioned was the launch of the laudable Rhythm & Blues Association of Great Britain. This was founded in January 1969 with an organising council comprising Mike Raven and Stuart Henry (Radio 1 DJs), Dave Godin (*Blues & Soul*/Soul City), Trevor Churchill (Bell Records), John Abbey, fellow specialist journalists Roger St Pierre and Norman Jopling, plus Tony Cummings and me from the *Shout* editorial staff. The idea was to bring together all factions of the UK soul following to form a unified body to support and promote the music. There was a first annual poll to recognise commercial and artistic contributions, and I recall an inaugural dance at Ilford Palais, but despite being advertised and promoted in all the right places the association floundered and died quite quickly. Perhaps this was because of the difficulty in gathering any more than two people for meetings, or perhaps because the UK soul world has existed relatively happily through the decades despite or because of the varied factions involved, fighting a common cause from different and diverse directions.

Back to the magazine: there were now three consecutive issues of major consequence. February 1969 brought a telephone call from Jeffrey S. Kruger, owner of Ember Records (UK) and of the Flamingo Club in Wardour Street in London's West End. As *Shout* (and *Soul Music* before it) had been giving keen support to soul and R&B records released on Ember, and was also giving enthusiastic support to touring US soul artists, he asked if we would like to co-promote a season of soul nights at the club, now rebranded as the Pink Flamingo, in an attempt to soften the image for the new generation of mod soul fans.

We were invited to a meeting with Mr Kruger at his Knightsbridge office suite, and presented with an enviable roster of stars booked to tour during the year. Our part of the deal was to promote these one-nighters with magazine editorials and advertising flyers, and to attend the club every Friday night from March to July, either to promote and introduce the performers or to run a *Shout* Disc Show soul disco on the nights without live shows. The roster of artists included the Fabulous Platters/Steinways, Garnet Mimms, Mary Wells, Howlin' Wolf, Otis Rush, Inez & Charlie Foxx, Freddie King and Solomon Burke. We said we'd be happy to do our bit, and were delighted to see these promoted in the press as 'The Pink Flamingo and *Shout* magazine proudly present . . .'.

This arrangement was publicised in *Shout* 42, and issue 43 appeared with the usual mixture of editorial content, record reviews and new jottings. Issue 44 came two months later, with a cover photo of the Watts 103rd Street Rhythm Band, and a further major change with the departure of Tony Cummings. Taking his place in the editor's chair was . . . Clive Richardson. Tony went off to live a more normal life, and likewise Charlie Gillett's name disappeared from the editorial page: he had been commissioned to write a weekly column for *Record Mirror*, which was to lead him into other journalism and media, starting with *Let It Rock* magazine and the noted *Honky Tonk* radio show on BBC Radio London. So began the new era of *Shout*.

Having total control of the magazine made things a bit easier regarding the logistics, if more time-consuming in production – and writing. Given the fairly primitive mechanics of wax stencils and duplicating machines there were no problems with layout. Filling the twelve pages was simply a matter of copy-typing the various record and concert reviews, interviews and discographies, though the latter was fraught with complexities because of the format, abbreviations, master numbers, disc numbers and the like. All of this was fronted by an editorial page and the front cover, which remained single-sided for several years because of the physical problems of running art or photocopy paper through the duplicator.

By this time I had bought a duplicating machine, and had moved the production office from the spare room in the Philibert household at Crystal Palace to my own bedroom in Chislehurst. The duplicator rested on the floor of my wardrobe when not churning out pages of the magazine, and my bedspread became the collating bench and stapling table.

The circulation and subscription list was small. I don't think the paid subscriptions ever went above 200, and distributed shop sales were a couple of dozen, courtesy of Dobell's record shop in Charing Cross Road: the print-run was a fairly constant 250. I don't think these figures ever reached the public domain: nobody made any enquiries so we never volunteered any figures. I suppose it really didn't matter: after all, a review of a record that is read by 200 dedicated fans is likely to generate as many sales as a review amid a sea of general releases. The support we received from record companies was through specialist personal contacts rather than through corporate press offices. Trevor Churchill was 'on the inside' at EMI, handling Bell product including samples of US releases as well as co-ordinating UK releases like the *Bell Cellar of Soul* LP series, and a colleague of his was Alan Warner, handling ABC and Stateside product before he moved on to Liberty/United Artists, and it was through these channels that compilation LPs like *Sweet Soul Sounds* and others containing tracks from ABC, Tangerine and Modern Records were generated. Alan went on to co-ordinate the *Many Sides of Rock 'n' Roll* multi-LP series on UA, a precursor of Ace's Golden *Age of American Rock 'n' Roll* CD series, before moving to the USA and cementing a reputation as a movie historian and music consultant on numerous reissue projects.

Also giving active support to the magazine and its crusade were Jeffrey Kruger, heading Ember Records as previously mentioned, and David Kassner (son of label owner Edward, who had the good business acumen to be publisher of the song 'Rock Around The Clock', the mechanical royalties from which reaped rich reward) at President Records, who were then licensing material from Vee Jay, the Leaner Brothers' One-der-Ful/Mar-v-Lus combine in Chicago, and Bronco Records from Hollywood, which launched the fledgling Barry White and also scored UK chart success with Felice Taylor. We gained active and advertising support from Phonogram Records, more specifically label managers Nigel Grainge (who was assisted in repertoire selection by James Hamilton) and Leon Campadelli, for whom I wrote more liner notes for Platters' reissue LPs than I care to remember.

Though the volume of subscription sales for *Shout* may have been modest, the readers were a faithful bunch and also globally quite widespread, with the magazine being sent to the USA, Australia, Japan, Holland, Germany, Switzerland, France and Scandinavia. The sophisticated subscription system comprised hand-written index cards, and the mailing was done in cheap manila envelopes for which the addresses were handwritten for every issue – no multi-label sheets from PC printers in those days. Shop sales were handled by me – copies to Dobell's in a large envelope, delivered during my regular Saturday morning record-hunting/junk-shopping trips.

Back to the editorial side of the magazine. For a while we attempted to list all UK soul releases, which proved to be a double-edged sword. As the popularity of soul music grew in this country, so did the quantity (if not always the quality) of singles and LPs released – so that issue 45 contained 50 per cent record reviews along with the Johnny Ace and Bettye LaVette discographies and a page of news jottings from *Billboard*. By good fortune, around this time Jacques Perin, a *Shout* subscriber living in the Paris suburb of Levallois-Perret, launched a French equivalent entitled *Soul Bag*, using Paris-domiciled Kurt Mohr for discographical material, a network of local soul fans for editorial material and good photo-files. Jacques published his intention to provide a comprehensive list of all new US soul singles, which helped me to make the decision to restrict review coverage in *Shout* to discs actually received.

Then came *Shout* 46, featuring the newly discovered Patti Austin, whose amazing debut UA single 'Family Tree' had been sent to me by Alan Warner to review along with a short biography and a session discography by Kurt Mohr, and a debut contribution by Bob Fisher of the Leicester Blues Society, reviewing a Lowell Fulsom gig. This was the first step in a career in the music industry which has taken him to many and varied executive positions and labels. The next issue brought blues authority Alan Balfour into the fold, reviewing Paul Oliver's combined book and double LP opus *The Story of the Blues*, while the tragic death of Roy Hamilton prompted Bill Millar to write a biographic appreciation. September 1969 saw Wilson Pickett in town, supported by Erma Franklin, and the concert review suggests that soul had become somewhat self-parodic, with both performers more interested in getting the audience to sing along than in entertaining those who had paid to watch and listen. The magazine reached a landmark issue 50 in December 1969, Bill Millar contributing a lengthy review of the Johnny Otis biography *Listen to the Lambs*, while American subscriber Lynn McCutcheon provided an overview of the Dells, augmented by Kurt Mohr's full session discography. Lynn was an East Coast college graduate, and his musicology pedigree was also enhanced by his book *Rhythm and Blues*, offering a sociological background to the doo-wop music style.

Blues & Soul

The contents of the first few issues of *Home of the Blues* give a good indication that John Abbey was a man of many talents, tastes and contacts. There were numerous tours by soul and R&B artists at that time, partly because of the legendary *Ready Steady Go* TV show which was broadcast by ITV every Friday evening from 1963 until its demise in 1966, and for which producer Vicky Wickham booked a host of R&B talent to do short live sets. There was a thriving circuit of music clubs – I'm not sure if they would be accurately described as discotheques at the time – which featured knowledgeable disc jockeys who were also keen record collectors and played a mixture of soul, R&B and blues dance records, and also booked live acts to perform on often tiny stages. Central London had several such clubs, including the renowned Flamingo, the upstairs Whisky-a-Go-Go and Tiles in a Oxford Street basement. John Abbey seems to have been a regular visitor to these, including reviews of the Drifters, John Lee Hooker, Sugar Pie DeSanto, Lee Dorsey, Alvin Robinson, Patti LaBelle & Blue-Belles – and that was just in issue 2! Other issues included Don Covay, Ben E. King, Roy C, Jimmy Reed, the Orlons, Billy Stewart and Rufus Thomas, and John also managed to get short interviews with many of these, while also indicating his other love, for country music, with reviews of Johnny Cash and Jerry Lee Lewis concerts and some country 45s.

John was also a globe-trotting music fan. I seem to recall that he worked as a travel agent at that time, which might have explained an editorial comment in *Home of the Blues* 5 stating that he would be in the USA for three weeks. He clearly put the trip to good use, as the November (no. 6) issue of the magazine included features on the Five Stairsteps, Percy Sledge, Bobby Powell, Bobby Hebb and Linda Carr, following a visit to their show at the Harlem Apollo. His US contacts also provided a regular source of review copies of new soul releases, and John provided a (for the time) comprehensive list of new releases and a Top 50 chart. He was also keen to promote all avenues of soul fandom in the UK, and published regular lists of fan clubs for soul artists, most of which also published small-scale newsletters and magazines.

March 1967 brought a striking change to the magazine. The physical appearance changed, as mentioned above, with the whole thing printed on glossy art paper, a colour photo on the cover and a masthead on page one revealing a team of publishing assistants and, more significantly, the legend 'Published monthly by CONTEMPO PUBLICATIONS'. Full page ads from EMI might be a clue regarding the capital investment in the magazine, though the contents were not tied to EMI releases. There was a feature on Prince Harold, then hot with new Mercury 45 'Forget About Me', a discography of the Corsairs, concert reviews of Little Richard, Alvin Cash and the Soul Sisters, and a page of news snippets called 'Dust My Blues'. Issue 9 of April 1967 went on to devote three pages to lists of favourite artists and records from 'Poll '66'. Fifty male artists are listed, from Otis Redding, Wilson Pickett and James Brown in the top three to Muddy Waters, Brook Benton, Chuck Jackson and Roy Head at the foot of the list, though there are only ten female singers (Irma Thomas, Carla Thomas and Dionne Warwick just a whisker ahead of Gladys Knight, Brenda Holloway and Baby Washington), twenty groups and ten instrumentalists. There were reviews of live shows by the Four Tops, Chuck Berry and Inez & Charlie Foxx, a feature on Gene Chandler, full-page photos of Chandler and James Carr, a double page review feature of Pye Records' Blues & Soul marketing promotion, a host of reviews of US 45s, and adverts from UK R&B independents President and Ember, together with US Stax.

Perhaps the most significant contents were a full-page advert for Soul City, the landmark record shop opened in Deptford, south-east London, by Dave Godin, David Nathan and Rob Blackmore, which was to become a legend in its short lifetime. The shop contributed Top 20 R&B singles (UK releases) and LPs (mixed imports and UK issues) together with a US Top 50 singles chart. There were some wonderfully eclectic entries in the Soul City lists: you had to wonder how many copies of Aretha Franklin's CBS LP *Soul Sister* sold when her Atlantic debut *I Never Loved a Man* sat atop the US Top 50, and whether the inclusion of Esther Phillips's *Country Side of* and Ketty Lester *When A Woman Loves a Man* were testimony to David Nathan's predilection for the soul divas. In any event, the charts provided plentiful targets for our spending money, and in the era of Soul City there was an accessible source for buying these gems.

Home of the Blues 10 was a strange creature, promoting its coverage of the Stax Revue in England and carrying a whole-page statement (in idiosyncratic grammar) from Polydor label manager Frank Fenter lauding this coverage, then running just short biographies of the stars and musicians involved but not including a review of the Revue, though there are feature reviews of Bo Diddley, Ben E. King, Fats Domino and the Soul Sisters. Charts and record reviews flesh out the magazine. *Home of the Blues* 11 takes the contents into a wider realm, with articles about Mabel John, Jimmy Holiday and Brenda Holloway and review features on Garnet Mimms and Clyde McPhatter. A significant new addition was the first Dave Godin column, entitled 'Girls with soul are the greatest', and while this was not a regular feature to start with, Dave's contributions to John's magazine were to become legendary in the annals of soul journalism.

The new era was born in October 1967, when *Blues & Soul Monthly Music Review* 1 appeared, the cover graced by a sepia-tinted, close-up photo of John Lee Hooker (perhaps to give credence to the blues element of the title, as the blues content has always been minimal). The only mention of Hooker in the magazine was (perhaps accidentally) a miniature photo of his then-new ABC/Bluesway LP *Live at the Café a go-go* in the back page ad from EMI, though to be fair Little Milton and B.B. King did feature. Critical biographies of Sam & Bill, the Isley Brothers and Aretha Franklin took pride of place, then there was a ska column from Island Records director David Betteridge, perhaps a reflection of the Mod predilection for Jamaican music as well as soul, 'welcome' ads from President, Polydor/Atlantic, Speciality/Ember and Sue/Island, which also hints at the source of funding of the new-style journal. Charts and reviews of UK LPs and UK and import 45s completed the contents, the UK 45s actually given star ratings. The editorial spent a few paragraphs explaining the history and background of the magazine and the reason for the name-change: 'We felt a little restricted using "Home of the Blues". The new title, although perhaps a little less personal, is without doubt more acceptable to the public in general.' While few fans at the time had any problem with the change of name, the question was and remains these forty years later why the new name wasn't *Soul & Blues*, given the style of the content, general editorial policy and change of public taste in music following the rise of Motown and Stax. Perhaps it was because B was nearer the beginning of the alphabet and thus towards the top of the distributor's stocklist!

Most of the editorial content up to this point had been written by John Abbey, with an occasional contribution by Peter Trickey, but *Blues & Soul* 2 announced the arrival of one Derek Lawrence to the editorial team, which also listed David R. Ryan, Art Director Thomas W. Baum and promotions man Brian Saunders. I didn't (and still don't) know anything about Mr Lawrence, but a helpful panel in the magazine listed his achievements as producer of London-recorded tracks by Garnet Mimms and a couple of local Brit-soul bands for EMI labels, which serves to support thoughts of EMI funding for the magazine. That *Blues & Soul* 2 and many subsequent issues carried features on artists on Bell and Stateside, and review features on many Bell and EMI group singles, gives a nod in a similar direction.

Aside from the editorial contents, another key factor advertised in *Blues & Soul* 2 was the relocation of Soul City from the depths of south-east London to the West End, and a good location at 17 Monmouth Street, WC2 (multi-digit postcodes were still years in the future), just a short walk from Charing Cross Road and Soho, music focal points at the time.

Blues & Soul continued to meet its monthly schedule, the pages filled with the usual range of features, show and record reviews, together with some fine full-page black and white photos, contributions from Bob Peacock, Roger St Pierre and Charles Yeats, and from Soul City co-owners David Nathan, Rob Blackmore and, from May 1968 in issue 8, the *Blues & Soul* debut of the periodic Dave Godin Column, in which Dave managed successfully to combine his views on music, politics, sociology and philosophy in a way that helped to enrich the reader's mind. The July issue (no. 10) focused on the sharp practice discussed in detail above, in which American black vocal groups were backed for UK tours as, for example, the 'Original' Drifters, the 'Fantastic' Temptations, 'Ruby & the Romantics', the 'Fabulous' Isley Brothers and the 'Fabulous' Platters. 'Fraud' was the editorial headline as *Blues & Soul* exposed this practice, and to make its readers aware of the duplicity involved. While this activity was not in breach of the law, it was recommended that readers approach such gigs 'with an open mind'.

Changes and developments were afoot by September when the magazine announced an imminent relocation from its historic home in John's Edmonton flat to 'more spacious premises outside London', and also published an advertorial regarding the launch of the Action label from B&C (Beat & Commercial) Records in north-west London. The item states that '"Blues & Soul" will be kept well in the picture with things at Action', which was not surprising as the same man was running both!

The new address in suburban Bishops Stortford was published in the next issue, along with John's statement of his involvement in Action, and a half-page ad for the first batch of releases, some eight singles mainly sourced from Duke/Peacock Records – a brave venture! Next came the first LP releases from Action: Fantastic Johnny C, Barbara Mason and Brenda & the Tabulations, again quite eclectic and far from guaranteed sellers, and the start of *Blues & Soul*'s only venture into session discography: Peter Burns joined the editorial panel to contribute the Curtis Mayfield story and the Impressions discography, to be followed by a likewise in-depth appraisal on the Drifters.

The year-end credits and acknowledgements in December's *Blues & Soul* 15 made interesting reading, as along with thanks to regular contributors and a host of record company press officers and label managers (including Trevor Churchill, Andrew Lauder and Alan Warner from EMI) is the name of Bob Killbourn. Though this meant little at the time, the significance increased greatly when John Abbey opted to move to the USA in 1971, following the chart success of Tami Lynn, his wife at the time, with 'I'm Gonna Run Away From You'. He left the editor's chair to Bob, who remained editor until July 2007; he is now consultant editor for the online music magazine *Black Sheep*. March 1969 saw the start of another brave venture when Roy Simonds joined the editorial panel to team up with Peter Burns in launching 'Disc Info USA', an in-depth research column transferred from *Record Mirror* to provide a specialist discographical service to a dedicated soul readership. A question regarding different takes of an Elmore James song being used on a UK LP and a US Chess 45 give an indication of the detail discussed in this forum, which was to run for the next year as the audience for soul music grew larger and the readership of *Blues & Soul* blossomed.

If the previous year-end editorial was notable, that for December 1969 was more so. *Blues & Soul* was to double its output and publish fortnightly from Friday 2 January 1970, and to add to the impact of this announcement page 18 was dedicated to providing a further insight into what was coming. The headline news was the launch of the Contempo Record Club, offering a mail-order service 'at no extra cost' to supply UK and US releases, the inception of the *Blues & Soul* R&B chart, compiled from records 'selling in R&B areas', and the launch of 'What's Happening Stateside' as a full news service and new release listing. Other features were to remain from the 'old' *Blues & Soul*, including a periodic 'Disc Info USA' and the ska section as a four-page supplement. Thus the magazine continued to progress, as it has done through the subsequent decades, even if the musical content and consequent terminology is a universe removed from those early years.

The physical style of *Blues & Soul* changed from glossy art paper to more cost-effective newsprint; the front covers were very colourful and the contents remained soulful, though the quality of illustrations dropped somewhat. But the market was clearly growing, which was good for us all. During the early '70s the offices of Contempo moved to the West End, occupying the first floor of offices above a shop in Hanway Street, which runs in an arc linking Oxford Street to Tottenham Court Road. They were open to readers for record sales – the small front office would get quite crowded on Saturday mornings. *Blues & Soul* 63, of 9 July 1971, carried a half-page map of Contempo's location, and a full-page advertorial inside the back cover detailed the cost of new UK and US 45s and LPs. It also promoted an offer of '10 different R&B singles on US labels for £1.00', along with a discounted volume bargain of '50 singles for £4.00', and this offer was soon extended to 100 soul 45s for £10. These so-called soul packs were a random batch of 100 imports, cut-outs and deletions sourced from major wholesalers. They were also available from numerous mail-order suppliers, often post-free, and were invaluable for building collections. In any batch of 100 there were usually a handful of oldies (Oldies 45 from Vee Jay and Flashback from Bell/Fire/Fury among others), off-the-charts hits, obscure gems by unknown artists, a couple of duplications, a few discs which were musically rubbish but on pretty, interesting or colourful labels, and one or two items which had been broken in transit, but for a net cost of 10p per disc it was unbeatable value for money. A smaller supply of deleted LPs trickled into the country and filtered into dump-bins in major stores, market stalls and some High Street general stores. These cut-outs were denoted by drilling through the label of 45s and drilling or clipping the corner of LP sleeves – so that US dealers couldn't return them to distributors for full credit. I mention this as younger record-buyers, who may not have encountered much vinyl in recent years, are now asking why some vinyl is drilled or clipped!

Soul City

There is a certain irony in that many of the singles that turned up as cut-outs in soul packs would have been the staple diet of visitors to the Soul City record shop a couple of years before. Soul City opened in Deptford High Street in a heavily multicultural area of south-east London in the late summer of 1966, and my first memory of the shop is buying two notable singles on the day of their UK release: Lorraine Ellison's 'Stay With Me' on Warner and Prince Harold's 'Forget About Me' on Mercury. I made regular journeys to the shop in the ensuing months, collecting catalogues and records alike while chatting with Dave Godin and David Nathan – though I never really knew the third partner, Rob Blackmore. The shop out-grew Deptford and moved to Monmouth Street in Central London in late 1967, where they launched the Soul City record label (distributed through Island Records), on which the first release appeared in March 1968: Don Gardner and Dee Dee Ford's 'Don't You Worry'/'I'm Coming Home To Stay', originating from Bobby Robinson's New York-based Fury Records and licensed from EMI. SC 102 was to change things a bit, however – Dave Godin licensed the 1965 Constellation single 'Nothing Can Stop Me'/'The Big Lie' by Gene Chandler, which had been a modest-selling single on Stateside Records, from EMI. DJ Tony Blackburn had the breakfast show on the recently launched BBC Radio 1 (of which more shortly) and began to play the new Soul City 45. The record became a major UK chart hit, and the financial rewards gave the label a solid foundation on which to build a catalogue of singles and some LPs.

The Soul City singles catalogue was a patchwork quilt of big names (for the soul world) and unknowns – great and otherwise. If Sylvia and Chuck Edwards were eclectic figures, the Valentinos and Billy Preston had enviable pedigrees, while though the song 'Go Now' was well known as a pop hit (the Moody Blues), the Bessie Banks original on Tiger and Blue Cat was an underground favourite which enjoyed considerable demand – and nowadays commands more exposure than the hit cover version. Shirley Lawson and Thelma Jones's names hardly raised an eyebrow (the latter went on to enjoy more success on Columbia in the '70s), and Chris Jackson was a young prodigy of Van McCoy who was being eased onto the UK market before being launched in his homeland, but further licence deals with CBS (OKeh and Epic) and EMI (Bell) yielded bigger names for the roster in Billy Butler, Major Lance, the Staple Singers, Erma Franklin, Mighty Sam, Chuck Brooks and Allen Toussaint.

The Soul City album catalogue was based largely upon material licensed from Sam Cooke and J.W. Alexander's Sar Records and the Derby subsidiary – *Double Barrelled Soul* with the Valentinos and Simms Twins was a collectors' item then, let alone now. Billy Preston's *Greazee Soul* and *Roots of Johnny Taylor* were from that source, while the Packers' *Hole In The Wall* was from the Magnificent Montague's Pure Soul label in Los Angeles, and Mighty Sam's Mighty Soul, from Bell via EMI. I mustn't forget the *Soul From the City* sampler, a whole array of tasters from the 45s catalogue with the added bonus of thumbnail photos of each artist.

Deep Soul was the elite label from Soul City, a handful of eclectic releases that would have been financial suicide without the benefit of a huge overdraft, and a virtual guarantee of early death even with such support. 'Soul As Deep As You Like . . . and then some' was the legend on the label. Five of the six releases were slow, tortuous ballads – Jean Stanback's 'I Still Love You' from Peacock, the Ad Libs' 'Giving Up' from Share via Van McCoy, the Emotions' 'Somebody New' from Epic, Jimmy & Louise Tig's 'A Love That Never Grows Cold' from Bell, and Roy Hamilton's 'Dark End of the Street' from AGP via Bell. The sixth was a political anthem by Nicky Lee, 'And Black Is Beautiful', which would have appeased Dave Godin's social conscience. Along similar lines, Chuck Brooks's 'Baa Baa Black Sheep', which had little to do with nursery rhymes or farming, was rumoured to be the probable next single on Deep Soul, but the demise of the Soul City business overtook this project. This ensured that most of the output from all the labels involved would become future treasures. As a postscript, it is fitting to note that a number of tracks released under the Deep Soul banner also featured on the Ace/Kent CD series *Dave Godin's Deep Soul Treasures...from the Vaults*, which ran to four volumes before Dave's tragic death in October 2004. It might be churlish to recall that the parchment scroll-style logo on the Deep Soul label was once described by Charlie Gillett as being, somewhat ironically, of similar style to the personal letterhead of a deep-south plantation owner – which would have been the opposite of Dave Godin's political ethos!

Soul City also (bravely, in view of the probable costs) published printed catalogues, of which I have a compact C5-size folded and stapled booklet with white print on a blue cover, dated "68 –'69', and an undated supplement printed on foolscap paper. The booklet included a preface which highlighted one of the complexities of retailing and cataloguing at that time: the four different numeric sequences in the LP listing, which allowed for mono and stereo pressings of UK and US releases. Never mind the problems of deletions and suchlike. Each catalogue included the US label of origin, and there were certainly some obscurities to be found. It seems odd, however, that the 45s at least did not retain their catalogue number from one listing to the next: Bessie Banks's 'Go Now', for example was no. 105 in the bound catalogue but no. 100 in the supplement. No matter, these listings are a valuable reference source of their time, and give a good indication of the varied stock range of the shop.

CHAPTER FIVE

RECORD SHOPS AND JUNK SHOPPING

I've written about Soul City already, but this chapter is a collection of memories of my quest in other shops for R&B and soul records old and new since discovering the music in the early '60s. While my initial thirst was quenched by the trickle of new releases to be found on London and Stateside, then by Pye International when they gained the rights to the Chess catalogue, and subsequently the flow of singles and the occasional LP from the Motown and Stax labels, it soon became clear that this was the very small tip of an enormous iceberg, and my search widened to locate back-catalogue material and new US imports.

I can't remember where I first heard about Transat Imports – perhaps an advert in the music press, perhaps word of mouth from another fan, but this basement treasure trove in Lisle Street in London's Soho was open on Friday lunchtime and Saturday. I didn't have much money to spend, but it was worth going down that rickety wooden staircase into the cellar with walls adorned with sleeves of import LPs, many on Duke (Bobby Bland, Junior Parker) and King (James Brown, Bill Doggett), and it was like wonderland handling the thick board sleeves and heavy shellac (I'm not sure that vinyl had been adopted in Houston or Cincinnati at that time). I don't remember actually buying much at Transat other than *James Brown Tours the USA*, which was a must-have LP if only for the hyper-energetic 'I Got Money', with its manic drumming and the earth-shaking horn riffs.

The weekly visit to Transat took me into London's West End, quite an experience for a teenager (OK, early twenties) from the suburbs, but also brought me into contact with three major sources of records in Alex Strickland's Soho Record Centre in Old Compton Street, where could be found a weekly batch of new soul import 45s in a cardboard box on or under the counter; Imhof's, a major store at the junction of New Oxford Street and Tottenham Court Road, which had a good stock of jazz, blues and European imports in these categories, and where the prospective buyer was given the disc to take to a personal listening-booth, then trusted to either return it to the counter or pay for it; and last but far from least HMV Records next to Bond Street tube station on Oxford Street. In the basement of HMV was a massive browser/counter full of singles, EPs and LPs, all filed in alphabetical order with large browser dividers, and the appeal was that the browser boxes contained not only current release material but *all* available back-catalogue discs by all artists – enabling me to catch up on the seven volumes of EPs issued on London American entitled *This Is Little Richard* and countless singles, as each visit gave me the chance to search through another letter of the alphabet.

Shortly after this I began a weekly tour of London junk shops and market stalls which, with regular repeat visits to some, probably lasted five or six years. This began with two shops in the south-eastern suburb of Catford just a couple of miles from my home, to which I was first introduced by a schoolfriend with whom I talked about records, and he took me on a circuitous bus ride on route 124 to Sangley Road. Both shops were effectively storage units for the disposal of house clearance goods and furniture, and both had huge browser boxes on their counters containing hundreds of 7-inch singles, all without their paper sleeves, and largely junk as far as a voracious collector of soul and R&B was concerned. Dozens of discs on Decca, Pye and countless minor labels camouflaged the odd tasty morsel on Top Rank (The Bell-Notes' 'I've Had It', Johnny Adams's 'Come On'), London (Gerry Granahan's 'No Chemise Please') or green label Columbia (Chan Romero's 'Hippy Hippy Shake'), not forgetting the occasional orange label Parlophone (Hank Ballard's Let's Go Let's Go Let's Go), mauve label HMV (Quotations' 'Imagination') or early Stateside (Johnny Thunder's 'Loop de Loop').

Waking early on a Sunday morning also became part of the routine, either driving or taking the train and tube to the major street markets close to Liverpool Street station in the City, where Petticoat Lane in Middlesex Street, and Club Row, a short walk away along Brick Lane, were a fruitful source of rock 'n' roll and soul singles and LPs (Carl Perkins's *Dance Album* LP on mint London for 75p, which dates that particular expedition at soon after February 1971, when decimal currency arrived in the UK) for several years. The main problem was finding a particular stall again, as their sites changed week by week.

Around that time (early 1968; it was later reprinted in an updated form that included many provincial towns) Chris Savory, then publishing the SMG fanzine from his Sheppey, Kent, home, and an inveterate junk-shopper, published a fairly comprehensive listing of London street markets and shops that sold old records – not necessarily junkshops and charity shops but sometimes general electrical dealers who sold a few records, but probably had no sale or return deal with their supplier and consequently held on to old stock in perpetuity – or until a collector happened by. This triggered wider record-hunting in remote parts of London often badly served by the tube network. The rotation of journeys included Dalston Market at the far end of Kingsland Road for a stall selling oldie singles (which may have been connected with soul collector Jim Wilson, who also ran a mail-order sales list), East Street market, running between Walworth Road and the Old Kent Road, not far from the Elephant & Castle, a music shop in Walthamstow, about a twenty-minute walk from Blackhorse Road tube station on the newly opened Victoria Line and with a wealth of jazz and blues LPs piled high on bookcase shelves, and Whitechapel Market, right outside Whitechapel tube station in the East End. The legendary Paul's for Music record stall was by the tube station entrance and a compact shop was a couple of hundred yards away in Cambridge Heath Road. Paul sold only LPs, and largely cut-outs, but had regular deliveries and a seemingly inexhaustible source of King material. Paul was a medium height stocky guy with short, greying hair and a permanent benign smile. I never knew his full name, but he was quite a figure in London music. I bumped into him several times at soul/R&B gigs during those years, and all these years later when I mention Paul's for Music to a work colleague there will be smiles and nods of recognition. There was always a cheery greeting as I arrived at the stall to browse, probably because he knew he was guaranteed to take some money from me. He was shrewd enough to sprinkle new discs among all the browser boxes, so that some 'maybes' from a previous trip would confront me again and temptation would triumph. Rain or shine, warm or freezing, the weather was of little consequence to an intrepid record-hunter, and I can recall flicking through the boxes while blowing on freezing fingertips, sometimes through woollen gloves, in search of the new stuff, with perhaps a quiet gasp when coming across a Hank Ballard & Midnighters LP and a broad smile when spotting Little Willie John's *Talk To Me*, Willie clutching a sturdy tree-trunk and flashing a wide grin at his girl, then the treasured find of an Ace LP by Huey 'Piano' Smith & the Clowns, *The Night Before Christmas*, the purple sleeve adorned with Christmas baubles and probably worth its weight in platinum. My collection is certainly richer for the Whitechapel years.

There were also good finds of a more modest nature in a shop near Lewisham railway station (Nathaniel Mayer's *Village of Love* on UK HMV) and another in Penge market (Hal Paige & the Wailers on Blue Beat), but as the value of the Saturday morning treks diminished so we entered the era of bulk quantity cut-out 45s from the USA, which began with countless Chess/Checker singles turning up in multiple quantities at every shop or stall which had a browse-box on the counter, then became more formalised, cost-effective and excellent value for money when the first soul packs hit the market.

CHAPTER SIX

LIVE MUSIC

The mid-'70s saw the emergence and rise of the new Philly Sound, replacing that of the twist-era Cameo Parkway of the previous decade, also from the Windy City, as the sophisticated dance and ballad productions of Kenny Gamble and Leon Huff on their Philadelphia International label came to dominate the charts. This prompted Arthur Howes, veteran of the rock 'n' roll era package shows, to assemble a cast comprising the O'Jays, Billy Paul and the Intruders to tour in 1975 (as far as I can remember without climbing into the loft yet again to check my files of *Black Music* magazine – why do so many concert programmes omit any date reference amid the reprinted PR handouts, photos and airline ads?). Soon afterwards – if about two years qualifies as 'soon' – Kennedy Street Enterprises booked a UK tour for the major missing element of Howes's Philly showcase, namely Harold Melvin & the Bluenotes (there can't be many groups through the years in which the featured name was not the lead singer), but by the time of this 1977 tour the Bluenotes had lost the majestic lead baritone of Teddy Pendergrass, replaced by David Ebo, and also added a female element in Sharon Paige to join Melvin, Jerry Cummings, Dwight Johnson and Bill Spratley (not that you would know from the photos in the programme, of which all except a token shot show five men) and moved from PIR Records to ABC. Support for this show were the (superior and original) Manhattans, thus providing a fine overview of harmony groups of the era. Once I got 'this' close to seeing the great Teddy Pendergrass sing solo in concert. I had a ticket for the second house of his show at Croydon's Fairfield Halls during his 1982 UK tour, and was waiting in the lobby for the auditorium doors to open after the first show, only to hear an announcement that the second house was cancelled as Teddy had been taken ill.

The '70s also saw London host two major musical events with more general Black music content, perhaps bravely seeking to appeal to a growing specialist audience. Wembley Stadium was the venue on 5 August 1972 of the Rock 'n' Roll Revival Show, for which the *Evening Standard* souvenir edition programme listed, 'subject to availability', such Brit acts as Billy Fury, Screaming Lord Sutch, Wizard and Gary Glitter (whose first hit 45 was blandly titled 'Rock 'n' Roll Pts 1 & 2', and whose previous persona of Paul Raven had been a formative Brit rocker), contrasting American groups the Coasters, the Platters (neither of whom I remember seeing on the day) and MC5 (a rock band, whom I remember walking out on!), and genre giants Bo Diddley, Jerry Lee Lewis, Bill Haley & the Comets, Little Richard and Chuck Berry. The first three of these were excellent and memorable, as was Chuck, who closed the show in the darkness of the evening, with a sea of arms waving glowing cigarette lighters as can be seen on a DVD of the show *London Rock & Roll Show*, released by MVD in 2009. Sadly Little Richard chose to wear his infamous mirror-suit, and spent about half of his stage-time prancing around on top of a PA speaker trying to tear his jacket to shreds to throw to the audience while the band persevered with a monotonous twelve-bar vamp. He was met with a chorus of jeers for his efforts.

At the other end of the decade, from 17 to 22 July 1979, the Capital Radio Jazz Festival took place. Capital was launched in October 1973 as the first music-based station in the newly formed ILR (Independent Local Radio), following in the wake of the Labour government's Marine Offences Act which outlawed pirate radio without providing an alternative – despite the BBC's gallant attempt to reach the pop market with Radio 1, and the subsequent (perhaps consequent) move by the succeeding Conservatives to deregulate radio and introduce a commercial strand funded by advertising revenue. Capital Radio did very well in the new market, and having established its footing in the commercial world took the brave and adventurous step of enlisting the skills and acumen of George Wein to organise a London version of his long-established, highly rated and very successful Newport Jazz Festival, held annually in Newport, Rhode Island, USA. There is a lack of available suitable open space in Greater London, so the choice of Alexandra Palace, some way from a convenient tube station and midway between and a bus-ride from Wood Green, Turnpike Lane and Highgate, was probably from a limited choice of venues, but it worked out well despite the travelling problems.

The festival ran with a couple of performance stages and an assortment of concessions and comfort areas, and with a roster of performers not assembled before or since. It combined the best of British and US jazz, ancient and modern, and the cream of blues. I don't recall going to much more than a couple of days of events in view of the distance from my South London home, but the festival programme indicates an opening day featuring Humphrey Lyttelton, Rockin' Dopsie, Jay McShann with Illinois Jacquet, and Herbie Hancock and Chick Corea as a duo – along with other local acts and a jazz combo featuring Ruby Braff and Vic Dickenson. Through Wednesday, Thursday and Friday the schedule featured Sonny Stitt & Milt Jackson, B.B. King, Stéphane Grappelli, George Shearing, Ronnie Scott, Dick Morrissey, Woody Herman's Band and the Lionel Hampton All Star Orchestra, while the weekend brought Dizzy Gillespie, Dave Brubeck, Stan Tracey and Spyro Gyra, and a headliners' showcase final evening including Muddy Waters, Chuck Berry, and the Lionel Hampton Orchestra to close. As if the music wasn't enough, I managed to get my programme signed by Chuck Berry and Muddy Waters, and a treasured photograph of Chuck and Muddy standing together off-stage beside a slim blonde lady wearing a diaphanous black blouse. It's amusing to note that Chuck ain't looking at the camera, he's too busy admiring the lady's cleavage!

This was a masterpiece of organisation and phenomenal entertainment, and it's likely that one reason (cost apart) that it was never repeated was the unreliability of London weather: it was too risky to subject so many musicians and so much electrical gear to the vagaries of our climate. Over the years, though, Capital has continued to present summertime concerts showcasing topline jazz musicians as well as the token bluesman, sadly closer in style to the glitz of Broadway than the heritage of Beale Street.

One or two other artists snuck in to do well-attended but often under-publicised shows, mainly in Central London, and at that time, thanks to my journalistic up-grade from *Shout* fanzine to *Black Echoes* establishment status, I was honoured with invitations to some press events, which while being almost useless for getting anything other than 'quickie-quote' interviews (the knack was to find a contact name and fix up a private interview later), were great for witnessing private concerts, including the chance to see and hear Little Esther Phillips at Ronnie Scott's (the only time I've ever been inside Ronnie's), the Coasters (UK issue on CBS of 'Soul Pad' in about 1970), whose press show I managed to capture 'for private listening' on a pocket cassette recorder!, and the Persuasions, masters of a cappella, at the launch of Capitol LP *Street Corner Symphony* in 1971.

The pleasures of Esther Phillips's vocal talents were on public display at the tiny Royalty Theatre, off Kingsway, in 1975 when she was promoting her Kudu hit 'What a Difference a Day Makes', and the same venue also saw the first London performance of Professor Longhair, bravely promoted by John Stedman in 1978 and recorded for his JSP label, featuring 'Fess playing solo piano with his conga player Alfred 'Uganda' Roberts. Eclectic!

From major-league package shows to one-off concerts at backwater venues, one constant through this era – and in fact throughout the period covered by this book – was James Brown, whose recording career progressed from King via an interlude on Smash to Polydor, with a succession of US hits and a steady stream of UK releases. His consistent popularity, albeit mainly limited to specialist circles, made him a regular visitor to England, and specifically London. This also serves as a handy indicator to the development and progression of musical styles, as James was very much the leader rather than a follower, and he and a number of his disciples helped us to trace the steady move from R&B to funk.

CHAPTER SEVEN

FUNK

Originally 'funky' was a Black ghetto-slang term for the smell of sex. The first 'funky' song titles appeared in the late '60s, with hits like 'Funky Broadway' (Dyke & Blazers before Wilson Pickett), 'Funky Street' (Arthur Conley), 'Funky Way' (Calvin Arnold), 'Funky Donkey' (Pretty Purdie) and 'Funky Fever' (Clarence Carter), and while these discs were largely up tempo they weren't funk as we have come to know it: Dyke's 'Broadway' was perhaps the closest. The turn of the decade saw funk move towards the heavy, thudding bassbeat and resultant heavy backbeat drumming which has come to exemplify it, and it is fitting that 'Ain't It Funky Now', released by James Brown in November 1969, was a title and style-setter to herald the new decade. The style had arguably been started by James as long ago as August 1964, when he cut 'Out of Sight' for Smash, and this was soon echoed by the landmark 'Papa's Got A Brand New Bag' in the summer of 1965 and 'I Got You' at the end of that year. Both used jazz-tinged vamping horn arrangements along with a heavy bassline and thumping beat at mid-tempo.

James Brown continued to use the key elements of what was to become funk in hits through the late '60s: 'Ain't That a Groove' (spring 1966), 'Bring It Up' (early 1967), 'Cold Sweat' (mid-1967), 'I Got the Feeling' (spring 1968) and the anthemic 'Say It Loud (I'm Black and I'm Proud)' were precursors of his soon-to-be trademark style, which begat a new strand of bands and groups who were to build their careers on the foundations of funk.

The acceptance of funk in the UK in general and London in particular was slow, even among the specialist soul cognoscenti – partly because it was a very 'Black' music form, and essentially made for dancing rather than just listening. Brit audiences had been generally quite reserved in their responses at soul concerts, particularly in seated theatres, except in exceptional circumstances like the Motown and Stax revues and James Brown concerts, all of which drew more dedicated soul fans rather than appealing to a wider audience. Northern Soul fans were also very vocal and enthusiastic in their response to witnessing their heroes' stage shows, though on some recorded concerts the audience reaction made it hard to hear the music – no reflection on the fans or their favourites, but not always appealing to the casual listener. The Motown Revue prompted a more vocal response from an audience than had been seen (or heard) since vintage rock 'n' roll stage shows, and the Stax Revue was greeted with an even more animated reaction, with the entire audience standing, swaying, clapping, shouting – this from a largely white attendance. This became more usual at James Brown's shows, which drew a more mixed-race (and consequently more demonstrative) audience.

Booker T & the MGs played a seminal funk style, driven first by Louis Steinberg and then by Donald 'Duck' Dunn's bass and Al Jackson's snappy drumming, which the Meters from New Orleans took a stage further with George Porter's bass and Ziggy Modeliste's drum patterns pushing Leo Nocentelli's guitar and Art Neville's keyboard into the pure rhythm/beat style of 'Sophisticated Cissy', 'Chicken Strut' and the captivating 'Look-a-Py-Py'. As the Stax empire changed with the machinations of big business, and the MGs lost direction after the murder of Al Jackson, so the Meters saw the doors of a wider world opening for them. The demise of Josie Records and a deal with Reprise brought their *Cabbage Alley* LP, an awkward compromise of funk and rock, and a visit to Europe along with their hometown legend Mac 'Dr John' Rebennack early in the '70s.

That these two groups/bands emerged from the deep south of Memphis and New Orleans may have been a nice coincidence, but the geography and ingredients of funk were about to change with an injection of brass and jazz from the east and west coasts. Kool & the Gang, on DeLite Records from New York, emerged with their eponymous 'Kool & the Gang' hit 45 at the end of 1969, and went on to make their mark through the '70s, soon followed by Earth Wind & Fire, from Los Angeles, whose first LPs on Warner came to my attention because of the group's personnel, which included veteran Vee Jay R&B singer Wade Flemons – whose 'Whoops Now' and 'Here I Stand' are collectors' items – and Maurice White, a writer and arranger from Chess Records in Chicago. These bands, along with the Crusaders on Blue Thumb and the Commodores on Motown, caught the ear of a new generation of record buyers and soul fans, and their impact on the evolving UK soul scene became evident first through coverage in *Blues & Soul* and the newly launched *Black Echoes*, and later with a stream of eager punters asking for their records during my time at the Black Wax record shop in Streatham.

It was also through Black Wax that a new element of funk was brought to the British public when we discovered stocks of the Fatback Band's Perception LP *Street Dance* and hit 45 'Njia (Nija) Walk' on the shelves of our supplier of 'cut-out' stock. These sold by the dozen, as did their new release singles on Event Records, the floor-shaking 'Keep On Steppin'' and thumping 'Wicki Wacky'. As might be reasonably assessed by these titles, there was little of lyrical merit about the recorded output of Johnny Flippin, Bill Curtis and company – just solid dance rhythm and beat drenched in funk!

As one who had come to appreciate soul music in a different era, although I was pleased to see the growing interest in soul purely as dance music, I became disenchanted when, on Friday afternoons with a delivery of new import 45s and LPs to play to counter-customers in Black Wax, I found that most punters made a decision after hearing as little as thirty seconds of a track (the time it took to catch the ear of the crowded masses on the disco dancefloors), with no concern nor interest in how the track grew from the intro. This extended to albums when the first release by Brass Construction arrived, and *Movin'* (UA Records) sold as many copies as a hit single. Despite the band's name, the focus of the music was the synthesiser, and this, sadly, set the tone and style during the next couple of years with the onset of the disco era. Indeed, the next couple of years – 1974 into 1975 – saw the beginning of a massive change to soul music, the music of Black America, as producers from Europe and Japan began to integrate a dance beat into their work, and a lot of modern jazz musicians saw a move towards the dance market as a way of earning more money. Soul fans had no problem in principle with the latter (though our jazz fan cousins had a tough job accepting the new style of musicians like Herbie Hancock and Donald Byrd, two of the prime movers of the emergent jazz-funk style), but many took issue with the former – as the basis of soul dance music was diluted and, arguably, terminally polluted. Records such as 'Love To Love You Baby' (Donna Summer) and 'Fly Robin Fly' (Silver Convention), both with a German production pedigree, began to dominate our (Black Wax) record sales and the charts, along with jazz-funk by an array of Japanese musicians and any number of names from different musical fields. We were selling singles credited to Canadian jazz-trumpeter Maynard Ferguson and Lalo Schiffrin (renowned for movie music), among others, plus more bona-fide new-wave dance music by George McCrae, KC & the Sunshine Band and others from Henry Stone's TK Records in Miami, and while the latter were good vehicles for soul singers and musicians to make their marks in the new style, acceptance of the style by the former told me that the time was right to distance myself from involvement in any element of the disco world in my day-job!

The extent of pollution by this disco malaise is exemplified by two specific cases. One is the Average White Band, a vocal and instrumental group hailing from Scotland who managed to register no less than a dozen *Billboard* R&B chart hits between 1974 and 1980, initially with funky, brassy tracks 'Pick Up The Pieces' (1974) and 'Cut The Cake'(1975). In 1977 they were adopted as a bona fide soul unit when Ben E. King cut an LP with them, produced in New York by Arif Mardin for Atlantic. In fact Atlantic cautiously credited them simply as 'AWB' on most of their hit 45s, and this gave rise to a parodic answer-band, the AABB (Above Average Black Band), produced by James Brown, whose 'Pick Up the Pieces One by One' appeared on the Identify label in 1975.

The other was the Bee Gees, brothers Barry, Robin and Maurice Gibb, who were born in the Isle of Man to English parents, but grew up in Australia before returning to England to advance their pop-singing career. Their music was featured in 1977 movie *Saturday Night Fever*, which created a reputation as a landmark of the disco era: both 'Stayin' Alive' and 'Night Fever' reached the US R&B Top 10 in 1978.

A British artist was a major catalyst in raising the awareness of the US market of its native talents, when in the autumn of 1975 glam-rock star David Bowie, born David Jones in Bromley, Kent (my own birthplace) a year after me in January 1947, rose to the top of the Billboard Hot 100 and no. 21 in the R&B chart with his funky 'Fame'. In response to the success of the JB-styled 'Fame', James Brown (who had endured a fallow year in the Hot 100 in 1975 despite R&B chart hits with 'Hustle', 'Superbad', and 'Hot') recorded the belting 'Get Up Offa That Thing', with the triumphant opening yell of 'I'm Back, I'm Back'. This thumping chunk of funk hit the R&B chart in June 1976, climbing to no. 4, and also restored the name of James Brown to the top half of the Hot 100.

Another consequence of the impact of Brit-funk on the US charts and the upsurge of disco was the tendency for some hard funk groups to adapt, maybe even soften, their sound for acceptance by a more catholic market. Examples are the Fatback Band, which changed from the gut-bucket 'Wicky Wacky' and 'Keep on Steppin'' to the broader appeal of 'Spanish Hustle'; Kool & the Gang, which went from 'Funky Stuff' and 'Jungle Boogie' to 'Love & Understanding'; and the Commodores, from the heavy funk of 'Machine Gun' and 'Slippery When Wet' to the balladry of 'Sweet Love' and 'Just To be Close To You'.

New labels emerged along with TK to cater to the new craze

with an identifiable brand, though in some cases, particularly in the jazz world with Blue Note and Fantasy, the music was so radically different from their norm that they were accepted as new labels anyway! There was also a move towards greater playing time for disco tracks, most running for at least double the regulation three minutes, in recognition of the fact that radio airplay was no longer the main vehicle for promotion. So came the club scene, and with it a new order of playing, following and hearing music. Club DJs were ready and happy to buy LPs for just one or two tracks to get their punters onto the dancefloor, and record companies were quick to realise that if there was insufficient comfortable playing time on one side of a 7-inch 45rpm single (there was no point in splitting a track over two sides), then there was a need to issue long tracks on 12-inch singles. Thus 'twelves' became fairly commonplace both in the US and the UK. Unfortunately there was no apparent norm regarding the playing speed, and I have a small collection of 12-inch singles which play variously at 45 rpm and 33 rpm – and it doesn't always tell you which on the label!

The focus on the club scene brought a new avenue for promotion of records and artists with the PA tour, in which a singer came to the UK to make brief personal appearances at clubs and discos to sing along with their hit record. For obvious (logistic and financial) reasons this was usually but not exclusively a vehicle for solo artists or the featured name with a group, with Loleatta Holloway (Goldmind Records, 1977) and Sylvester (Fantasy, 1978) being regular visitors and Frankie Beverly of Maze doing the circuit in 1978 to promote their 'Golden Time of Day' 45 and LP, though I also recall seeing the trio that was Lanier & Co. crowding onto the tiny stage at a local venue in Welling, Kent, in 1982, to sing their Larc 45 'After I Cry Tonight' over a backing track, and interviewing Al Goodman of the Moments (along with Harry Ray and Bill Brown) at a London hotel. George McCrae was another who benefited from a hectic travel schedule. A big name whose career was boosted by his ability to integrate into the new wave music style was Ben E. King, a frequent UK visitor who got on board with Tony Sylvester and Bert De Coteaux and hit with the appealing 'Supernatural Thing' early in 1975.

There were also concert tours by the major stars of the era which became cult events. One such was the aforementioned Maze, an eight-piece band originally from Philadelphia but domiciled in San Francisco, fronted by vocalist Frankie Beverly, who scored a 'club' hit with 'Golden Time of Day' (Capitol) in 1978, then championed and promoted on-air by soul presenter Robbie Vincent. Robbie was primarily a radio man who also dabbled as a live DJ, with feature spots in London clubs, and his relentless plugging turned the US B-side, a live version of 'Joy and Pain' into a UK anthem. Maze played to a full house at Hammersmith Odeon for six consecutive nights in a 1985 tour. In a similar musical groove, this was reminiscent of the response when Ashford & Simpson made their UK debut at the Dominion Theatre in 1982, hot with 'Street Corner' (also on Capitol) and the storming 'Solid (as a Rock)', the audience voracious to absorb and savour every beat and semi-quaver of their soulful favourites.

Just as Maze straddled the decades, so did Millie Jackson. Millie's career blossomed and flourished in parallel with her label, Spring Records in New York, whereon the lilting 'My Man A Sweet Man' and bitter-sweet ballad 'Hurts So Good' charted in 1972–73 before she teamed with producer Brad Shapiro to record the concept album *Caught Up* and its follow-up *Still Caught Up* in 1974–75. Both LPs were issued in the UK on Polydor, gaining enough critical and buyer-reaction for Millie to be booked on a UK tour, the first of several, and a learning curve in terms of performance and repertoire. I can recall seeing her on stage three times, which was perhaps once too many – as she developed her act and material to favour the risqué and overtly sexual. Having made her name singing dance songs and some great ballads like 'If Loving You Is Wrong' and 'Loving Arms', she decided to extend the rap element and take it into the bedroom. This may have had the desired shock effect on the casual listener, but only served to alienate her original fans, many of whom chose to join me in the queue for the exit while Millie sank to artistic depths in her 'Phuck U Symphony' – no matter how you adapt the spelling, the pronunciation remains the same.

Worthy of mention here is radio presenter David Simmons. David had a regular mid-week evening specialist show on BBC Radio London which endured through the mid-'70s, variously as *Soul '76*, *Soul '77*, etc. His two-hour programme was a pioneer in giving regular air-play to records by Jimmy Castor, George Clinton (in Parliament and Funkadelic modes) and Millie Jackson, along with funk, deep-soul and blues artists, and he was a pioneer in playing what became world music: percussive Caribbean tracks and funky and jazzy items from African musicians like Fela Kuti, which indicated the roots of James Brown's style, as well as opening a chicken or egg debate about whether Fela's bass-laden, brassy African music was the leader or follower in the origin and development of funk. David also took his musical tastes and adventure on the road, along with a range of world music percussion instruments, and involved his club audiences in participation, playing, tapping and shaking the various items in time with the records.

Rap

Rap, or is it now called hip-hop? While this extension of black music has a part in the scheme of things, I considered it to be but an appendix to 'London soul' until I was persuaded that it warrants a mention in this tome.

Rap was originally the term accorded to the spoken section of soul records, appearing on some tracks by Joe Tex, Millie Jackson, Isaac Hayes, Love Unlimited and others. I wonder if it also applied to Deek Watson's rumbling bass-voiced interludes to Bill Kenny's soaring tenor lead vocals in the Ink Spots' hits like 'Whispering Grass' and 'If I Didn't Care' in the late '40s.

The spoken lyric came to the fore in 1979, at the tail end of the disco era, first with hits by the Sugarhill Gang, a trio of guys from Harlem signed to Joe and Sylvia Robinson's New Jersey-based Sugar Hill Records, effectively a continuation of their All Platinum/Stang/Vibration label empire which gave us the mellow harmonies of the Moments and the intense balladry of Linda Jones. The Sugarhill

Gang scored no less than eight R&B chart hits, of which their debut 'Rapper's Delight' is the only one I heard (and I consider it no great loss to my musical education that I missed the others). This entered the *Billboard* chart on 13 October 1979 and spent nineteen weeks in climbing to no. 4, but a week earlier Fatback made perhaps the first rap breakthrough with 'King Tim III (Personality Jock)', as Tim himself took the mike to deliver his vocal encouragement in fairly simplistic rhyming couplets over the band's characteristic bass-heavy funk beat topped by vamping brass. The disc stayed in the charts for eleven weeks to reach no. 26, and listening to it as I write this I'm reminded of a very similar disc of a decade earlier, when Pigmeat Markham reached no. 4 in the R&B chart and no. 19 in the *Billboard* Hot 100 with 'Here Comes The Judge', a catchphrase borrowed from the popular TV show *Rowan & Martin's Laugh-In*, a rap record before anybody invented the term.

Also from 1979, and released on Philadelphia International, was a ditty called 'Rhythm Talk' by Jocko. It was a little less in-your-face than the New York records just mentioned, and perhaps presented a more accurate root of the rapping style. The record used the rhythm track of the McFadden & Whitehead hit 'Ain't No Stopping Us Now' as the music-bed, and the lyric was a series of nonsense couplets with rhyming end-syllables – along the lines of 'ooh poo pah do, and how do you do'. It was, I suspect, done with tongue firmly in cheek. Jocko was none other than legendary radio DJ Douglas 'Jocko' Henderson, a veteran of the golden years of American rock 'n' roll radio, who spent seven years during the '50s commuting daily between WDAS in Philadelphia and his late-evening *Rocket Ship Show* on WLIB in New York City. He later made his base in the Fairmount Park, Philadelphia, studio of WDAS, broadcasting live from there while taping his show to syndicate to Boston, St Louis, Detroit and Miami. Hence the pedigree of Jocko, an originator of rapping rhymed couplets as radio links; this art was simply transferred to vinyl for 'Rhythm Talk'. It gained UK release on PIR Records in 1979, as did the aforementioned Sugarhill Gang, with Sugar Hill distributed through Pye Records in the UK. Jocko died, aged eighty-two, in July 2000.

James Brown delivered 'Brother Rapp' towards the top of the R&B charts in May 1970, and his involvement had a two-fold impact – first in setting a musical benchmark for a music form that would rely heavily on his influence, and second in providing – sometimes unwittingly – an unwitting foundation for years to come, as his rhythm patterns were subsequently sampled (physically copied and pasted from his record, with or without credit or permission) or re-created by other musicians.

The doors were thus opened to a subculture of black music from which I have managed to largely distance myself, although aware of its existence and growth. Rap and hip-hop (an expression apparently derived from the rhythmic sound of soldiers' marching feet) crossed the Atlantic during the '80s to take up residence in London's clubs and on pirate radio. The genre developed into verbal social expression, the music element stripped down to a basic rhythm. Words (lyrics might be a generous term in this context) seemed to comprise comment on and reaction to socio-economic situations, often in harsh and/or abusive terms, by young people who had contributed little to either but had expectation of comfort and sustenance from both.

The rap and subsequent hip-hop culture, which has evolved into music, dancing and art, has become something of a lifestyle for a generation that has multi-ethnic origins, and is somewhat removed from its black musical roots. It is a domain which you now need to make an effort to enter, having its own strand of specialist radio and not usually being included on the schedule of numerous soul-based broadcasters on the internet, its own designated areas in retail outlets, be they physical High Street stores or web-based dealers, and its own magazines. Another consequence has been the emergence of sub-categories within the spectrum of soul music, including garage, house, two-step and even R&B – not to be confused with old-fashioned rhythm & blues – all rooted to some degree in what was once simply soul music. No doubt the culture has merit, but to paraphrase the Groucho Marx quip it's a club I'd rather not be a member of!

The author outside Harlem's Apollo Theatre, 2000.

Allen Toussaint browses discographies in *Shout* magazine, 1972.

Bettye LaVette signs a CD for a fan(!), London, 2005.

The author with wife Barbara.

Soul Explosion package show, London, 1969.

The first show promoted by *Home of the Blues,* 1967.

Aretha Franklin's first UK tour, London, 1968.

James Brown's first UK tour, London, 1966.

Chuck Berry's first UK tour, London, 1964.

Dionne Warwick and the Isley Brothers' first UK tour, London, 1964.

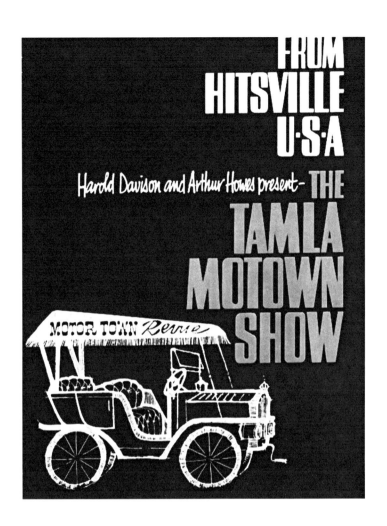

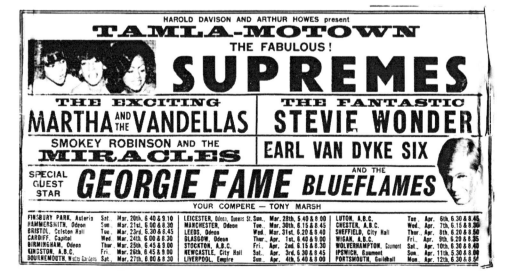

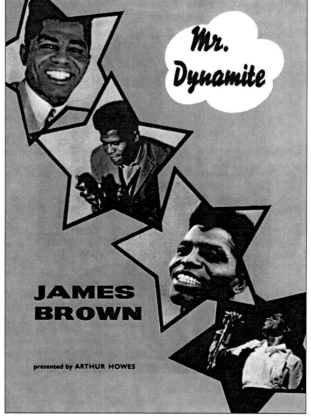

POP SINGER'S MOCK 'FITS' SHOCK VIEWERS

By MIRROR REPORTER

Brown... "a new act," says his manager.

AMERICAN rhythm and blues singer James Brown threw four "fits" on television's "Ready, Steady, Go!" beat show last night.

Scores of viewers phoned in to complain about his "disgusting behaviour."

What they didn't know was that the "fits" were part of his act.

A spokesman for Associated Rediffusion, who present the show, said: "the highlight of his act is a mock seizure."

Viewers complained after seeing Brown "collapse" several times after working himself into a frenzy.

He was led off the stage several times, covered in a gaudy cloak which was thrown over him by members of his supporting group.

Reserved

But each time he returned, to scream, screech, leap about the stage and roll on the floor during his thirty-minute act.

The 31-year-old singer's manager, Ben Bart, said last night: "I realise that the English people are reserved and may be astounded by James's act.

"It is a completely new act, and I suppose you can't please everybody

Bear Brand Pure Honey sets you up for the day

Daily Mirror report of James Brown's TV appearance on *Ready Steady Go*, 1966.

Sunday 26th November 1967

Compere Peter Stringfellow

THE TANGERINE PEEL

GEPY & GEPY

CHRIS CLARK

FELICE TAYLOR

INTERVAL

SOUNDS INCORPORATED

EDDIE FLOYD

phone: RED 2600
BRIXTON

STAGE . ONE NIGHT ONLY . SUN 13 MAR . 6 o'c & 8.30

FROM AMERICA - MR DYNAMITE

JAMES BROWN
and the FAMOUS FLAMES

AND ALSO FROM AMERICA

BARBARA LEWIS

| MIKE COTTON SOUND | MARIONETTES |

BRITAIN'S ACE COMPERE - DIRECT FROM BBC'S POP INN

KEITH FORDYCE

BOOK NOW   7/6   8/6   10/-   12/6   17/6

The author interviews Johnny Adams, New Orleans, 1982.

Denise LaSalle and Johnnie Taylor pictured in casual mode by the author, London, *c.* 1988.

Bobby Bland photographed by the author, New Orleans Jazzfest, *c.* 1982.

The author as match sponsor at Charlton Athletic v MK Dons, 2010, with brother Andrew (left) and Addicks host Mark Penfold (right).

The author (front row, second left) playing in a charity football match at The Valley with Charlton legends Mark Kinsella (front row, third from left) and Paul Mortimer (front row, second right).

ATLANTIC RECORDING CORPORATION
1841 BROADWAY, NEW YORK 23, NEW YORK
AREA CODE 212 PLaza 7-6306

May 4, 1966

Clive Richardson
Chislehurst, Kent
England

Dear Clive:

Thank you for your letter of April 23. We are glad to hear that Don Covay has acquired such a success in England.

Enclosed are some photographs and a biography of Don, as well as an Atlantic-ATCO catalogue.

As for advance information on records to be released, I would advise you to get in touch with our English representatives, Polydor Records.

As for fan clubs, as far as we know there are no Don Covay fan clubs in the USA.

Wishing you lots of success,

cordially,

Robert Rolontz
Publicity Director

RR/em
Encls.

TALENT

England on a Soul Spree, Reports Returning Atlantic 'Soulist' Covay

NEW YORK—Soul music is taking hold in England. The most fanatic and loyal soul music fans are located in England, reported Atlantic Records artist Don Covay, who returned recently from a month-long promotion tour of England's TV and nightclub circuit.

"They've got soul music fan clubs all over England," said Covay, "and they let every American soul music performer know about it when he visits there. Every time I arrived in a town, hundreds of young fans would be in front of the club waiting for me. Sometimes they would parade up and down in front of the club with placards and signs saying 'Welcome Don Covay,' or 'Greetings to Our Favorite Soul Singer'."

Covay also pointed out that these fans put out leaflets and booklets that circulate through-

DON COVAY

out England about soul singers. He said, "They have stories about me, Solomon Burke, Otis Redding, Joe Tex, Wilson Pickett, Bo Diddley, and other soul artists. They review the latest releases, singles and albums, and they print lists of all the records these artists recorded. They meet their favorites at airports, railroad stations, night clubs, and elsewhere, and they set up press conferences wherever they can. They really dig soul."

While in England, Covay played at a flock of top rhythm and blues clubs, like Blaze's, the Whiskey a Go Go, and the Flamingo in London, as well as clubs in Manchester and Birmingham. He also was featured on the TV show, "Ready Steady Go." He visited the disk jockeys at all of the pirate radio stations and discovered that they were soul fans, too.

Covay's visit helped spark one of the new English dances called "The See-Saw Dance," based on his hit record of "See-Saw." Another dance that was started there, according to Covay, was the "Sookie Sookie," which stemmed from his recording of the same name.

The author broadcasting as Clive R, Solar Radio, 2005.

The author holding the Division 1 championship trophy with Charlton Athletic chairman Richard Murray, 2000.

Clive R 'on air', Solar Radio, 2010.

'Honky Tonk' trippers at Floyd Soilleau's Record Store, Ville Platte, Louisiana, 1980. Left to right: the author, Maureen McQuillan, Rob Hughes, Geoff Suich, John Broven, Paul Harris.

Esther Phillips at a press show, Ronnie Scott's Club, London, 1975.

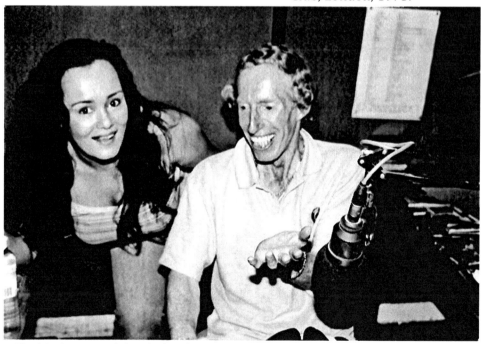

Flashlight Records' Isabel Roberts is interviewed by the author, RTM Radio, c. 1994.

Huey 'Piano' Smith at a private party, New Orleans, c. 1981.

Irma Thomas photographed by the author at the New Orleans Jazzfest, 1981.

The author with Johnny Adams, Festival Hall, London, 1987.

Cosimo Matassa leaving the 'office', Sea-Saint Studio, New Orleans, 1980.

Johnny Adams in action, New Orleans, 1987.

The author gets close with Fern Kinney, London, 1980.

'By Royal Appointment'? The author meets HRH the Princess Royal during the official opening of Dillons Bookstore, the day-job at the time, *c.* 1985.

The author, co-hosting Charlton Chat at RTM Radio, meets 'Miss Charlton Athletic', *c.* 1994.

Marshall Sehorn, Sea-Saint Studio, New Orleans, 1982.

Reunion of the *Shout* magazine editorial committee, November 2010. Left to right: Dave McAleer, Tony Cummings, the author.

Something to SHOUT! about from 2007
www.shoutrecords.co.uk

A veritable alphabet of classic rhythm & blues re-issues...

A JOHNNY ADAMS "Chasing Rainbows" SHD 36

B BARBARA BLUE "By Popular Demand" SH 33

C OSCAR TONEY JR CONTEMPO sessions "Loving You Too Long" SH 40

D DELLS "Always Together - Great Chess Ballads" SH 38

...Exciting Further releases by vocal Groups.....

RIVINGTONS "Papa Oom Mow Mow" SH 35

SPELLBINDERS "Chain Reaction" SH 39

....great Hand-clappin' gospel   ....and Iconic Grammy-winning blues

FIVE BLIND BOYS OF MISSISSIPPI "Something to Shout About" SH 34

T-BONE WALKER "Good Feelin'" SH 37

..and into 2008 with Little Milton (SH 41), Doris Duke (SH 42), Lloyd Price (SH 43), Roy Hamilton (SH 44)

For details of all releases, visit www.shoutrecords.co.uk.   Order online or phone 020 8740 4208

Solar Radio chairman
Tony Monson, 2005.

The author with
Radio Medway DJ
Tony 'Shades'
Valence, *c.* 1980.

Wardell Quezerque, New
Orleans Jazzfest, 2000.

The author and friends in New Orleans in 1985.

CHAPTER EIGHT

MORE MAGAZINES

*S*hout went monthly in January 1970 with issue 51 (Ember (US) label listing and Bobby Freeman discography) and the cover price increased to 2*s*. Issue 52 brought bad news with the death of Billy Stewart on 17 January and Slim Harpo on 5 February. We had managed an exclusive interview with the former under unusual circumstances. I was walking up Wardour Street towards the Flamingo when I encountered Tony Cummings rushing out of a pizza bar. 'I've found Billy Stewart having some dinner,' he said. We walked in, and there was Billy, tucking into a pizza while answering our questions! There was mixed reaction to a January 1970 package show unfortunately billed as 'Soul Together', owing to the withdrawal of Clarence Carter early in the tour and Joe Tex later, with replacements for neither, leaving just Arthur Conley and Sam & Dave in the East Ham show of Monday 9 February, though the chance to see the great Joe Tex stage show in the Croydon concert was very welcome, and Jon Philibert took the opportunity to do an in-depth interview with Conley. The next issue brought news of the death of Tammi Terrell, and in April Darrell Banks's obituary was another sad inclusion. On a brighter note, the May issue saw the first contribution from Bedford-based subscriber Roy Stanton, mentioned earlier. His first input was an interview and show review for Ben E. King, and he was later a valuable contact with George Clinton and Parliament, and perhaps more importantly the Dells.

In June history was made when the first paid ad appeared in *Shout*: a full-page from Ember Records' Speciality label was on the inside front cover, promoting the release of LPs by King Curtis, the Jodimars, and a compilation named *All The Blues All The Time*. There was also an editorial thanking Mr Jeffrey Kruger for his kind financial support. An LP review and full discography of Screamin' Jay Hawkins also graced that issue, following which I had the pleasure of a long conversation-cum-interview with Jerry Butler at the BBC studios while he was rehearsing for his *Top of the Pops* appearance on 26 March 1970 (performing 'Hey Western Union Man'). Next came another price increase, with August's issue (no. 58) costing 2*s* 4*d* – and the change to decimal currency took this to 12p. The editorial of that issue carried news of the closure of the Soul City record shop, this loss mitigated to a small degree by jazz and blues specialist shop Dobells expanding their stock range to include some soul albums; but a valuable source of import 45s was no more. There was another momentous occasion for *Shout* when Creedence Clearwater Revival toured the UK in July 1970, bringing with them as support renowned North Carolina one-man-band bluesman Wilbert Harrison. This time I went through proper channels to secure an interview, having first watched his brief set from a balcony near the roof of the Royal Albert Hall. With the help of Jon Philibert I conducted an interview that ran to three pages of quarto paper in *Shout* 59, October 1970, and may still be unique in R&B annals. Interview snippets with Delmar Evans, Margie Evans and trombonist Gene 'Mighty Flea' Connors, from the touring Johnny Otis Revue, featured next, in November. Then came another major scoop.

I mentioned earlier the invaluable contacts made by Roy Stanton with key personnel at the USAF base at Chicksands. It was in November 1970 that I had a phone call from Roy from the lobby of a London hotel. He simply said, 'Get your ass over here: we have an interview with the Dells!' Thus, cassette-recorder in hand, I caught the train to Charing Cross station and walked briskly over to the Trafalgar Hotel, adjacent to the National Gallery, to talk one-to-one with Marvin Junior, Chuck Barksdale, Micky McGill and Johnny Carter. Sadly Verne Allison was asleep in his room, so we didn't get a chance to talk to him, though cousin Marvin Junior tried to reassure us with 'Verne don't say much anyway!' The interviews and some thoughts and opinions from the guys filled issue 61, the cover of which was graced by my Kodak Instamatic photographs of the group, dressed in floral patterned shirts with floppy collars that were typical of fashion of the time. It was their first interview anywhere.

Shout 62 included a book review of *The Sound of the City*: Charlie Gillett's serialised university thesis had finally metamorphosed into a published paperback, later to be upgraded to hardback in the UK by Souvenir Press. That issue also included a feature on Candi Staton, though the lack of a by-line suggests it was based on a high-quality press-release rather than a first-hand interview. This was supported by my review of the UK Capitol release of her *I'm Just A Prisoner* LP from Fame and a cover photo of Candi which was not one of my better choices for half-tone printing: a mass of black hair and dark garment dominate the small patch of facial features.

February 1971 brought a postal strike in England and a UK tour by Stevie Wonder, supported by Martha & the Vandellas. I saw the show at Lewisham Odeon – or at least the first half, as my review is of the Vandellas and an admission of dashing off home to watch a blues programme on TV rather than staying 'to see the much overrated Stevie Wonder'! Label listings and discographies tended to dominate the content of the magazine, though *Shout* 65 saw the arrival of Sweden's Jonas Bernholm as a contributor with a profile on New Orleans singer Curly Moore, sometime member of Huey Smith's Clowns. Jonas went on to gain considerable repute at the helm of a family of Swedish R&B reissue labels. In the next issue I interviewed Rosetta Hightower, ex-lead singer with the Orlons, who had a string of hits on Cameo-Parkway Records ('South Street'/'Don't Hang Up'/'Wah-Watusi', etc.), and was then domiciled in England – having married CBS record producer Ian Green.

Summer of 1971, and another odd occasion. Heavyweight boxing champion Joe Frazier had followed his old adversary Cassius 'Muhammad Ali' Clay from boxing ring to recording studio, and also travelled to London for a couple of concerts including an entertaining evening at Tooting Granada. The main interest, however (with the greatest respect), was not the vocal talent of Mr Frazier but that the tour support was Epic Records star Vivien Reed, who had reached the Top 50 of the US *Billboard* R&B charts in June 1966 with 'Yours Until Tomorrow', and with whom I managed a short interview. Then I snatched a few words with Frazier's band, the Knockouts, before seeing their short but rewarding stage show. *Shout* 68 featured a Marvelettes discography and a Gone label listing, plus a book review section that included a glowing mention of *The Drifters*, the first published work by *Soul Music/Shout* regular contributor Bill Millar, and an integral part of a series entitled Rockbooks from Studio Vista Books. Another old friend in print was featured in issue 69, with a review of Mike Leadbitter's *Nothing But The Blue*, a hardback compilation of articles and artists' biographies as published by Mike in the first fifty issues of *Blues Unlimited* magazine. The issue also carried the tragic news of the murder of King Curtis Ousley, the legendary R&B/soul sax man who was stabbed to death on 13 August 1971.

October brought issue 70, and comprehensive coverage of Huey 'Piano' Smith, comprising a four-page interview by Jonas Bernholm and a similar length discography from the combined files of Kurt Mohr, Ray Topping, Mike Leadbitter and Jonas. There were more contributors aboard a month later, with Chicago's Cary Baker providing a profile on Vee Jay owners Jim Bracken and Vivien Carter, and Peter Burns an appraisal of Baby Huey, the giant of a man who was James T. Ramey, and who had died just a year earlier with little recognition. Bob Fisher sent a feature on Little Milton Campbell – an overview of many of his great recordings – and a Johnny Adams discography sowed the seeds of my hero-worship of this great New Orleans singer. The main impact of this issue, however, came in the editorial by Roy Stanton. It was headlined 'Pye Gets Crusty', and detailed an incident in which a coachload of fifty or so London soul fans made a journey all the way to Blackpool with the intention of sampling the merits of Northern Soul at the Mecca, only to be told at the door by the manager, a Mr Bill Pye, that the shoulder-length hair of one of our party Terry Davis was 'not acceptable'. We contested the decision, were refused entry *en masse*, and had to kill several hours in Blackpool's pubs before our coach driver was available for the return journey. After some correspondence in the weeks following the trip, Mr Pye was gracious enough to refund our coach fare. Rumours have bounced around for decades regarding the background to this saga. Among the tributes to Dave Godin published after his tragic death in November 2004 was the information that he had phoned Mr Pye and told him to exclude us as we were 'out to cause trouble'. Tony Cummings had published his (not very complimentary) views on Northern Soul, crossing journalistic swords with Dave on the subject, and as he thought (incorrectly) that Tony was the brains behind our intended adventure, Dave felt we were a potential threat to the Mecca clientele. Roy's editorial alluded to this without naming names.

December 1971, and a veritable plethora of live shows. Roy Stanton and I enjoyed Ronnie Dyson supporting the Supremes, then comprising Mary Wilson, Cindy Birdsong and Jean Terrell, but walked out on the latter as they alternated Broadway hits with one-verse medleys of their own hits. Soon afterwards I went to a show promoted by John Abbey and *Blues & Soul* at Finsbury Park. I'd forgotten that I'd seen Phillip Mitchell, who impressed then as now; Tami Lynn's act is described as 'an abomination' – she may have been an regrettable inclusion in proceedings by John, but next on the bill were Bloodstone. What a revelation for a London audience who had not previously witnessed a soul harmony group in person. The show was closed by Al Green, not, it was reported, in either the best of health or voice. *Shout* 72 also included a Ric-Tic label listing, and my own file copy of the magazine is signed on the front cover by J.J. Barnes, who came to London for a great gig at the 100 Club in 1974, and a feature on Edwin Starr.

Another *Shout* scoop opened the new year when we were granted formal permission to meet and interview Funkadelic. That the interview took place in a downmarket hotel in a side street off the Edgware Road did nothing to devalue this unique occasion, and the cover photos, taken with my Instamatic camera, are testimony to the bizarre humour of George Clinton and his group. There was a small child's tricycle in the hallway of the hotel, and George insisted I take a photo of him lying on his side on the floor pedalling it! Between us, Roy Stanton and I managed to interview ten group members including Clinton himself, Fuzzy Haskins, Bernie Worrell and Eddie Hazel, and we were intrigued to find that they had a strong strand of doo-wop and vocal-group pedigree.

More journalistic pathfinding soon followed. I had a phone call from Dave McAleer, label manager at Pye Records, telling me that his company had made a new signing. It seems that the UK A&R man walked into Mack's office and mentioned that he'd signed a Tommy Hunt. 'THE Tommy Hunt?' 'You mean there is a THE Tommy Hunt?' We set up an interview with the sometime Flamingos baritone and Wand Records chart star, and again Roy Stanton and I set off for a remote London hotel to meet Tommy, his new English wife Leah, and their delightful fourteen-month-old son Nile Pharaoh. A comprehensive interview took place and was published in full in *Shout* 74.

Sadly a regular feature in *Shout* was the obituaries column. While it could be expected that some bluesmen and R&B pioneers of advancing years would be travelling towards the Pearly Gates, there has been a high incidence of premature deaths in the world of soul through the years. All come as a tragic shock, of course, be it the murders of King Curtis and Darrell Banks or the travelling accidents which took Otis Redding and Billy Stewart, but some have an even more poignant impact. One such instance was the brain tumour that killed Tammi Terrell, and another was the death from diabetes of Linda Jones, aged just twenty-seven, reported in *Shout* 75 along with a tribute and a discography. That issue also published the results of the first (and only) readers' poll, with Bobby Bland, Aretha Franklin and the Dells winning the prime categories, and the Chantels edging the Supremes into second place in the girl groups section. Another obit followed in issue 77 with the June 1972 death of Clyde McPhatter, the original lead voice of the Drifters whose subsequent solo career spanned two decades and several labels, latterly including material recorded during his domicile in London; his last LP was the excellent *Welcome Home* for US Decca. Cause of death was initially attributed to a heart attack, with subsequent reference to a degree of alcohol abuse. A full tribute and biography by Bill Millar followed in the next issue, along with Ray Topping's session discography.

Back to the live acts, and Eddie Floyd was in town for a London concert and a fruitful and interesting interview in a Hammersmith hotel. Not so rewarding was an attempt to talk to Jackie Wilson before a Contempo-promoted show at the Finsbury Park Astoria – rebranded as the Rainbow to comply with '70s psychedelic tastes. I went along at the arranged time in the company of the enthusiastic Lou McDermott (sadly long deceased – a young man who drew massive inspiration from his love of soul and R&B in an losing battle against personal problems), only to find that things were running late and Jackie, who was due on stage at 10pm, had arrived at 9.35 – and no-one could find the key to the dressing room. The interview was necessarily brief (though I managed to talk to Jackie at length at the 100 Club some years later), but his performance was dynamic.

Shout 81, in November 1972, was an issue busy with interviews, live reviews and 'domestics'! The problem arose when I received a bitter letter from Kurt Mohr, who accused fellow-discographer Ray Topping of being 'a crook and a thief', quoting a number of cases where a discography published in *Shout* and credited to Ray included 'the same gaps and the same inaccuracies as sheets I had sent out' and doubting that the material submitted was 'wholly his own work'. There was a pressing need to resolve this issue, with Ray and Kurt being the key contributors of discographical material to the magazine. One source of the problem was traced to a discography of Hank Ballard & the Midnighters which had been submitted by a third party, passed to Ray for scrutiny and erroneously credited to Mr Topping by an embarrassed editor, unaware that the third party had originally received the information from Kurt Mohr! The situation was defused in a diplomatic editorial by yours truly, in which the situation was reviewed and both parties were appeased.

In the same issue we also published the brief interview with Jackie Wilson, and also a more in-depth feature on a cappella group the Persuasions, who had come to London to promote the release of their *Street Corner Symphony* LP on Island. Lou McDermott and I had managed to conduct the first comprehensive interview with the group, comprising Sweet Joe Russell, Jerry Lawson, Jay Washington, Herbert 'Tuobo' Rhoad and Jimmy Hayes. We were also privileged to attend a press gathering at a West End club and witness an exclusive live stage show by the group, a small portion of which was also committed to cassette for private enjoyment later. The other live shows covered were Ike and Tina Turner at the Wembley Pool – scheduled for two shows but cut back to one, which started late, had lousy sound and used the same repertoire as their previous tour; and the Stylistics, who managed a whole thirty-five minutes on stage at the Sundown club/theatre in Charing Cross Road. Small ads in this issue included *Bim Bam Boom*, the emergent doo-wop magazine from New York, *Hot Buttered Soul*, Chris Savory's new magazine venture built around Stax and modern soul, *SMG*, a fanzine covering a pot-pourri of musical styles and run by the late Barry Lazell, and Black Wax Records and mail-order company. The next issue included mention of the launch of *Black Wax* magazine, had two paid ads from Phonogram Records and an inside front cover photo signed by the great Johnny Otis, who had made his first visit to the UK.

The new year of 1973 started with a Gladys Knight & the Pips interview at Lewisham Odeon, after a commendable show promoted by Jeffrey Kruger and Arthur Howes, with New York lounge singer Carol Woods as support, and achieved through the more usual *Shout* technique of door-stepping rather than bothering with PR agents. Part of the knack was to find out the name of the tour manager and ask for him at the stage door: this worked well at Lewisham, and gained me access to the Pips' dressing room and an enjoyable and fruitful interview with Gladys and the group. A useful tool to assist with this was the group's discography, recently published in *Soul Bag*, which served to dispel some myths and correct some inaccuracies. Fats Domino's band came to town and I managed to take some photos backstage to use on the magazine cover, then came a visit from Sonny Terry and Brownie McGhee (and a fine interview by Bob Fisher) and a New Orleans invasion by the Meters, Allen Toussaint and Mac 'Dr John' Rebennack, which played at a remote theatre in Edmonton. The Meters had edged towards rock with their *Cabbage Alley* repertoire, Toussaint is a great pianist but never a singer, and Mac is an enigmatic, if talented, performer, so the long trek from south London was hardly rewarded.

August 1973 brought the UK release of Don Covay's first Mercury LP, *Super Dude 1* (reissued on 'my' Shout label RPMSH 292 in June 2005), suitably heralded in the magazine editorial and with an advert from Phonogram. *Shout* 88 also featured a contribution by Mike Leadbitter, when he found that an article on Norman Thrasher and (Hank Ballard's) the Midnighters didn't sit comfortably in the editorial content of *Blues Unlimited* magazine. A new but short-lived project emerged at the end of the year when issue 91 published a 'songography' of Jerry Leiber and Mike Stoller – a list of all songs written by the duo, listed alphabetically by the artists who had recorded them, and including the catalogue number and date of release. I suspect that a project like this would be relatively straightforward these days, with a search of BMI and ASCAP files for a given writer, but in those days this pioneering effort was quite a task. One might have hoped the idea could have gone on to include such as Rudolph Toombs, Helen Miller and Rosemary McCoy (who were featured in *Juke Blues* 26) and the like, but perhaps that's for the future.

1974 opened with a comprehensive interview with Bloodstone, whose recent tour had yielded a contract with UK Decca, and an LP, produced by erstwhile fanzine editor turned recording studio wizard Mike Vernon, from which came hit 45 'Natural High', one of the first 'sweet soul' harmony tracks to aspire to the UK charts. The singles reviews section also mentioned the UK release of 'Hey Now' by Little Wayne Anthony on Jay Boy (from President Records). A Vee Jay radio-station copy of this Northern Soul favourite was found by Tony Cummings and me in a London street market, and subsequently taken to David Kassner at President by me and fanzine editor and radio presenter Chris Savory; the single was duly released in the UK. Writing of friends in high places, late 1973 had brought a London visit by Kenny Gamble and Leon Huff, as a precursor to the UK launch of their Philadelphia International label through CBS, and I had received an invitation to a lunch in their honour at the plush Quo Vadis Restaurant in Soho. This very pleasant event was followed by a kind letter sent by Kenny Gamble that thanked me for joining them. This I published in *Shout* 93, along with a front-cover collage of 'personality pics' taken on the trusty Instamatic camera with Gladys Knight, J.J. Barnes, Allen Toussaint, Esther Phillips, the Persuasions, and the aforementioned Gamble and Huff.

The next landmark came with *Shout* 96, in which German contributor Norbert Hess combined resources with Kurt Mohr and Mike Leadbitter to enable me to produce a special issue devoted to Little Esther Phillips. Norbert provided a stunning cover photo and some archive shots for the back cover as well as an in-depth biography cum career appraisal, while the discography included input from diverse sources including Esther herself. The songography venture continued in the next issue, with new contributor Rob Hughes having done a fine job researching the works of Bert (Russell) Berns; and the death was recorded of Ravens' bass lead voice Jimmy Ricks.

A small modification to the editorial credits of *Shout* 98 in September 1974 was the precursor of some changes that were still in their formative stages. As well as my home address in Chislehurst, a London office was now included – 12 Mitcham Lane, Streatham. It was no coincidence that this was a (fairly hefty) stone's throw from *Soul Music*'s birthplace, as it was the home of Black Wax Records, a shop run by Soul Music founder Tony Cummings's ex-wife Hilary and sometime *Shout* contributor Roy Stanton, who had moved from Bedford to Streatham, and had initially set up a record mail order operation in a flat in Greyhound Lane. I'll talk in more detail about this business later. For now, suffice to say that it looked good to have a London office address for the magazine.

The landmark event of *Shout* 100 duly arrived in December 1974, for which I dug deep into the bank vaults to produce a litho-printed, wire-stitched magazine. The list of contributors testified to the loyalty of soul fans, as almost ten years down the line the same guys who were flying the flag in the early '60s were still promoting and publicising the music. Kurt Mohr and Ray Topping provided discographical material on both the renowned and the obscure; John Broven, whose first book, *Walking to New Orleans*, had recently been reviewed, contributed a biographical and musical appraisal of Willie Tee, and all of the present and past editorial team wrote short eulogies – as did long-time friend and soul-brother Dave Godin. It was quite a compliment to be described as 'fearlessly abrasive' by Dave in respect of my often blunt comments and reviews. Looking at the editorial of *Shout* 99, I commented to my wife, Barbara, that little has changed in my attitude over the last thirty years: in October 1974 I wrote, 'Must've been a quiet month – I can't think of anything to moan about!' Sadly, issue 100 was tainted with the sorrow of the news of two deaths: R&B singer/pianist/pioneer Ivory Joe Hunter, whose discography was already scheduled for publication and was joined by an obituary, and closer to home was the early death of Mike Leadbitter, a pioneering blues researcher, writer and fan, who co-founded and edited *Blues Unlimited* magazine and undertook early field research into blues in Louisiana, writing several booklets that drew on the fruits of his travels, interviews and experiences.

Into 1975, and back to normal. Sadly there was another obituary of a major R&B pioneer, with the death of Louis Jordan, but more positively a lengthy interview with Allen Toussaint. Then came another special issue devoted to Don (Harris) and Dewey (Terry), courtesy of Norbert Hess with some fine vintage photos, critical biography and comprehensive discography. Quite a lot happened during the summer, including a visit from Jerry 'Swamp Dogg' Williams Jr, another visit by Jackie Wilson to sing at the 100 Club in London and play some provincial gigs, and a package tour of '70s Atlantic stars the Spinners, the Jimmy Castor Bunch and Sister Sledge. There were also two deaths to report – Aaron T-Bone Walker at the age of sixty-five, and that of rock 'n' roll, when Little Richard went on stage at Lewisham Odeon in a pink cat suit and was booed throughout his forty-minute set while most of the audience walked out! Also imminent was the death of *Shout* magazine, though at the time the future looked promising. Issue 104 appeared in August 1975, resplendent with a cover photo signed by Jackie Wilson and including my interview with the great man conducted at the 100 Club, along with a session discography of Dave 'Baby' Cortez (though not including his vocal group tracks with the Pearls). The editorial, however, heralded the end of an era, with my monthlyish quarto-size mag being upgraded to a periodic A4 magazine to be produced by Paul Pelletier, whose Record Information Service produced a series of UK specialist label lists, covering the likes of London-American, Stateside, Top Rank and others with predominantly US R&B/soul repertoire.

Thus into the new era, and *Shout* 105 in October 1975. The business address moved to Paul's home in nearby Catford and the usual array of contents was enhanced by Roy Stanton's ambitious attempt to list all soul/R&B singles and LPs ever released in the UK. There were good interviews too: I don't remember meeting Gary Bonds, but I interviewed him, along with Shirley Goodman, who came to the UK to promote the emergent All Platinum Records, along with her own disco smash hit 'Shame Shame Shame', which reached no. 6 in the UK Top 40 in February 1975, and the (Buck Ram) Platters, then led by the somewhat theatrical tenor of Monroe Powell and supported by Tommy Ellison – who may have been the same guy who sang gospel with the Five Singing Stars on Hob, but I never got to ask him! Onwards with a Scepter label listing, Roy Stanton's attempt to catalogue the use of soul/R&B music in movies – which may have borrowed heavily from a more comprehensive published work by Alan Warner, and Roy Simonds's fine phone interviews with Arthur Alexander and Chuck Jackson. Predictably Roy's plans to list every UK soul music release proved over-ambitious, given the resources available at the time, and this was dropped along with the cover price of the magazine, and subscription over-payments were compensated with gift vouchers to be redeemed against other items published by Paul. The publication of *Shout* 109 in the summer of 1976 saw the bulk of the work back in my hands again, as I typed the stencils and handled the admin while

Paul used his duplicator for the physical production and gathered in the subscription revenue, but the next issue carried an editorial announcing the end of the management involvement of RIS. The magazine also carried an interesting discussion between soul journalist Cliff White, Bo Diddley and Johnny Watson taped during their European tour in November 1975, a reprint of a Peacock label listing previously published in the hard-to-find *Record Research* magazine some fifteen years before, a Garnet Mimms discography and the continuation of a James Brown discography.

By the spring of 1977, and with the publication of what turned out to be the penultimate issue, I had files of discographical information and photographs but precious little else, apart from continued enthusiasm. Paul's involvement and the use of his RIS resources had coincided with the launch of a new venture in black music journalism, namely *Black Echoes*, a weekly tabloid-size paper covering soul music and also blues and reggae. I applied for a full-time staff position, but as my production and layout skills were limited to typing on a wax stencil and filling twelve pages I was not successful. Instead I was offered the opportunity to become a contributor on a regular freelance basis, which I gratefully accepted. As a consequence my *Shout* time was limited. By this time I was no longer working at Black Wax, as the business had closed – more on this later.

Shout 111 included a live-show appraisal of funk-era James Brown along with another segment of discography, an in-depth interview with Jerry 'Swamp Dogg' Williams, courtesy of David Yeats, label-manager at DJM Records, Peacock and Pzazz label listings and a Kip Anderson discography. Then came the final issue, in July 1977. I reached July 1970 with the James Brown discography, managed a comprehensive interview with Harold Melvin, delving into the Bluenotes' history with the interesting revelation that 'I'm glad I'm able to let the public know that there were no Bluenotes on the Gamble/Huff sessions. Kenny Gamble and myself, we were the Bluenotes on record – the only person I took in the studio was Pendergrass: I cut his voice and me and Gamble were the background. All the other guys were just for the stage shows.'

Preston Love, Duke Records and Roosevelt Grier, a couple of book reviews and three pages of record reviews... here endeth the history of *Shout*.

It is likely that Roy and Paul saw the magazine as a source of revenue, and in theory the production element could have combined into the schedules of Paul's label listing projects. Once the production chores had been taken from me, I was left with time and inclination to expand into the wider journalistic opportunities provided by the launch of *Black Echoes*. However, when it was realised that there was little profit to be made from *Shout* and that the production was somewhat laborious, the magazine reverted to me. My circumstances had changed, though, and perhaps the era had ended anyway.

Black Echoes and the Progress of Fanzines

The door to wider journalistic exposure was held open for me by *Black Echoes* editorial staff like Chris Gill, Lindsey Wesker (son of playwright Arnold Wesker), Debbie Kirby and Chris Wells, along with publisher Paul Phillips. I was offered the opportunity to make regular freelance contributions covering vintage soul and R&B (though writer and teacher Mike Atherton cornered the market for blues). I was able to contribute LP and concert reviews, and through my friendship with record dealer/DJ/radio pioneer Tony Monson was able to provide reviews of import 45s on alternate weeks. More importantly I was asked for suggestions for vintage soul material, and this led to two major projects. The first, a history of the saxophone in R&B music, ran in two parts in successive issues, giving me the opportunity to research the territorial jazz bands of the '30s, the big band era of the '40s, and the emergence of numerous jazz-based tenor-sax men as featured soloists in the R&B era of the '50s, along with the rise of Louis Jordan with his alto sax and small combo jump blues. This also gave me an insight into the progression of the musical careers of saxmen including Sam 'The Man' Taylor, Red Prysock and Big Al Sears, who had graduated from big-band beginnings to become bastions of the 'honking' rock 'n' roll era, and the emergence of soul talents that included King Curtis and Jimmy Castor.

The second project was an open-ended feature which began when some old names from the R&B past returned to the scene with new single releases in the mid-'70s. I called this 'Yesterday's Hitmakers, Today's Hopefuls', and included the likes of Solomon Burke, the Jive Five, Brook Benton and Sylvia (Robinson). It ran for a couple of years, giving me copious column inches in which to propagate the qualities and heritage of vintage R&B singers and groups to a new and younger audience. Looking back, it is quite remarkable how many artists and vocal groups (or group members) who had been chart names in the '50s and early '60s enjoyed a revival in the mid-'70s. The fact that I had access to a full range of import singles and LP releases, and that *Billboard* was still cheap enough to buy regularly, certainly helped this eagle-eyed fan to spot the names from the past in lists of new releases, regional charts, advertisements and small news items. Equally helpful to the cause was the fact that *Black Echoes* in Newman Street, *Billboard*'s office in Carnaby Street and my day-job office in Gower Street were all within a half-mile or so of each other, and for a year or so I was able to collect a complimentary copy of *Billboard* from Carnaby Street, scan through for relevant names and news jottings for my column 'A little bit of something', lifted from *Shout* to *Echoes* to provide bullet-point snippets of soul/R&B/blues information, then deliver the column-copy and the *Billboard* magazine to *Echoes* office – and get paid for the news-jottings and 'Hitmakers' columns.

My freelance role also led to commissions for books (biographies of B.B. King and Ray Charles, specialist tomes on New Orleans music and the sociology of soul music), film reviews (Diana Ross in *The Wiz*, the *Soul to Soul* extravaganza in Africa) and concert reviews (too many to cite examples!), interviews with vintage artists who toured the UK (including Johnny Otis, Jackie Wilson and Roy Brown), and the chance to publish (lengthy) reports on my first couple of trips to the New Orleans Jazzfest – which I will talk about in more detail later.

Black Echoes continued as the publishers, first Alan Thompson, then Paul Phillips, bravely fought for a niche in the specialist market as a weekly tabloid, later adapting a monthly glossy format, but now solely a web-based venture.

Black Music

IPC launched *Black Music* in December 1973 as a glossy and comprehensive monthly competitor to *Blues & Soul*, though with a far wider musical remit to cover reggae and jazz alongside mainstream and specialist soul, and also rode the disco wave of the mid-'70s. It survived until spring 1983 with a roster of staff and freelance writers which now reads like a who's who in establishment soul journalism, including Tony Cummings, Cliff White and Geoff Brown, under the editorship of Ray Coleman and Alan Lewis, veterans respectively of *Melody Maker* and *New Musical Express*.

Issues of *Black Music* were never given sequence numbers on the front cover, being identified by month and year until you turned the page to find the number on the masthead. I note from the March 1975 issue (actually 'Volume 2, no. 16' – most odd for a monthly publication!) that Dave Godin and Ian Levine are listed as contributors in a month where the mailbag was full to overflowing with reactions to Tony Cummings's features on the Northern Soul scene, which were akin to asking the leader of the Labour party to write about the merits of a Conservative opponent: the basic premise of their national loyalty was the same, but their methods of governing the nation are radically opposed – as was Tony's opinion of the followers of Northern Soul despite their sharing a black music root. 1975 also saw major features on Memphis stars Al Green, Shirley Brown and Willie Mitchell, on Dionne Warwick, the Hues Corporation and James Brown, Solomon Burke, the contrasting funk of the Ohio Players and Kool & the Gang, All Platinum stars Shirley Goodman, the Moments and Whatnauts, percussive disco musicians Bohannon and Paul Humphrey, and an expansive feature on Barry White. The magazine could boast an impressive roster of writers and contributors, so it is curious to note that a number of the main feature interviews carried no by-line other than photo credits to Dennis Morris.

While *Black Music* continued to fly the flag for mainstream and traditional soul during the disco era (along with its coverage of more diverse black music forms), it accommodated market needs from time to time. In August 1975, for example, it published a feature by Tony Cummings on gay soul, led with a photo of Valentino, whose 'I Was Born This Way' eased into the dance charts in both the USA and UK on its floating beat. Tony traced the gay appeal back to the effeminacy of Charly & Ray's 1957 Herald US R&B hit 'I Love You Madly' and through the eras of implicit gay soul hits – the Meters' 'Sissy Strut', for example – to the Dynamic Superiors on Motown and the affinity of gay soul fans for emotional ballads by girl singers. This time TC did not offend, and the mailbag in the September issue included two letters complimenting him on the style and content of his feature – though that's not to say that the editor hadn't spiked a number of letters with a different opinion!

Tony took over the editor's mantle from Alan Lewis in May 1976, and there was a move towards contributions of an investigative nature about reggae, dance and drug-related issues, along with major features on Candi Staton, the Spinners and Marvin Gaye. Then it was into 1977 with Stevie Wonder, Jerry Butler and Grover Washington, before Tony published a focus on Britain's soul scene in May. Reading through the nine-page epic, it's interesting to note that a number of the names Tony mentioned are still involved in the scene –Tony himself (now an executive with Crossrhythms, an online Christian radio and media organisation), Dave McAleer (now a music consultant with Universal Music Group), Ian Levine (now a major co-ordinator of multi-media projects on Northern Soul), and me! It is perhaps rather ironic and indicative that media figures, including DJs, and musicians mentioned are no longer actively involved in the world of soul music. This feature was the last for Tony as editor, with Geoff Brown being promoted to that role in June and Tony listed as the magazine's American correspondent, while Davitt Sigerson was enlisted as disco editor, perhaps recognising that while a percentage of Black music could be categorised as disco, not all music played in discos had its origins in the soul culture.

For the remainder of the year the contents of *Black Music* maintained a balance of contemporary and classic soul, reggae and jazz-funk, with cover names including Ernie Isley, Archie Bell and Ben E. King, Eric Gale and George Benson, and even Fats Domino plus some reggae stars. 1977 closed with Smokey Robinson (November) and Stevie Wonder and Marvin Gaye (December) providing a Motown focus. Also notable in December was the absence of Tony's name and also that of erstwhile disco editor Davitt Sigerson from the contributor credits. It is thus somewhat ironic that the new year began with the January 1978 issue boasting a cover photo of disco diva Donna Summer to accompany the published review (by Geoff Brown) of her October UK concert, the magazine also including a feature on Boney M, those Munich-based bastions of disco soul!

The first few months of 1978 brought a predominance of female soul to the magazine, following Nona Hendrix, Dorothy Moore, Eloise Laws and Betty Wright with Millie Jackson, Patti Austin and the Emotions. An editorial in March heralded a greater diversity of content from April with a name-change to *Black Music & Jazz Review*, together with a larger format – a quarter-inch deeper and an inch wider, destined to play havoc with filing systems! The expanded name, explained the 'Blackchat' editorial, was to accommodate jazz-funk and soul-jazz as 'the more recent additions to the vocabulary' of Black music. Thus the names of Sam Dees and Phillip Mitchell shared coverage with Weather Report, John Surman and John McLaughlin, and a front-cover strapline boasted 'soul-reggae-jazz-disco', which probably explains why my archive collection of the magazine has gaps hereafter, as I became selective in the destiny of my monthly 40p. It was tested almost to the limit in October with Etta James and Freddie Hubbard balanced with Ira Kere, and likewise in December with the Temptations, B.B. King and Latimore competing with John McLaughlin (again) and Joe Zawinul, the somewhat avant-garde keyboard player with jazz group Weather Report.

There were further changes in 1979 when *Black Music & Jazz Review* left the corporate realm of IPC to become part of the empire of its historic rival *Blues & Soul*, moving home to the latter's Praed Street offices, with *Black Music* regular contributor Chris May as editor reporting to long-time *Blues & Soul* staffer Jeff Tarry as managing editor. The physical aspect of the magazine also changed, reverting to the more usual A4 size of its original naissance. *Black Music & Jazz Review* came to look like a sibling of *Blues & Soul* in the quality of newsprint, fonts, style and layout, and by early 1980 had reverted to its original *Black Music* title, with *and Jazz Review* relegated to a subtitle strap, often hidden behind an overlaid part of the cover photograph. The list of contributors now included barrister cum soul scribe Clive Anderson, knowledgeable fan John Armstrong and Richard Wootton, an R&B fan who has enjoyed a long career as a music publicist, with *Blues & Soul* veteran writer David Nathan also contributing from his New York home.

Soul content now dominated, with the occasional nod towards jazz-funk and Brit-soul, the latter an emergent facet of the music with jazz-funk and disco or dance-based music played by British-born black musicians like Light of the World, whose talent and popularity are beyond question but sit more happily in a history of dance music rather than as part of soul music in London.

A further subtle change followed when the editorial of the February 1981 issue (for some reason given as 'Volume 3, issue 10' on the masthead) revealed that with effect from the next month the magazine would be retitled *BM*, subtitled with the full strapline *Black Music & Jazz Review*, on the grounds that 'for eight years people have been calling us *BM* anyway', a logic that clearly had not been applied to host-journal *Blues & Soul*, which has been known as *B&S* almost since its birth yet has always maintained its full title on the cover. Anyway, the first issue of *BM* duly appeared in March, graced with an out-of-focus cover photo of Marvin Gaye carrying his overcoat over his arm. It was mainly filled with charts, news items and album reviews, apart from the Gaye feature promoted on the cover and a detailed discography of James Brown's LPs and singles, contributed by Cliff White. The last issue in my files is from April

1981, and is filled mainly with reggae and African content, apart from the continued James Brown discography and a nice three-page spread on Eloise Laws. Although *BM* continued to be published for a further two years, until May 1983, I decided that my money and time was best used elsewhere.

Other Magazines
I was pleased to receive copies of several soul fanzines from overseas, and *Soul Bag* continued to fly the flag for in-depth discography, also turning to glossy and colour production. Then came *Voices From the Shadows*, launched in 1986 by Rod Dearlove and subsequently funded by snooker champion and soul fan Steve Davis. It was blessed with bounteous editorial copy, record reviews, fine photographs, art paper production and colour cover. *Voices* also ventured into record mail order and was sustained through more than a decade – though the latest date I could find on Rod's website is 1998 – as a comprehensive vehicle for soul research and journalism. This mantle was later assumed by *In The Basement*, published since 1995 by David Cole from Brighton and probably the definitive magazine for classic soul and Southern Soul. I'm happy to say that David was a subscriber to *Shout* all those years ago, and clearly ingested the bug for publishing interviews and reviews. Blessed with the tools generated by new technology, David networks with supreme skill to rediscover artists, and his resultant interviews are sympathetic and revealing, the discographies comprehensive and the copy eminently readable. The magazine takes its title from the Chess hit single by Etta James and Sugar Pie Desanto, and is now a quintessential journal in its field.

Of equal literary and musicological quality – and even greater pedigree – is *Juke Blues*, presently at issue 69 as I type this in November 2010, with amazing production and layout quality and contents that cover the broadest spectrum of blues and related musical styles, including soul, gospel, Cajun, zydeco and blues-rooted jazz. The magazine was born out of the demise of *Blues Unlimited* following the tragic and premature passing of editor

Mike Leadbitter in 1974 (although *Blues Unlimited* carried on, albeit somewhat sporadically, until 1988). Cilla Huggins and John Broven took up the mantle to continue Mike's work, and the new title hinted at a more catholic approach to the broad world of blues. Blessed with the photography skills of the much-travelled Paul Harris to provide a wide variety of illustrations, and a list of contributors that is a veritable who's who of (mainly UK-based) blues fans, *Juke Blues* sets and surpasses high targets for the quality of its contents, and the CD reviews keep many a credit card in frequent use.

Treading a similar path is *Blues & Rhythm*, which is kind enough to pay tribute to the influence of *Shout* on its website, and the magazine's editor Tony Burke was of immense help in producing the later issues of *Shout*. For some reason, though, I never got into the habit of buying the magazine – perhaps because the contents tended to include blues of the more vintage style, which I like to hear but tend not to read much about. The *Blues & Rhythm* website now promotes the fact that their coverage ranges into 'old timey' and western swing, musical paths diverging from the soul and mainstream blues that dominate my tastes.

CHAPTER NINE

SLEEVENOTES AND MORE

As with a lot of things in life, it was a combination of circumstances and people that led to my big break into the world of LP sleeve-notes, which has long since metamorphosed into CD booklet notes and the growth market for memorabilia. It would have been in about 1973 that the office phone rang with a call from Nigel Grainge at Phonogram Records. Mike Leadbitter was working with Nigel on the compilation of the Genesis box sets of early Chess blues material, and this had prompted Nigel to compile a series of LPs containing R&B and some blues into the soul era, covering the years since rock 'n' roll broke the Chess label into a wider market and focusing on 1956–66, entitled the Chess Golden Decade. These LPs, a series of eight, were compiled with a lot of assistance from James Hamilton, and James was also the major catalyst in pushing Phonogram to the fore during the subsequent disco era, when their licence deal with Joe and Sylvia Robinson's All Platinum company reaped a rich harvest – but that's another story.

While Mike had a comprehensive knowledge of blues, soul was not his forte, but his recent contributions to *Shout* prompted him to suggest that Nigel should contact me regarding notes for the Golden Decade series. I was happy to accept this first commission. Having just checked in my collection I find that I did the notes for vols 2 and 6 (the notes in vol. 7 were un-credited) in the series, which involved researching Big Al Downing, J.C. Davis, Dave Cortez, the Marathons/Vibrations, the Corsairs and others. This got me more involved with Phonogram – fruitful to the extent of several paid ads in the magazine over a couple of years – and with Leon Campadelli, the man responsible for working with back-catalogue budget-lines. From this connection came the chance to do comprehensive notes for two definitive volumes of the *Best of the Platters*, followed by notes for several other LPs of the group's bounteous Mercury repertoire, some of which were pleasant rather than essential listening.

There was also an intriguing double LP entitled *The Rock 'n' Soul Story*, issued on Phillips' International Series (6640 006), which gathered together an odd but interesting range of Mercury and other material, ranging from the Contours and Del Vikings, the Champs and Bill Justis, Freddy Bell and Jerry Lee Lewis to Rufus Thomas and Johnny Thunder.

Further benefit from the liaison with Leon was the chance to suggest other LPs for reissue. UK Mercury LP *Rhythm & Blues Party* (Little Richard/Sil Austin/Red Prysock, etc.) from a dozen years earlier was reissued on Philips International (6436 023) with a modern sleeve (and minus Lee Allen's 'Walking With Mr Lee' for licence reasons), and we managed to mark the tragic death of Louis Jordan with *Choo Choo Ch-Boogie* (6336 246). This reissued a dozen of his best Mercury recordings, some being re-runs of his Decca hits but not lacking in quality, and at that time (February 1975) it was the only Jordan LP in the catalogue. With the agreement and co-operation of Nigel Grainge I also managed to manoeuvre a *Best of the Dells* LP into the schedules on the Checker budget line, which was an early adventure in selecting the repertoire *and* writing the notes, though one Michael Farrell was credited with the dreadful sleeve design of thumbnail cameo heads of the group drowned in an ocean of garish colour – but then, this was the '70s. While there were other monograph LPs from Phonogram (Bo Diddley/Chuck Berry/Little Milton 'Golden Decades') and a comprehensive trawl of the Chess catalogue from the early '50s to the mid-'60s divided up into eight compilation LPs. These were marketed in a series reasonably titled 'Chess Golden Decade', which actually covered more than that. They were packaged in rather grand gatefold sleeves, each with a top-quality sleevenote from a leading expert of the style or era. There were also some compilations aimed at the disco market, where the budget (and need) for sleevenotes was limited.

My next commission came out of the blue via another industry connection, and took me into a potentially bigger and wider market. I first met Alan Warner in the mid- to late '60s when he was label manager for EMI Licensed Product, compiling LPs of ABC and Kent/Modern material like *Soul Sixteen* and *Soul Supply*, then moving to Liberty/UA whom he followed to the UK, originating the 'Many Sides of Rock 'n' Roll' series of double albums. The latter gained sufficient profile for the idea to be picked up by World Records, a mail order operation of the time who advertised multi-LP boxed sets in various styles in the national press. 'The Golden Years of Rock 'n' Roll' was a World project in 1975, and as Alan was busy with numerous other things related to his skills, knowledge and enthusiasm as a music and movie historian, he kindly delegated to me the task of writing notes for the six-album set, which encompassed elements of vintage pop, rock 'n' roll, R&B and formative soul, and for which it was also necessary to incorporate some information on world affairs during the eras covered. It was rewarding to see the finished article and the resultant cheque for my labours, but I have no idea how many units it sold! This networking also brought me into contact with budget company Pickwick, for whom I wrote notes for LPs of Booker T & the MGs, Ray Charles and the Everly Brothers, even moving into the realms of pop music for a long-forgotten double album including the Troggs and the Honeycombs amid a few more acceptable R&R/R&B names.

My first step in originating compilations and doing notes had come in 1973 when old friend and *Soul Music* co-editor Dave McAleer was label manager for licensed product at Pye, which had recently acquired the rights to Florence Greenberg's Scepter/Wand labels from Decca. *Hot Buttered Soul* fanzine editor Chris Savory and I approached him with an idea for doing a deep soul anthology from material in the Greenberg catalogue. Dave was receptive to this, having in the pipeline an LP of Northern Soul from the same source compiled by Ian Levine, and interested in comparing respective sales. Thus the three of us sat down and pored over label lists of Scepter and Wand singles releases, focusing on known soul names alongside the usual fans' instinct for great unknowns, obscure or eye-catching artist names and titles with impact. The masters were duly ordered and Dave and I sifted through the resultant material, refining the possibles down to two sets of sixteen tracks. We formulated batch one into a running order that included a variety of styles, ranging from the New Orleans funk of Warren Lee, the Motownesque beat of Nella Dodds and the deep soul of the Masqueraders, Katie Love, Johnny Moore and Marvin Preyer, through the hits of Dionne Warwick, Theola Kilgore and Tommy Hunt, to the retro doo-wop of the Ti-Tones and the Jokers. We made an attempt at giving our selection the longest-ever LP title, but *Not just another soul album, but probably the best soul from the '60s compilation LP ever...* was truncated to a somewhat immodest *Best Soul From the '60s* for the benefit of the sales team and graced with an anonymous-looking sleeve photo of a black girl in a royal blue cardigan photographed in dim light. Visual impact was about minus eight on a scale of one to ten. I doubt it sold more than a couple of thousand copies, and we were never asked to prepare the second volume for release. The main benefits for me were the pleasure and credit of being involved in the project, getting paid for it and being given a treasured acetate containing some ultra-rare tracks that we didn't get to use on the issued or unissued compilations.

Later in the decade came the beginnings of Ace Records, which led to commissions to write notes for LPs/CDs of Bobby Bland, the Staple Singers and Eddie Floyd among others, but in the mid-'70s it was my involvement in *Black Echoes* which led to another chapter in the book of life.

First came a call from Bill Millar, prompted by Phil Hardy and Dave Laing, his editors at Studio Vista publishers who were working on his profile of the Drifters. Phil and Dave were embarking on a major project which would come to fruition through Panther Books in paperback as *The Encyclopaedia of Rock*, divided into three volumes as 'The Age of Rock 'n' Roll', 'From Liverpool to San Francisco' and 'Sounds of the Seventies', for which I was contracted to write about fifty entries on soul acts at lengths varying between 100 and 200 words. It was a challenge to write at such precise (lack of) length, but very satisfying to see my name in print in a proper paperback book, though the venture was also published as a copiously illustrated magazine-format partwork, also in 1976 and also entitled *The Encyclopaedia of Rock*. Along a similar path, my name on the list of contributors at *Black Echoes* led to another commission for entries in *The Illustrated Encyclopaedia of Black Music*, published in November 1982 by Salamander Books, in which general editor Mike Clifford collated contributions from a range of black music writers, grouping the results in musical eras. My contributions totalled around a hundred names in the '50s and '60s sections, though sadly no entries carried a by-line.

The passage of time continues, and further opportunities have arisen through networking (that management buzz-word that derives from the old concept of knowing a man who knows a man). I've been involved in some interesting reissue projects, which have involved both the selection of repertoire and writing notes. The name of Dave McAleer crops up yet again, with two projects that came to me through his role as consultant to the Universal Music Group. Dave had passed me some booklet-note commissions for CDs on Junior Parker (Mercury and Duke material) and psychedelic era Temptations (someone has to do it!), and then during 1999 came an invitation to compile twenty-track *Best Of* CDs for Bo Diddley, Howlin' Wolf and Muddy Waters, issued in 2000, which allowed me the freedom to include some personal favourites and hard-to-find items. Following on from this was the opportunity to select tracks from the Chess catalogue of blues for a forty-track double CD to be issued on a combined HMV/Universal logo and distributed through HMV stores. Knowing that many casual buyers would be unfamiliar with some Chess big names anyway, and that collectors would steer clear of anything containing too many classic gems (which, great as they are, have mostly been reissued to death) I went through the Chess/Checker catalogue with a well-aimed pin and a good memory and selected a combination of lesser reissued hits and classics, singles tracks by blues names like Jimmy Rogers, Lowell Fulson and Billy Emerson, and some left-field soul/blues items that had never been reissued (Jesse Hill, McKinley Mitchell, Eddie Bo and Little Miss Cornshucks. I sequenced the running order, wrote the notes and forgot about the project until I eventually found a browser rack in a local HMV store that contained their own-brand discs. I remembered that my old mate Tony Cummings had compiled a gospel collection for the same series, and with a bit of diligent rooting around I found that as well as mine – and bought them both. The lesson to be learned is that the time between originating a reissue project and seeing finished copies can be as much as two years.

Another phone call came out of the blue early in 2004, from another networking contact. This time it was Steve Brink from Prism Records, a major leisure company that deals in multi-CD packs of all music styles (as well as the whole gamut of movies/videos/DVDs). The plan was to compile 3CD boxed sets of 'Southern' Soul, Blues and Gospel. The repertoire was the combined resources of the Malaco and Charly catalogues. The hurdles to clear were persuading each of the two companies to pool their catalogue with that of the other company, and to gather together just short of 200 tracks from the original selection. This was a nightmare, and achieved only with countless substitutions. We battled on, however, and the end product was excellent value for money, at £10 for sixty-six tracks per boxed set, and rewarding for me financially as well.

The other project in which I've been involved is Shout Records, the *raison d'être* and history of which deserves its own chapter later on.

CHAPTER TEN

RECORD COLLECTING AND RETAILING

Black Wax Records

I went to work at Black Wax Records, which sold exclusively black music, late in 1974 and left early in 1976. The shop, in Mitcham Lane, opened when the mail order record business run by Roy Stanton and Hilary Cummings began to show a healthy profit, which persuaded Roy to give up his job in the food processing industry and Hilary to relinquish book-keeping duties in a local office. I was close to both of them, and to the growing fortunes of their business, through their involvement in *Shout* and through Roy's enthusiasm with *Black Wax* magazine, and was also happy to move from the tedium of clerical work in mail-order bookselling to the excitement of specialist record retailing. I ran the dispatch side of the mail order business and helped in the shop at busy times. While the wages were at pauper level, the source of records at trade price was appealing, and as I had a typewriter and stencils to hand for the record lists we came to an arrangement that I could spend some time during the working day producing *Shout*.

To the best of my knowledge, the bulk of Black Wax's initial stock came from John Anderson's Soul Bowl warehouse at King's Lynn, Norfolk. When I arrived at the shop it was fitted out with steel shelving units, with a plastic strip curtain dividing the counter area (with its home-made LP and singles browser bins) from the mail order stock and the work tables where Hilary did the accounting and opened the mail, and where I set up the dispatch and packaging area. Another shipment of 45s arrived from Soul Bowl to bolster the stock a bit, and Roy had also made contact with a US supplier on the west coast, which yielded some rather left-field soul gems – including discs by Richard 'Dimples' Fields, who was to become a cult figure before his untimely death, and, on the Bay-area Jasman and Fog City labels, singles by Johnny Talbot and Sugar Pie DeSanto. More LP stock was obtained from van sales by an East London wholesaler who carried a range of UK and US deletions. Nolan's LP on a Probe deletion became a steady seller to Northern Soul fans, and it became a standing joke for whoever took phone orders to replace the handset at the end of a call and say "'ave you got Nolan?' in as broad a regional accent as could be imitated! There were also plentiful copies of cut-outs on All Platinum and Stang. The whole range of Linda Jones's LPs became core stock, along with the Fatback Band LP on Event.

While the mail order business provided what might be called in footballing terms a solid mid-field, there was the need to stock and supply new releases. It was Roy's (idealistic) intention to stock at least one copy of every soul/blues/gospel UK release, and as many import singles and albums as could be obtained or afforded. The former was achieved by poring over *Music Week* each week, scouring the trade paper for listings and adverts for new releases, and subscribing to an independent weekly news sheet listing new singles, which developed into MusicMaster. This published quarterly, building into its first (yellow-bound) annual volume, and became the bible of record retailers. Subsequent annual volumes were bound in different and distinctive primary colours, including dark red and blue, and the publication has grown over the years to become an essential industry tool, now as RED MusicMaster and with an online research facility.

The next trick was to find a wholesaler who would supply small orders, initially on a cash on delivery basis, but later with credit terms and willing to wait sixty days for settlement of a seven day invoice. This was managed by using two or three dealers plucked from the classified ads in *Music Week*, then rotating between them when cash was available or when we were off the stop list for credit. US imports, which proved to be the basis of revenue for the business, came from two main sources – both of which relied to a degree on personal friendship and business goodwill.

The legendary specialist soul record retail and wholesale outlet Record Corner was about a mile away in Bedford Hill, Balham. It was run by Dave Hastings, a friend from the *Shout* team, with Reg and Eric (whose last names I never knew) and with Terry Davis handling the import ordering and sales. As I recall, the weekly delivery of new imports arrived on Thursday morning, and it was among my duties (as the only one with transport – a Reliant Regal van) to drive over and collect the standing order of five copies of each new 45 and one of each new LP. The basement of Record Corner became a hotbed of record-collecting friends, fans and dealers on those Thursday mornings, with the chance to look at other new material, be it R&B, blues or other offerings, and also to browse through the racks of stock and dealer returns. This was where the eye of the seasoned collector and record-hunter came into its own, the glimpse of a title, odd name or hint of R&B or blues in a title being sufficient to warrant further examination, often with an arrangement to take the disc on chance and bill it later or return it the following week. Not many were returned: one of the perks of my job was a growing collection of gems bought at trade price.

The second source of US imports was Tony Monson's company, located in Orpington, Kent, just a couple of miles from my home. We found his name among the classified ads in *Music Week*. Tony has come to be a major factor in my life in recent years – the last twenty-five to be accurate – but at that time I'm not sure that any of us (other than Hilary who wrote the cheques to pay the bills) knew the name of his High Supply company, just that his white van arrived at regular intervals and Roy picked the necessary stock. I maintained contact with Tony after the Black Wax era and made frequent visits to his home/stockroom, partly in search of odd copies of US gems and later, during the *Black Echoes* era, to select 45s for review, which we did on a week by week rotation basis. Tony had a good ear for hit material, while I managed to root out some more unusual items, deep soul obscurities and the like. Tony was also a key factor in London radio – but that's for another chapter!

Typing lists of records onto wax stencils for a lot of the time, picking and packing records for dispatch for some of the time and answering the phone to take orders for a little of the time . . . and serving in the shop for as little time as possible was the average working day. Serving wasn't too bad to start with, with the novelty of playing short clips to prospective buyers but, while I like the funkier stuff, being obliged to listen to some of it repeatedly soon saw my limit exceeded. Indeed, it was some ten years before I was able to listen to some tracks by Brothers Johnson, the Fatback Band and Parliament/Funkadelic without reaching for the off switch, particularly the latter, given George Clinton's quirky sense of humour and indulgence in audio effects – and Roy Stanton's seemingly inexhaustible appetite for these. It was to get worse, as my time at Black Wax coincided with the emergence and rise of disco, which apart from the sound meant that the goalposts moved with regard to the ethnic origin of the records we sold: the Black of Black Wax began to refer to the colour of the discs rather than the racial origin of the artists, which had been the original intention.

The mailing list was going global, and I learned a lot about packing and preparing parcels of records for overseas insured dispatch, becoming good friends with the counter clerk at the local post office as he realised I knew what I was doing: the handover time for a dozen parcels dropped from about an hour to just a few minutes! As well serving other countries (Australia, Japan and Holland being voracious markets for deep soul and bluesy ballads), we also established some big name clientele in the home market. A number of Northern Soul DJs were regular customers, and even now I pick up on the names of various London club DJs who were apparently regular visitors to the shop on Friday afternoons (the hot time for selling new imports) and on Saturdays, when Roy had the shop to himself. It was pleasing to deal personally with the needs and accounts of two media DJs of note. Robbie Vincent had a weekly soul show on local and national radio, and also lived in Beckenham, handily on my route home. I stopped by Vincent Towers once a week with a bag of new releases on firm sale for him. Also on the mailing list, at his farmhouse in rural Suffolk, was John Peel, and it was my pleasure to be greeted by his dulcet tones on the telephone once a month as he placed an order from the new list and asked for my recommendations from the recent new arrivals. We enjoyed an empathy of taste in good soul and blues, and never was a disc returned nor adverse comment made.

From time to time the front window of the shop was submerged in deep shadow as a large Land-Rover parked on the pavement outside, and Black Wax was graced by the presence of John Peel and his producer, John Walters, who would flick through the bargain bins, listen to a few new singles, ask about some obscure LPs in stock, settle their bill, exchange a few amicable words on the state of music, then disappear off to central London. My friendship with John Peel endured beyond the Black Wax era, and the last time I saw him, which must have been around 1990, he shouted a cheery 'Hi Clive' across the broad pavement of Tottenham Court Road as we walked in opposite directions.

With a small retailer cashflow is always a problem, and this is exacerbated when you venture into specialist areas: you have to maintain a turnover of stock to prompt continued interest and sales. We were fortunate in that we had a finger in the pie with the Northern Soul scene – some of our stock items were Northern staples, some discoveries came our way at bargain prices and some new releases became in demand as Ian Levine took to playing what were known as 'Philly floaters' in the Highland Room at the Blackpool Mecca. Even something as mundane as 'Fly Robin Fly' by Silver Convention sold by the box-load (twenty-five per box) when it was issued in the UK on Magnet. We didn't ask questions; we were just happy to take the money. The disco era then emerged, blossomed and flourished, with singles of varying aesthetic merit but consistent tempo flying out of the shop in eager hands almost as fast as they could be unpacked from the delivery carton. LPs had always sold steadily to the club clientele, as DJs were all keen to make their own discoveries of potential floor-fillers from album tracks, more so with the increasing flow of jazz-funk material: even the mighty Blue Note and Fantasy labels came to realise that there was cash in them there zipping cymbals and thudding bass-lines,

Those were the positive elements. The bad bit came in paying for the stock. As mentioned earlier, we obtained new UK releases from wholesalers by rotating orders between those whose cheques had cleared, and a similar situation prevailed with SP&S, our LP cut-out supplier. When their van arrived Roy would be waiting in the hope that Hilary had robbed Peter to pay Paul, and mustered enough funds from the accrued cheques in the morning mail to enable us to pay the outstanding account. The imports pushed the boundaries of old friendships to new limits, with both Tony and Dave allowing far more credit than would or should have been the case, but were generous and realistic to realise that without new supplies to sell, albeit in reduced quantities, there would be no cashflow to meet liabilities.

The combination of the dilution of our soul principles in the disco era, the need to earn a living wage and put a foot back on the ladder of normal business life with career prospects, and the knowledge that a management policy which basically equated to buying more than there was money to pay for or the hope of selling was a recipe for disaster meant that I contacted Dillon's Bookshop in central London in the summer of 1976 to apply for a job as an order typist. Two interviews led to a job offer and twenty years of continuous employment. Sadly the business strategy described above, together with dwindling takings, eventually reached its inevitable conclusion. Not long after I'd left Black Wax Hilary and Roy visited the local Citizens Advice Bureau armed with the accounts and related paperwork, and were advised that as Black Wax was not a limited company and there were no consequent directorial responsibilities, the best option given the level of debt and the lack of funds would be to close the shop one night and not reopen for trading – just disappear. This is exactly what happened: the doors were locked one night and never reopened. I've no idea what happened to the remaining stock: there can't be much market value in several racks of obscure soul 45s for which the demand had been exhausted over three years, and I expect any remaining imports were taken back by Record Corner. Hilary Cummings soon left suburban Streatham and returned to her Plymouth roots, where she still lives happily today: she is still a friend. Roy Stanton left Streatham and has never been seen nor heard of again – though there was an unconfirmed rumour some years ago that he had moved to Hong Kong.

As I said earlier, the main reason why I became disillusioned with life in a record shop was the realisation that people would buy a disc, be it a 45 costing £1 or an LP costing a tenner, on the basis of hearing less than thirty seconds of the intro of a track and had little regard for the musical quality of what followed. To give them their due, Northern Soul fans at least had a depth of knowledge about and loyalty to the whole concept of a song and/or performer, whereas most disco or club fans were loyal only to the beat (or beats per minute) of the latest hot import. That both will make money for the singers and writers was some consolation, but it's worth noting that few of the artists who emerged or charted in the disco era enjoyed sustained recording careers afterwards. The jazzmen who benefited short-term reverted to their root styles with money safely banked, but few enjoyed back-catalogue sales as, with the exception of a few Blue Note LPs, the funky beat was missing. There were established (veteran) artists who dipped their toes into the disco pool and soon reverted to the ocean of stability, but many folk have a selection of LPs and 45s in their racks (me included) by artists whose discographies run to just two or three lines.

CHAPTER ELEVEN

DJs AND GIGS

Mention of the various punters at Black Wax brings me to DJs, and the different worlds of club and radio jocks. There was good representation of both at the shop, with differing requirements and tastes to suit the respective audiences. I've had experience of both worlds, and have known people who were masters of one yet a fish completely out of the water in the other, while some work in both camps with consummate skill and ease.

For three years in the mid-'70s I played a half-hour session of new releases at a local club in Welling, Kent. It didn't much matter to me whether the audience of around 400 danced or not – clubgoers seem reluctant to accept or enjoy unfamiliar discs, though some tracks like Andrea True Connection's 'More More More', MFSB's 'Sexy' and Shirley & Co.'s 'Shame Shame Shame' caught on instantly – but to the main DJ, a confident and voluble guy named Mike Randall, an empty floor was a sign of failure. Mike was quite happy and confident talking at 400 teenagers at the club, yet when we went for a guest appearance on the David Simmons Show at BBC Radio London, with the microphone live but no visible audience, he froze and dried on air. Perhaps it was best that way, as over the years I've heard a number of big-name club DJs on the radio whose voices and style were really not right for a wider audience.

Having that limited experience of club work, a good track record of written journalism, a good record collection and a good memory, I was quite pleased to have an opportunity to gain some broadcasting experience. This initially came through the good offices of the aforementioned Dave Simmons at Radio London, on whose weekly soul show I became a regular guest from around 1977 for a year or so, taking to the studio various collectors' items from my collection together with the more R&B-styled new releases in what was still the disco era. Dave had a good ear for the Jimmy Castor style of soul, which combined elements of floor-shaking funk, sweet soul, R&B roots and a hint of Latin, and involved his club audiences in various records, like Castor's 'Bertha Butt Boogie', getting them to clap along with the beat and playing percussion instruments that he distributed. Somehow Dave also managed to arrange a PA by veteran soul singer Lenny Welch at the modest and remote venue of the Green Man in Plumstead, amid the terraced rooftops of the grimy Thames-side south-east London suburb, to promote Mainstream's 45 'A Hundred Pounds of Pain' in 1974.

Soul Mafia DJs

Into the '80s the club DJ began to be the focus of the music in the London soul world as, almost at the expense of the performers, as the 'Soul Mafia' began to emerge. The dominance of club DJs as the vehicle for promoting the music began as part of the Northern Soul scene, first in the original clubs like the Torch near Stoke-on-Trent and the Twisted Wheel in Manchester, then in the '70s in the Wigan Casino and the Blackpool Mecca. As the Northern Soul scene had its Russ Winstanley, Ian Levine, Keith Minshull and Colin Curtis, and some DJs with a peculiar penchant for covering the labels of the records they played and inventing new names for the obscure artists whose music they were using to generate a following. The London area had the likes of Chris Hill, Tom Holland, Sean French, Mark Webster, Chris Brown and 'Froggy', followed by Pete Tong and the late Steve Walsh. Just as the northern scene had its all-nighters, so the London Soul Mafia focused on all-dayers, and while it may have been a little odd trying to re-create a club evening in the afternoon of a sunny day, the atmosphere certainly worked well in my limited experience. I once spent a couple of hours on a Bank Holiday Monday inside the capacious ballroom of the Purley Orchid watching a floor full of people dancing, lit by the revolving strobe-light and virtually deafened by the booming music and the exhortations of the DJ. All-Dayers became Weekenders, at locations like Caister, near Great Yarmouth, starting in 1979 and enduring to the present day. Their popularity was phenomenal, necessitating the need to move to progressively larger venues and expand their schedules. Brit-funk bands like Light of the World were available to play the right music in the right place at the right time.

Gigs

The gatefold sleeve of *A Memphis Soul Night – Live in Europe* has great photos of David Hudson, Otis Clay, Ann Peebles and Lynn White, and what there is of the liner notes reminds me that I travelled north of Camden Town to the Town & Country Club to see the Waylo Records package brought to London by Willie Mitchell. The only clue to dates is that the tour played Berlin on 30 October 1989, which looks to have been the final date on the schedule after Rotterdam, Amsterdam, Hasselt and London. I remember doing a good interview with Willie Mitchell on a cassette which I don't think was ever transcribed, and the concert was a great event in the tradition of US soul revues, thankfully committed to vinyl on the 1990 Waylo double album. While I can remember shreds of action and reaction from the soul one-nighters of the '60s and '70s, I'm afraid that not much remains in my mental archive of the Memphis night other than having to stand for the duration of the show: the Town & Country had been a cinema but the seats had been removed to make room for the crowds at music events – though maybe there was a balcony with a few tables as well as the smoke-filled arena.

The London visit of the Malaco Revue took place in July 1989, according to an interview with Bobby Bland by journalist Barney Hoskins published in *The Times*. Along with Bland was Johnnie Taylor, who I had the pleasure of interviewing for *Black Echoes*.

He was a debonair gent clad in silk dressing-gown, smoking a huge pipe and looking thoroughly comfortable lounging in a hotel room. Denise LaSalle was also appearing alongside Bland, and I got to interview her in the less-congenial environs of the hotel bar. Songwriters and sometime performers (Sam) Mosley and (Bob) Johnson were also along, evidence of which I obtained by having them sign a paper napkin in the same bar. The concert was at the Hammersmith Odeon, and the audience was perhaps in awe of these three major black singers: the response wasn't quite what these soul legends would have encountered from a home-town, chittlin' circuit crowd, but they came to realise that rapt silence during a song and rousing applause at the end was the London way of showing appreciation. Having had the pleasure of seeing Bobby Bland perform before, once in London with B.B. King and a couple of times in New Orleans, I was aware that he tends to feed on audience response to build his performance, and he fell just short of doing a great show. Even then the trademark throaty squall that enhances some of his classic records was rationed to conserve his voice.

The third notable major soul event of the time was a New Orleans Night staged at the Royal Festival Hall by Capital Radio as part of their annual jazz week in the summer of 1992. I recollect a show featuring Dr John, Irma Thomas and the first London appearances of Johnny Adams and the white-suited, turbaned R&B pianist/songwriter Eddie Bo. Capital soul music presenter Peter Young was the MC that night, and I was pleased to be able to talk to Johnny Adams again, this time on my home ground, and also to be recognised by Irma Thomas as she walked from her dressing room – and to be waved inside by her husband Emile Jackson for a short reunion and friendly conversation. All performed superbly, and while the talents of Irma and Johnny were already widely known, the extrovert stage act of Edwin 'Eddie Bo' Bocage certainly drew the attention of many to the fact that he was far more than an obscure name in the writer credits of vintage R&B singles.

A final live musical memory of the decade is the appearance of Benny Latimore in 1990. Latimore was a long-time favourite of mine, from his Glades albums released in the UK on President in the early '70s and others that I found as import copies while working at Black Wax Records, on to later material of equal quality recorded during his long affiliation with Malaco. It was through the auspices of the latter label that he eventually made his London debut. The event took place at the Astoria Theatre, a modest auditorium at the Oxford Street end of Charing Cross Road, where I was honoured with some interview time. This necessitated climbing a narrow, winding staircase to a small room just like my vision of a prison cell. Benny was a good subject with a clear recollection of dates and places, and he related several stories of his sessions for Henry Stone in Florida. Then it was showtime, and cramped standing room only in the crowded performance area: the stage was where the cinema screen would have been, and we stood, crushed and swaying, in the limited space where there would have been about twenty rows of seats. I presume he played with a small combo or rhythm section, but I was close to the stage and couldn't see much beyond the glare of the stage lights. It was a great musical evening, despite the circumstances.

CHAPTER TWELVE

EXCURSIONS TO THE PROMISED LAND

New York

To the young London soul fan of the '60s, the thought of a trip to the USA was the equivalent of a pilgrimage to a holy venue – be it Mecca, Nazareth or any other. As a member of the Tamla Motown Appreciation Society, I remember reading with immense envy the diaries of Dave Godin's adventures in Detroit, but it was almost twenty years later that I made my first journey to the USA. This was the result of friendships originating in the 'fanzine' era when, following the evolution of several minor-league (in publishing quality rather than in quality of contents) soul journals in England – as mentioned before, my own *Shout* had been joined by the likes of *Hot Buttered Soul*, *Black Wax* and *SMG* – this trend was matched in the USA by the emergence of a number of magazines covering the history of doo-wop music.

I think *Record Exchanger* was first, followed by *Bim Bam Boom*, *Yesterday's Memories* and *Time Barrier Express* – as well as others I have just rediscovered courtesy of Google: *Whisky, Women and . . .* and the more wide-ranging *Goldmine* – which started out in fairly modest formats just like the duplicated and stapled pages of *Shout*, but evolved into more durable journals, litho-printed with lots of photos.

I made reciprocal arrangements with the editors of these magazines to exchange complimentary copies of each issue, and through this developed further communication with my new

American friends, including an exchange of letters with Marcia Vance at *Yesterday's Memories*. Marcia, ex-wife of singer/musician Kenny Vance (an original member of Jay & the Americans), lived in Brooklyn, New York, and it was a chance remark in a letter to her about cheap accommodation in New York which led to her kind offer to stay at her place in the spare bedroom. A visit to a travel agent, a quick decision and a small deposit later I was booked onto a transatlantic flight for my maiden trip to the US of A!

Marcia told me to take a cab from the airport to her house in Brooklyn, but with my experience of the cost of London taxis and youthful naïvety, I decided to take a bus ride from JFK Airport to the bus depot in mid-town Manhattan, then get a cab from there. Mistake. I soon found that Manhattan cab drivers knew Manhattan but little else, and when I finally found a driver who didn't look the other way when I gave a Brooklyn address, I didn't know that I was about to become a lost stranger in a strange land for the best part of an hour while the guy drove across the Brooklyn Bridge and out of Manhattan with little idea of how to get where he was going. A scenic tour of the gas stations of Flatbush and about an hour and a $25 fare later I finally climbed out of the cab to a welcoming hug from Marcia. Later I checked on a map to see where I had gone, and saw the error of my impetuosity. The return cab journey to JFK took about ten minutes and $6!

This would have been around 1976, and thirty years later much of the trip is a distant and faded memory. I recall spending the days on sightseeing trips around the Big Apple, mainly courtesy of Marcia's daughter Abbey, who I think had just graduated. She kindly took me on the Staten Island Ferry to the Statue of Liberty. I managed other trips on my own, though the family were dismayed that I'd walked from Broadway to the East Side Harbour to take a boat trip round the island. I stayed at home for the evenings, of which I recall little apart from two main events: one was the visit of a record dealer who brought a car-load of doo-wop LPs on Relic and other reissue labels, from which I took my pick for a very modest price. The other was a house-call by Marcia's friend Paul Evans – he of 'Seven Little Girls Sitting In the Back Seat' and – more recently

– 'Hello This is Joannie', and also a fine pianist and great doo-wop fan. The result was a memorable evening sitting round the piano as Paul played through doo-wop hits as Marcia, other friends and I sang along as best we could. Of such things are memories made.

The New Orleans Years

Many music friends recommended to me the famed hospitality of the deep south, and more specifically New Orleans. The music of Louisiana had been the subject of pioneering blues journalism by Mike Leadbitter, both through articles and reviews in *Blues Unlimited* and through special BU booklets such as *From the Bayou* (the story of Eddie Shuler and Goldband Records from Lake Charles, Louisiana) and *Crowley Louisiana Blues*, dealing with Jay D. Miller and his Excello label. There were also appetising stories crossing the Atlantic about the New Orleans Jazz & Heritage Festival, held every spring in the Crescent City's Congo Square, and after 1972 expanded to the Fairgrounds Race Track on Esplanade Avenue. 'Jazz & Heritage' could be readily expanded to include a host of local acts in the R&B category, from old-time bluesmen to modern soul stars and hopefuls, so it was a fine showcase for as many local singers and musicians as could be scheduled into two weekends at the end of April and beginning of May.

It would have been in the late '70s when Charlie Gillett, one-time co-editor of *Soul Music* and then playing two hours of R&B-related music on Sunday mornings on BBC Radio London, mentioned a group holiday to New Orleans to see the Jazzfest (as it is generally known). The organiser was a young lady named Lesley Stanford, who lived with her husband Ken in Hammersmith, west London, and had done the groundwork for taking a party of Londoners on what turned out to be the holiday of a lifetime. Taking its name from the promotion vehicle that was used to gather potential trippers, the Honky Tonk Trip to New Orleans gathered pace over the following months, with the payment of deposits and much saving to pay the remaining balance, and it must have been in about March 1979 when some fifty trippers gathered at Nelson's

Club at Wimbledon Stadium to meet each other for the first time. We somehow organised ourselves into groups of four room-mates, so we could share at the Vieux Carre Travel Lodge on North Rampart Street on the edge of the French Quarter in New Orleans.

The small world of soul fanzines and their readers bore fruit, as my name was known to a couple of guys, and we kindred spirits got together, managed to find a fourth gent of similar taste, and were thus settled and ready for departure day at the end of April. In the company of John Broven, Paul Harris and Phil Reeves, I set off on a journey to the musical paradise that is South Louisiana. Some readers will recognise the name of John Broven as a recognised authority on the music and traditions of the area, and author of the pioneering book *Walking to New Orleans*, first published in 1974. It is still available in a revised edition, under the title *Rhythm & Blues in New Orleans*, and chronicles the history and lives of many singers and musicians from the city and surrounding areas. It was my good fortune that John had just been commissioned by local publisher Pelican Books to write another book, this time covering the broader range of Louisiana music. The benefits of this were two-fold: John had already set up a number of interviews with key figures in the state, and he also had a wealth of contacts through whom further interviews could be arranged when we arrived. Furthermore, he was already a veteran of at least two previous trips to Louisiana, and was well versed in the state's geography!

Thus during my first trip to what was to become my second home within a decade (I returned to New Orleans six times during the '80s, then made my eighth pilgrimage in 2001 to introduce my wife to the pleasures of southern hospitality), not only was I able to watch and hear a number of my musical heroes and heroines in their own parish, but also to meet and talk to a number of legendary figures from the world of rhythm and blues, and see first hand some of the recording studios and locations in which the music was made.

We spoke to (or more accurately John interviewed and I listened intently) a number of people in New Orleans, some of whom were happy to travel to our hotel and sit in air-conditioned comfort with a cool glass of beer, including Joe Barry and Johnny Adams and

George 'Tex' Stephens, formerly R&B DJ on WJBW and WMRY, who spoke at authoritative length about radio and local music, and invited us to guest on his radio show. This involved a midnight trip to Canal Street to a studio at the top of a skyscraper. We walked there and back and thought nothing of it, but were later told that doing so had put us in mortal danger.

We also travelled out to Clematis Street to talk to Marshal Sehorn in his capacious office at Sea-Saint Studios. I have an enduring memory of the phone ringing during the interview, Marshall pressing the desk intercom button, leaning back in his luxurious leather swivel-tilt executive chair, and hollering 'Talk to me!' at the receptionist connecting the call. One irony of the visit to Sea-Saint was that the first person we met while sitting in the reception lounge was fellow (ex-pat) Brit John Abbey, ex-*Blues & Soul* editor, who was running Ichiban Records from his home in Atlanta, Georgia, and was producing the Staple Singers at the studio – who we also got to meet briefly. Also passing through reception was a tall, well-built black guy in T-shirt and jeans, employed as a maintenance man, who was Sansu recording artist Lee Bates.

Looking through the appendices to *South To Louisiana*, wherein John lists the dates and locations of the taped interviews, I am reminded of the timetable of our tour, and that it included two trips out of New Orleans to Cajun Country. At the time this seemed to be an expensive addition to the initial cost of the holiday, but it turned out to be priceless. We spent the weekends in the city absorbing the wide array of music at the Jazzfest, then ventured off along Interstate Highway 10 towards Lafayette for the midweek. On 25 April 1979 we were in Lafayette, visiting Johnnie Allan on his homestead (what else do you call a beautiful house where the backyard includes a paddock with two horses set amid a clearing in the surrounding trees), and meeting Rod Bernard and Warren Storm in a break from their day jobs. That first evening was also eventful. Having checked in at an cheap motel, we were told that a local band would be playing at a lounge just down the road – so mid-evening saw four intrepid Brits walking briskly along the Evangeline Thruway towards said lounge, only to be apprehended by cops! A police car pulled up alongside and asked what we thought we were doing. Informed that we were going to see a band, we were advised to be very careful and to have a good evening. It seems nobody walks in the deep south if they have a car, even for a couple of blocks, hence the concern.

We reached the lounge, found a table and seats, bought a round of drinks (again and again: they don't like to see people with empty glasses!) and sat back to enjoy the band. We didn't know what to expect, so were pleasantly surprised when the first few songs were soul oldies and swamp-pop favourites – then we found that we were watching Lil' Bob and the Lollipops, a renowned swamp-soul band with an LP and singles on La Louisianne Records. The set went on late into the night. Also in the audience was local country rock singer Scooter Lee, a shapely blonde wearing tight pants and a welcoming smile!

It was back to Cajun Country the next week, when we spent a day at the tiny, rural Lake Charles, home of Eddie Shuler and his Goldband Records. Shuler had a wealth of stories, all told in best down-home style, and while we were looking around his legendary studio, where a host of great rockabilly and formative R&B tracks were cut, along came Katie Webster (she and Eddie are both now sadly deceased). An enthusiastic, vibrant person, Katie was a splendid interviewee for John and subject for numerous photo poses for Paul Harris (dubbed 'Shutter-bug' by Shuler that day). After talking with us Shuler first played us master tapes from Katie's recent session (subsequently released on Goldband, and years later on UK Charly), then Katie sat at the piano and proceeded to play a jam session of blues and R&B songs for about half-an-hour. Pure magic, followed by magic of a different kind as we were given the freedom of Eddie's attic-cum- storeroom for an hour or so, which was quite long enough in the stifling heat, to rummage through boxes of 45s and LPs for which we were asked to pay but a modest price.

We were back on the I-10 again the next day, this time the shorter journey from Lafayette to Crowley, for a lunchtime meeting with Jay D. Miller of Excello Records. Mr Miller showed us around his office, and opened a large filing cabinet to show us dozens of bundles of receipts – to verify his statement that far from being paid no royalties on their hits, the bluesmen on his roster like Lazy Lester, Moses 'Whispering' Smith, Lightnin' Slim and Slim Harpo had actually been in his debt for numerous expenses in liquor, cars and suchlike! Another novelty here was that Miller had a video camera, and shot a short session with us in the acres that were his back garden, later playing back the resultant movie on a TV screen of about 40 inches – this in an era when our biggest domestic TVs were about 16 inches! Our next stop gave us an immediate contrast between opulence to abject poverty as we stopped off briefly in the tiny hamlet of Rayne (seemingly just a couple of streets of single-storey prefabricated dwellings) to visit LeRoy LeBlanc. He recorded early Cajun music as Happy Fats, but this huge man was far from happy, in poor health with a bronchial condition and living in near-squalor in a converted caravan – though his memory was good after he dispelled his initial caution at talking to a group of strangers. John's knowledge of and familiarity with his music was the catalyst to more open conversation.

The last stop on our tour of South Louisiana took us just north of the Interstate to Ville Platte, the home of Floyd Soilleau's empire, comprising Jin and Swallow Records, Flat-Town Music (the publishing arm of the organisation, Ville Platte being French for Flat Town) and Floyd's Record Store. Floyd is a typical ebullient, good-living Cajun who enjoys life, food and music in similar measures. A fine raconteur, he responded in flowing quantity to John's questions and showed a near-photographic memory for details of the music in his catalogue and the performers concerned. We were treated to lunch at the nearby Pigstand eatery (not as grand as a restaurant but more than a café), then were allowed the freedom of the record store stockroom to choose our selection of home-grown discs at special price.

It was back to New Orleans for the weekend, spending around six or seven hours a day through Friday, Saturday and Sunday at the Fairgrounds imbibing the musical and culinary delicacies served up at the Jazzfest. I had written to the Jazzfest office in New Orleans a month or so before the event, with a letter from the *Echoes* editor that confirmed my identity and my role, and on arrival in the Crescent City a visit to the office on North Rampart Street yielded free-entry passes to each day of the Jazzfest and, equally beneficial, a coloured wristband that gave access to the privileged area between the crush barriers and the stage at each venue. This was a helpful convenience for local and minor acts who drew meagre crowds, but a significant benefit with major acts like Fats Domino or Allen Toussaint, from the city, or Bobby Bland and James Brown. Armed with two cameras – one colour, one black and white – I took a few photos with each, then watched the performance without being subjected to the mêlée created by the enthusiastic crowd. I also learned quickly how to photograph Black performers against a light background to avoid what became known as 'black blob syndrome' – pictures taken with the sky as background where no detail of the subject is visible. Thus I was able to take photos of people like Roy Brown, Percy Mayfield, Little Sonny Jones and Ernie K-Doe, who have since died, along with Huey Smith, Bobby Bland and Irma Thomas, who are musically big names but rarely travel abroad.

I liked what I saw and heard, and met numerous contacts in New Orleans – people like Tad Jones, Jon Foose and a guy calling himself the Duke of Paducah, a radio and broadcasting veteran who may have been the same guy who was well established in country music annals, Benjamin 'Whitey' Ford, named from his white hair. I never saw the Duke's hair as he always wore a huge stetson hat, whether he was doing stage announcements at the Jazzfest or broadcasting on radio at WWOZ. The inevitable result was that I returned to the city the following year, and for two years after that, still through the organising capabilities of Lesley Stanford, but with a different party of trippers each time. Through the benefit of my contacts in the city, and my reputation as a veteran soul fan, I came to be regarded (somewhat generously) as a fount of local knowledge, and this in itself bore reward because of the enjoyment my fellow trippers found in their experiences around town. I managed to organise trips to (and tours of) Sea-Saint studios, did an interview there with Ernie K-Doe, found our way to see the pink mansion home of Fats Domino on Marais Street, took an evening cab ride to Dorothy's Medallion Lounge, deep in the Black part of town, to see Johnny Adams sing, rode out to Senator Jones's compact office and did a lengthy interview.

A bunch of us also had an adventure at Prout's Club Alhambra, courtesy of the Senator, who was booking manager of the club – a large and opulent old-fashioned theatre building under the shadow of the Interstate flyover and way across the tracks, usually out of bounds for white folk. We heard a radio ad for Joe Tex doing a show there, so I phoned Senator Jones and asked if we could come along (I hadn't seen Joe Tex since his late '60s show in Croydon). I was told that the doors opened at about 8pm, so we arrived soon afterwards, not wanting to miss anything, and were courteously guided to a table on a balcony facing the stage. We were the only ones there, but during our first round of drinks more people began to arrive, many dressed in fine silk dresses and suits, and gradually filled the ground floor, which was primarily a dancefloor furnished with a scattering of tables and chairs. An hour or so on, with records playing over the sound system, Senator Jones came along to our table carrying an armful of 45s and several posters, which he generously gave to us to share around – many 45s on his own JBs, Hep'Me and similar labels, and posters for gigs by local singers. It was around 11pm when the Joe Tex Band eventually took the stage, by which time we were all exhausted, having spent the afternoon at the Jazzfest before our evening at Prout's. After just half an hour of Joe we came to a unified decision that, sadly, we'd had enough, so left the theatre with Joe in full swing.

As a postscript to these four visits, on the fourth trip my carry-on baggage for the transatlantic flight included a plastic supermarket carrier bag containing the complete manuscript of *South To Louisiana – The Music of the Cajun Bayous* by John Broven, who had kindly entrusted me with its safe delivery to Ms Frumie Selchen, editor for Pelican Books of Gretna, Louisiana. Upon my arrival in the Crescent City I telephoned the lady and arranged to rendezvous with her at the prestigious restaurant K-Paul's Louisiana Kitchen on Chartres Street. I wondered how I'd find the place, but its location was readily obvious because of the long line of folk queuing outside. There were no exclusive tables at K-Paul's: such is the demand that every seat was quickly filled even though it meant eating with total strangers. The bag with its invaluable contents was duly delivered, and soon afterwards published in full hardback glory.

Mo' New Orleans

One of the problems which had arisen concerning the music of New Orleans was relative stagnation following the boom years of the '60s. The big hits of Ernie K-Doe, Irma Thomas, Aaron Neville, the Dixie Cups and Lee Dorsey had dried up, largely as a result of local labels (like Minit/Instant) being swallowed by majors (like Liberty), which was rewarding for the owners but the kiss of death for the artists. Fats Domino and Clarence 'Frogman' Henry had come and gone as market leaders in a previous era, and other than a plethora of local acts being recorded by Allen Toussaint and Marshall Sehorn with little chance of breaking out from small pond to large ocean, things had ground to a halt. With the advance of the '70s, however, and the emergence of a more bass-driven funky style of music by such as Kool & the Gang, the Fatback Band and Earth Wind & Fire, led by the somewhat dramatic change of style by James Brown and his band, it was recognised that this percussive, bassey rhythm was also the foundation of the New Orleans Sound. This motivated the various members of the Neville family, then engaged separately in their local music scene, to pool their resources and form the Neville Brothers. When I first visited the city Aaron was singing at the Jazzfest and in gospel groups, while Charles was playing eclectic avant-garde jazz in coffee bars, while Art and Cyril were largely inactive; but by the end of the decade their eponymous debut LP was out on Capitol Records, comprising their usual mix of busy, percussive funk, rhythmic down-home N'Orleans, and a couple of ballad features to showcase Aaron's superb voice.

Between their emergence as a family musical unit and their major-league debut on vinyl, the Nevilles gained quite a reputation as a live act, touring the USA and even crusading into Europe.

It was during one such crusade that the Nevilles appeared at the Shaw Theatre on London's Euston Road, sometime in 1984, and while sitting at a table in the lobby before the show I found a distinctive yellow flyer from Festival Tours advertising an organised trip to New Orleans for the Jazzfest, this time including an optional midweek trip to Cajun Country. The price was attractive – still below £1,000 for a ten-day trip including flights and accommodation, with a discount for early payment – and after an abstinence lasting just a couple of years I decided to make a return to the Big Easy in spring 1985.

Having made a number of previous trips, and being a contributor to a specialist music paper, I contacted Festival Tours and spoke to Louise Bailey, who was handling the UK admin for the company on behalf of a lady named Nancy Covey. It turned out that Nancy was a veteran of the US west coast music scene in a booking and management capacity, and also the wife of a leading musician – England's own Richard Thompson (once of Fairport Convention but renowned for his solo work these past three decades). To cut a longish story short, I helped with the pre-trip publicity and marketing, and helped Louise a little with the admin, all for the reward of some discount on the main trip and the adventure into Cajun Country.

There was a difference between Festival Tours and the Honky Tonkin' set-up in that while the latter comprised entirely Brits, mainly soul and blues fans on a musical pilgrimage, the former, being a transatlantic organisation, drew its clientele from both sides of the ocean and as a consequence had a rather wider musical taste-base. Also, as many US companies allowed employees only ten days of paid vacation time per year (compared with twenty-plus days for most UK folk), the main Jazzfest Holiday lasted just one weekend and one week, so we Brits with time available to take in the second weekend of Jazzfest were accommodated with a special weekend extension. Having our American cousins sharing the New Orleans experience served to broaden our horizons, in music, cuisine and social style, enabling us to integrate more into the American way of life.

Nancy's musical connections were a key factor in the set-up of the activities that we enjoyed in the Cajun Country excursion. I had toured the area by car with John Broven in earlier years, but this time we had a tour bus, which gave us a more scenic view of the bayous and countryside while travelling along the I-10 and conveniently ferried us organised tourist attractions. These included a visit to the McIlhenny Company Tabasco Sauce factory, at Avery Island, some 140 miles west of New Orleans, close to New Iberia and Breaux Bridge, where a tour of the factory (with its intense smell of peppers) was balanced by a trip around the nature reserve. Next stop was a boat ride along several miles of bayous to catch sight of alligators, lured towards the boats with the contents of a bucket of raw chicken, hordes of egrets and trees almost smothered in Spanish moss, all of which was very atmospheric and photogenic. The ultimate destination, however, was Eunice, and first a visit to Marc Savoy's world-famous accordion shop on Highway 190, heading towards Lawtell. Marc was a shy and quite reserved Cajun gentleman and a superb musician, who gave us a quick résumé on Cajun music and the history and manufacture of the range of accordions on display. Then it was on to home, where a busload of about forty music fans parked in the driveway of the Savoys' spacious house, set amid delightful rural forest, where his wife Ann was waiting with other local musicians, who had gathered to provide a back-porch vintage jam session, including accordion and fiddle, guitar, washboard and triangle. Of such things dreams are truly made. The approaching sunset brought a crawfish broil, as the Savoys provided a veritable bathtub full of cooking crawfish, broiled in pepper sauce, and delicious with jacket potatoes, washed down with beer and soft drinks.

These decades later, it was pleasant to recount the events at Eunice with the Savoys' daughter Sarah, who would have been all of five years old at that time but is currently fulfilling a busy diary of dates around Europe with her Paris-based Cajun band Sarah Savoy and the Francadians (French Cajuns – geddit?).

The Cajun part of the trip also included a visit to the famous Mulates Club at Breaux Bridge, which brought us into contact with another legend of the music, Michael Doucet, fiddler extraordinaire, then the leader of cult-band Beausoleil, and later to join forces with his good friends from along the road in Eunice to form the Savoy-Doucet Cajun Band. In similar style to Floyd Soileau and Marc Savoy, Michael is a huge figure of a man, but with great humour and benign character, and we were given a warm welcome to Mulates to eat a big meal and then were encouraged to participate in the dancing: attempts to master the steps of the Cajun waltz or two-step after a meal and a couple of glasses of beer were something to behold! There was yet more honour for us as visiting music fans when we were invited first to attend a concert in Eunice Town Hall, then a civic reception to honour a great old musician well into his nineties, whose name escapes me. At the concert, which featured a mixture of Cajun (white) and zydeco (black), there was a block of seats taped off with red ribbon in the middle of the auditorium. We studiously avoided these as we walked down the aisle, only to be told that this was our seating area as *we* were the guests of honour.

I was also grateful for commissions to write feature reviews of my New Orleans trips, which were published variously in *Black Echoes* and *Juke Blues*. I hope these chronicles of my adventures may have encouraged other fans to take a look for themselves.

As a postscript to this, even at the time of my last '80s trip – in 1987 – there were significant changes in the city for the music collector. There were never many record stores in the city centre – the modest Canal Street Records on the main thoroughfare and Tower Records on Decatur Street, just a block away from the Mississippi – but in the former the browser racks of local product had reduced to a solitary row, drowned by the sea of rock dividers. Most of the stores in the French Quarter that used to sell records or CDs stocked only the easy-listening mainstream of Pete Fountain and tourist Dixieland, while out-of-town destination stores such as Leisure Landing had dropped soul in favour of rock, or gone out of business entirely, and the aftermath of Hurricane Katrina may have had an even more lasting impact on the scene.

CHAPTER THIRTEEN

RECORDS AND COLLECTING IN THE '80s

Record-collecting in the '80s had a different perspective from previous decades, and seemed to divide into elements of listening and dancing. As one for whom the former held more appeal, my wallet had a bit of a rest where UK product was concerned, though my various trips to New Orleans and the Jazzfest meant that the level of outlay was maintained through bagfuls of fairly obscure LPs being carried through HM Customs at Gatwick. The club scene was gathering pace, which meant that dance music began to dominate, and radio shows reflected this with the weekly output of presenters like Greg Edwards and his cult-show *Soul Spectrum* on Capital riding alongside Robbie Vincent on the BBC for mass popularity and huge audiences, these extending to a strong following at live shows such as the All-Dayers mentioned earlier.

By the mid-'80s the terminology was changing as well as the music, particularly in the dance music scene. Sub-genres came in, named after buildings, with house and garage followed by electronic extensions of these such as techno, where soul and rock met and were scrambled into a barrage of electronic noise with a thudding beat, also electronically created: real instruments were an unnecessary impediment. Then a quasi-sociological spin was put on the creativity of youth, and hip-hop emerged, perhaps the bastard cousin of what had been rap in the soul world.

Many of the younger generation decided at this time that the guaranteed hot and fine weather of Spain meant that this was the place to be for a summer holiday (as their parents' generation had done in the preceding two decades), and Ibiza became a favoured destination not only for punters but also for DJs, several of whom decided that this was a thriving venture with which to be involved. Thus the London club scene was exported bodily to Ibiza, and replicated on disc in the form of compilation LPs to remind the young Brits of what they were missing when they arrived home. Never slow to spot an earner, the London DJs involved in this holiday music bonanza were happy to endorse the albums and thus gain marketing exposure as well as a few quid.

The '80s also saw the birth of some notable sources of reissues in the wider field of rhythm & blues music. Ace Records originated at Ted Carroll's record stall in Golborne Road market, expanded into an annexe run by Roger Armstrong in Soho market and developed to include the astute industry background of Trevor Churchill. The label was initially named Chiswick but soon became Ace for R&B with the Kent brand for soul. It was based initially in Camden then relocated to canal-side offices in deepest Harlesden, north-west London. The first portion of the decade was entrenched in the vinyl era, but with the emergence of CDs later Ace and its numerous style-based subsidiaries grew and flourished. Ace began by licensing product from US labels, but developed this into a strategy of purchasing masters from some classic '50s companies, retaining ownership of labels like Specialty, Dootone and Modern. Their roster of consultants grew to include New Orleans and vintage R&B specialist John Broven, veteran soul, R&B, blues and rockabilly expert Ray Topping, and Adrian (Ady 'Harboro Horace') Croasdell, a knowledgeable soul collector, well respected on the Northern Soul scene, and the range of material being licensed grew wider as a consequence, with packages of catalogue material being licensed *en bloc* from Atlantic and Chess. A later arrangement with Fantasy Records gave Ace exclusive UK access to the Stax catalogue, though excluding material from the early years – which was still owned by Warner.

Meanwhile, south of the Thames, Charly Records was born as the result of a partnership between European jazz fans Joop Visser and Jean-Luc Young, and proceeded to build a reissue catalogue with material ostensibly licensed from, amongst others, King, Atlantic, Chess, Vee Jay, Scepter-Wand, Marshall Sehorn's Sea-Saint studio output and Bobby Robinson's Fire/Fury combine. Certainly a profusion of very interesting and collectable vinyl poured forth from their New Cross headquarters, with repertoire selection and compilations handled by soul aficionados Cliff White and Bob Fisher, with guidance on blues projects by Mike Rowe. There was, however, some question regarding their legal entitlement to the material released, and there was a complex chain of company affiliation with European subsidiaries. The eventual result was a lawsuit from MCA Records, who had by then acquired the rights to Chess from Sugar Hill via All Platinum, after Joe Robinson had bought the ailing company from GRT (following their purchase of the great name after the death of Leonard Chess and the exit of son Marshall).

Charly released numerous albums of soul, blues, R&B, doo-wop and gospel, with the owners pursuing their own jazz expertise and interest with releases on the Affinity label. As the decade rambled on, vinyl releases metamorphosed into CDs. I don't know how many or how few copies were sold, or whether the legal paperwork was completed in invisible ink, but sitting on my shelves years later are promotion copies of a six-CD box set of John Lee Hooker's *The Vee Jay Years* and *The Complete Muddy Waters, 1947–1967* in a nine CD box set, including a sixty-four-page booklet with full biography, appraisal of material and complete discography by Les Fancourt. Les, incidentally, was known to many London blues fans during the '80s as the man behind the counter in Dobell's record shop. I've mentioned Dobell's in passing already: it was a key part of the London specialist retail scene during the '70s and '80s (and way before then). It included a folk and blues department, and was located in Charing Cross Road until a combination of redevelopment and massively increased rent and overheads necessitated relocation in 1981 to Tower Street, just a couple of blocks away. Ray Bolden was the original guy in the blues department, but Les Fancourt took over after the move and remained with Dobell's until its closure in 1992.

CHAPTER FOURTEEN

GOSPEL IN LONDON

My contact with the growing gospel music scene in London Black churches probably came about because I was the only radio presenter in the capital who had a dedicated gospel music show; this was at 8am on Sunday mornings on Solar Radio back in 1984. As well as buying albums by the classic quartets like the Five Blind Boys (Mississippi and Alabama groups), Swans Silvertones, Dixie Hummingbirds, Caravans and the Soul Stirrers, I bought *The Voice*, the weekly newspaper for Black London, and found a gospel column written by Viv Broughton. Viv is a white Londoner who has done a significant amount of work over the years in developing and promoting gospel music, writing books, compiling albums and acting as a consultant.

Viv is from Hackney in east London, and has a keen ear for local talent. When he heard south London group the Spirit of Watts singing in churches in the area, he took them under his wing as manager at a time when gospel music was trying to move beyond the confines of churches to a wider audience. Spirit of Watts were named after Dr Isaac Watts, renowned hymn writer who developed a linear style of presenting spiritual music, and comprised Verna Wilks, Barry DeSousa, Leroy Barrett, Errord Jarrett and one Michelle Wallen, from Catford. This quintet built quite a following around the London music circuit, both sacred and secular, playing to large audiences in assorted halls, churches and theatres, often on a combined bill with their north London counterparts the Trumpets of Zion, the Escoffereys and soloists Shirley Fenty and Paul Johnson, sometime member of the London Community Gospel Choir. One such memorable occasion was recorded for posterity and issued on an LP *Gospel Joy . . . a Live Celebration* on the independent Ears & Eyes label, containing a selection of excellent music but graced with the most awful impressionistic sleeve illustration, which hardly served to attract interest.

There was such an increased interest in and awareness of gospel music in London that Capital Radio launched a gospel show, presented by Al Matthews, the Black American soul singer who had scored a hit with 'Fool (If You Think It's Over)'. He and I had frequent telephone conversations regarding the progress and popularity of the music. US classic quartet the Mighty Clouds of Joy flew in to do a concert at the Dominion, Tottenham Court Road, which drew an audience of mainly white, middle-class folk. Albertina Walker, from the legendary Caravans female quartet, visited us as guest of honour at a Black Gospel Association Annual Awards dinner, while Shirley Caesar did a promotional tour for a new LP, and I was privileged to meet and interview her. Also touring in about 1987 were husband and wife duo Phil and Brenda Nicholas, whose albums for Command Records sold well on import. I saw them in concert twice on consecutive nights at, I think, St James's Church near the Embankment in London. They played to a sold-out house on the opening night, but were confronted with an audience of about twenty people on the second night, to whom they played their full-length set with never a mention of the size of the audience. The final major gospel name to hit London arrived in 1990 when Vanessa Bell Armstrong, a delightful singer with a powerful and beautiful voice, played a memorable concert at the Dominion. Other major gospel performers who played London concerts were Andraé Crouch & the Disciples (including Andraé's sister, the dynamic Sandra Crouch) and the Clark Sisters, who nearly succeeded in blowing the roof off the Central Hall, Westminster, in a memorable show.

Amid the increased taste for gospel music, so the industry

discovered the quality of some of the voices to be heard in these groups and choirs. While some of these remained dedicated to the sacred cause – following the lead of US star Shirley Caesar, who practically made a career of recording inspirational albums that included songs chronicling the temptations to turn to a secular career, which she'd resisted – others chose to follow the road to possible fame and fortune. It was around 1986 when Viv Broughton mentioned to me that he was looking for a new lead singer for the Spirit of Watts, as Michelle Wallen had been approached to go solo. We discussed the limited available options, and the impracticability of importing the lead singer from a rival group (as they were essentially family units), and the search was on for a new lead when an invitation arrived in early 1987 for a launch party to be held in a Mayfair preview theatre for the secular debut of Michelle Wallen. Her name was changed, she was rebranded and smothered in industry gloss, and had become Mica Paris! A short while later, in a similar venue, came the chance to welcome Paul Johnson to the gold-paved world of pop music, though sadly without the same results.

CHAPTER FIFTEEN

RADIO DAYS

So now we had the means to read about the music, to buy the records we knew, both UK releases and imports, and the chance to hear some of our favourites singing live. But how did we get to hear some of the other gems we were reading about, apart from spending the odd hour in Soul City or Contempo? What about soul music on the radio?

For the London (or even UK) teenager of the early 1960s there wasn't much. BBC Radio was split into three networked stations: the Home Service, which essentially broadcast news, current affairs and academic speech content, the Third Programme, covering classical music and heavier academic content, and the Light Programme, light entertainment, popular music variety shows such as *The Billy Cotton Band Show*, *Two-Way Family Favourites*, a record request programme devoted to music for forces personnel in the empire, *Worker's Playtime*, *Henry Hall's Guest Night* and comedy shows starring such as Tony Hancock, Kenneth Horne and Peter Brough and Archie Andrews (possibly the only ventriloquist's dummy ever to feature on radio). Little scope, then, for R&B or blues records, other than the odd Muddy Waters or Leadbelly track which might squeeze into a jazz playlist on the Third Programme. The only other options were the sponsor-laden output of Radio Luxembourg, with quarter-hour or half-hour segment shows produced by companies like Decca, EMI and Pye Records, and the fading, static-filled transmissions of AFN (American Forces Network), broadcast from continental Europe and at least providing tantalising snippets of US chart hits.

If the lack of outlets wasn't bad enough, there was an agreement between the Musicians' Union and the BBC that served to restrict the number of records that could be played – hence the Billy Cotton and Henry Hall shows, which featured live band music throughout. A similar safeguard restricted the number of US performers who could tour the UK for live shows: for each American musician who was allowed to tour and perform here, a British musician had to go to the USA to do live work. This arrangement hindered our chances of witnessing some vintage R&B and soul acts at the start of the '60s, but the UK 'Beat Boom' in the USA, which started with the Beatles and their countless peers, meant that a flood of British beat-groups were booked to tour the USA – thus opening the doors wide for soul and blues performers to tour the UK and Europe (although it was detrimental to the sales of soul discs stateside). It's likely that but for the Beatles' domination of the US Hot 100 we might not have been blessed with the chance to see the Motown Revue, the Stax Revue, the Atlantic package shows and the various American Folk-Blues Festivals, all of which graced our shores in the early and mid-'60s.

But I digress a little. The lack of opportunities for record airplay was a frustration not only for fans but also for independent producers and other industry folk, whose opportunities to break into the establishment were limited. Ronan O'Rahilly was one who suffered thus, as manager of the emergent Georgie Fame, who was attempting to break his artist into wider recognition and acceptance. Becoming aware of Radio Veronica, a Dutch venture that broadcast from a ship anchored at sea in the early '60s, he launched Radio Caroline in March 1964 with the support of his record company and funding from his father. His first vessel was the *Fredericia*, soon to be joined by the better-known *Mi Amigo*, as Caroline North (moored in the Irish Sea) and Caroline South (moored off Felixstowe) respectively. The latter soon had the company of the *Galaxy*, housing the rival Radio London. Thus was born pirate radio in the UK, with these ships joined by some others, and some stations like King and 390 located on old war-time forts in the Thames estuary.

The result was radio anarchy, but in the most positive way as it provided a number of outlets for the new teenage music – which just happened to feature large doses of soul. Freed from the restrictions of playlists and the shackles of MU regulations, the new wave of radio stations played records day in, day out, with DJs who had learned their skills either in independent in-house radio organisations (like the UBN, United Biscuits Network), which played through private networks to their factory workforce, in hospital radio, or in American and Canadian radio. With the emergence in the UK of the Motown, Stax, Atlantic and Chess brands through the licence deals described elsewhere in this book, there was plentiful material available for promotion, and soul certainly reaped the benefit of this increased airplay.

At the time I was working in the local public library service in what was then Woolwich borough (now part of Greenwich), more specifically with the mobile library unit. This meant I had a little more freedom and less discipline than in the main library, with the result that I was able to listen to my transistor radio while tidying shelves and sorting out books – at a time when a twist of the tuner dial brought so many pirate options. I had many happy daytime hours listening to Radio Caroline and London, flicking from station to station to maintain optimum soul content, and also during those warm summer evenings when ballad gems like Percy Sledge's 'When A Man Loves a Woman' and Ben E. King's 'Goodnight My Love' became anthems of the era.

With such a plethora of stations on the AM waveband, it was sometimes interesting just to sit and turn the tuning dial and listen, sometimes briefly, to the music that came forth. It was in this way that I discovered Mike Raven, and I duly tuned in to King Radio on a Sunday night in September 1965. I was pleasantly surprised to encounter an hour of blues and R&B, beautifully eclectic and presented in scholarly yet enthusiastic style by Mike. There was material by Howlin' Wolf, Bobby Parker, Elmore James, Freddie King and others – a playlist to dream of in those days. I think there was some dodgy politics concerning the forts, their ownership and usage, and after the demise of King, Mike and his wife Mandy soon returned on Radio 390 with a programme of similar style and quality – a good introduction to the blues for the floating soul fan.

The radio revolution brought reaction from all sides. The listening public relished the chance to hear the wider range of music that was being broadcast, and buying habits changed accordingly. We also enjoyed the presenters' style: the BBC's 'old school' were bound by tradition and scripts, but the new wave of pirates were closer to the 'motormouth' style of American AM radio, with a greater affinity to the teenage ear and a greater appreciation of the younger music they were playing. At the same time the Musicians' Union began to realise that its membership now came from a wider base than just fading big-bands and seaside variety acts, and included the long-haired guitarists from beat groups, who were equally deserving of regular work and actually benefited from their records being played on the radio.

As well as allowing welcome exposure for the new breed of soul music, more independent pop acts began to break through, and the bestseller charts began to provide a more accurate reflection of varied musical tastes. Bob Dylan's folk hit 'The Times They Are a'Changing' was, indeed, indicative of the cultural revolution assisted by, if not generated by, pirate radio.

This dreamworld remained in place for some three years, during which time there were discussions at the highest levels between central government, the BBC and the Musicians' Union which were to result in the drafting and publication of the Marine (Broadcasting) Offences Act. This put laws in place to prevent any assistance being given to pirate radio operators, and a complete restructuring of British network radio by the BBC. The new law took effect in July 1967, and the BBC launched a new station, Radio 1, on 30 September 1967, also rebranding the Light Programme as Radio 2, the Third Programme as Radio 3 and the Home Service as Radio 4. Many of the pirate presenters were taken on board by the BBC as Radio 1 attempted to match the youthful enthusiasm of its illegal competitors, but while the general principle was absorbed by the Corporation, the spirit was not captured so well. Some soul music found its way into the playlists, but although there was a thriving underground soul scene in the UK there was only one show a week on BBC Radio 1 to represent it. Soul soon found itself shunted into specialist shows, which eventually disappeared. The single show was Mike Raven's blues show on Sunday evenings at 7pm, which included a healthy ration of soul music, Broadcast from 1 October 1967, it was billed as *The Mike Raven Rhythm & Blues Show*, and remained on the schedule until he was replaced by David Simmons in January 1972. David continued on Radio 1 until being laid off in January 1975, when he moved to BBC Radio London – as mentioned earlier. January 1977 saw the introduction to the Radio 1 schedule of *Alexis Korner's Blues and Soul Show*. Alexis was a great British bluesman and a consummate, erudite broadcaster. He brought us the chance to hear a vast array of blues and R&B styles, and we benefited from his vast knowledge and experience, even if his style tended to be scholarly rather than entertaining. Alexis continued broadcasting into the early 1980s (sadly he died in 1984), being replaced on Radio 1 in 1983 when Robbie Vincent moved up from Radio London, initially on Saturday nights before moving to Sundays. Another noteworthy character was Stuart Colman, a pub DJ who led a crusade for a rock 'n' roll show on Radio 1. With his friend and fellow pub DJ Geoff Barker he was given a Radio 1 rock 'n' roll show during 1976. When his national contract came to an end Stuart moved into the Sunday morning slot previously occupied by Charlie Gillett on BBC Radio London, and presented *Echoes* during the early 1980s. Though his main taste had been for rockabilly, Stuart fostered an interest in vintage R&B, specifically West Coast product, and became a great enthusiast and devotee of the work of veteran tenor saxman Plas Johnson. While never a great fan of soul music, Stuart was kind enough to invite me as studio guest on a few occasions, giving me the chance to introduce and play some bluesy new soul releases. His enthusiasm for the music was paramount, and he gathered a large and regular audience for specialist music. It's also worth mentioning Charlie Gillett again. First invited on air to play his kind of music by music presenter cum phone-in host Robbie

Vincent, Charlie's popular *Honky Tonk* Sunday morning show began in 1972 and continued until 1979, which opened the door to wider exposure for varying styles of Americana music, including the numerous regional styles of R&B along with Cajun, Tex-Mex, western swing, rockabilly and down-home blues, though not often the relative sophistication of soul.

Soul Spectrum

Some loved him, some hated him, but there was no doubting the impact of Greg Edwards on London soul radio in the mid-1970s. On 16 October 1973 Capital Radio was launched in London, with a schedule including Roger Scott's highly rated *Cruisin'* show on Friday evenings, perhaps the first taste Londoners had of rock 'n' roll radio, opening with hot-rod instrumental 'Stick Shift' by the Duals as its theme and including an enjoyable mixture of rock 'n' roll, R&B and pop oldies, delivered in American style with Roger's London accent! How appropriate was it that *Cruisin'* was on air at the time of the premier of *American Graffiti*, for which Capital and Roger organised a special preview showing. I was honoured to be invited as a studio guest on two occasions, joining Roger in the studio at Euston Tower to introduce my selections of favourite R&B oldies (I still have cassette recordings of these shows somewhere in my archives). Roger remained with Capital for fifteen years before moving to Radio 1 in 1988. He tragically died from cancer in 1989, aged just forty-six.

Having created an appetite for black music, in spring 1974 Capital brought Greg Edwards to the schedule with *Soul Spectrum*. Greg was born on the Caribbean island of Grenada and raised in New York, moving to London in 1969 to work for CBS Records, promoting soul music on licensed labels. He took his marketing expertise and product knowledge to the airwaves, and *Soul Spectrum* was part of the staple diet of Saturday night radio for a decade, lasting into the early '80s and playing the best in contemporary soul music of the time, including half an hour of down-tempo tracks during the 'bathroom call' section around 7pm as his young audience were preening themselves for a night out! Greg also worked out – which at that time referred to working in clubs rather than gymnasiums – featuring Capital's Best Disco in Town roadshow.

Concurrent with the success of Greg Edwards on Capital was the rise of Robbie Vincent as a soul presenter on BBC London. His weekly show was on air each Saturday lunchtime, and at the birth of the jazz-funk era Robbie was a crusader for that musical genre, building a huge following. His most popular drop-in ident was 'If it moves, funk it', presumably phrased to allow the listener to adapt it to an Anglo-Saxon alternative, and voiced by the gravelly tones of Bill Mitchell. Bill's taped package of similar idents was very popular with club DJs, and frequently used by the likes of Steve Walsh, Chris Hill and 'Froggy', who were also regular contributors to Robbie's radio show. Vincent also joined with them to work live at clubs and weekenders, becoming part of the Soul Mafia, whose reputation grew during the '70s and lasted into the early '80s. He moved to Radio 1 in 1983, and spent the next six years presenting first Saturday and later Sunday evening soul shows on the network.

Invicta and JFM
By the late '60s the first land-based soul music pirate radio stations were on air. Technically minded soul fans began to build small transmitters and, with the aid of cassette recorders and willing volunteers, started transmitting on a local basis over public holiday weekends. In about 1970 a group of enthusiastic soul fans set up a pirate station in London called Radio Invicta, broadcasting for just three hours on a Sunday. Despite the problems it faced across the decade, the station became more and more popular with its dedicated approach to the music. The weekly mailbag became huge. Tony Johns was Invicta's founder, and it is largely down to him that the soul radio explosion in the '80s occurred. Radio Invicta ceased broadcasting in 1984, but not before the next batch of stations came along. He ran the pioneering station by asking soul fans to prerecord their shows onto C90 cassettes which, with the aid of an auto-stacker cassette player, ran for about half a day. I was invited by

him to record a show, which was to be broadcast over a bank holiday weekend from a remote transmitter 'somewhere in Mitcham'.

In 1981 a station called JFM (generally accepted to be an abbreviation of Jazz Funk Music) took to the pirate airwaves, initially broadcasting through the whole of Sundays and sometimes into Monday mornings. Much as my first steps in sleeve notes and broader market journalism began with a telephone call, so did my introduction to working live in radio. My first contact came with a phone call from Brian Anthony, brains (and launch money) behind JFM Radio, asking if I would like to do a show once a month along with Terry Davis, playing soul oldies.

Brian had built a studio in the back of a car repair workshop off Wandsworth Road, near Vauxhall, basically in a garage at the bottom of a steep driveway, comprising two record decks, cassette players, microphones and an amplifier, all linked to an FM transmitter a short distance away. It certainly required smart detective work to locate the premises. A cautious knock on a corrugated shutter found Brian clad in overalls at a mixing desk built into a wood-panelled studio behind glazed soundproofing.

Thus began the defiance of the government's Department of Trade & Industry, which was responsible for policing use of the radio airwaves. Terry soon dropped out, leaving me with a free hand to build a regular radio show, and having battled through bad roads and bad weather for several months, it was great to find out that the studio was moving to a room under a lean-to stairway at a building high on Shooters Hill, near Woolwich, south-east London, just a fifteen-minute drive from my (then) home in Grove Park, near Bromley. This was to ensure a good signal and wide transmission area, and was less than half an hour's drive from my home. Part of the 'pleasure' of pirate radio at the time was the need to move studio premises fairly regularly to avoid detection by the DTI.

After moving to Shooters Hill I began broadcasting a two-hour programme that included '60s soul, '50s R&B, blues, doo-wop, and cross-decade deep soul ballads in a formula that has endured through some twenty five years into my present radio show with Solar Radio. My Woolwich studio tenure must have lasted through to the end of 1980, as I can recall going to the studio with my bag of records having come straight from watching football at nearby Charlton Athletic, and it was during that time that I was sometimes doing three two-hour shows per week, covering vintage soul, blues/R&B and gospel, with the occasional unscheduled standby if I was sitting at home listening and transmission went to dead air. As I was only a short drive from the studio, I would gather a bagful of records and step into the breach!

The station fast became a must for any serious soul, funk and jazz fan, and was probably best remembered for its thoroughly professional approach – many people thinking that it was a legal station. JFM concentrated largely on upfront new music, and many a huge crossover song started life on one or more of its shows. From 1982 into 1983 Brian built a solid roster of good presenters – including excellent club jocks like Graham Gold, Nigel Owen and Smokey Joe – so good that the station was able to take the brave step of moving from weekend broadcasting to seven days a week transmission on FM, opening at 6am and closing at midnight, using 'London Town' by Light of the World as the opening and closing theme tune and generating steady sales and near-legendary status for this track. There was a range of specialist shows each evening along with strong breakfast and drivetime programming, and a good line-up at weekends. Would that I had kept a full list of DJs on the station, but names that come to mind are such legendary names as Jeff Young, Pete Tong, Barrie Stone, Dave Collins, Marc Damon, Nigel Owen, Steve Jackson (sometime morning show DJ on Kiss FM), Terry Davis and Froggy. My Saturday evening slot of 6pm to 8pm was preceded by a youthful, fresh-faced, blond guy from nearby Orpington named Jim Colvin (longtime Smooth FM staffer), and followed by a chart-style show produced by Brian Anthony and presented by a very personable young lady, Lynn Parsons (now a BBC Radio 2 swing-jock, sitting in for presenters during holidays or illness, and a weekend presenter on Smooth Radio since 2007). Lynn recalls: 'Brian worked for a music shop at Tooting Broadway . . . I worked voluntarily for a hospital radio station (Radio 9) in Tooting and very kindly Brian used to renew our Top 20 singles every week, so we always had the chart songs to play: he did this free of charge. One day he asked what I was like at interviewing people and would I like to try an interview show at JFM . . . and that's where it all began for me.'

There was also Steve Walsh. Steve was one of a rare breed of DJs who were comfortable with both live work on the road and in club residencies and also as a radio presenter, though for the latter it helped to have a large studio and a strong chair. A big man with a big personality, Walshie had quite a following on JFM with his free-form and energetic style. He was wise enough to follow Brian Anthony's management guidelines. Brian, a diminutive figure but a wise businessman and hard taskmaster, knew exactly what he wanted from presenters on his station – and didn't suffer fools gladly. This included minimal 'jabbering' in on-air links: I recall at one DJ meeting he said, 'If all you have to say is "that was – this is", don't bother, wait till you have something worth saying.' To Steve Jackson, later a star on Kiss FM, who was having trouble reading out advertising matter, he said, 'Jacko, get some glasses and read the bloody announcements properly.'

Walshie cut it, though, and proved to be a main focal point in a brave venture that Brian organised. This was the JFM Soul Cruise, in which space was booked on a passenger ferry boat which sailed from Sheerness, Kent, to Vlissingen, Netherlands. Some 200 JFM listeners paid about £40 each for the voyage, to be entertained in transit by Steve Walsh among others. I don't know how Brian managed to get it all together, but as I recall, we JFM presenters read and played an ad promoting the trip, asking for cheques for prepayment. Listeners and DJs met somewhere in south London to board a coach that took us to Sheerness. It all went as well as these things can, and the JFM bunch were treated to a great soul record extravaganza as we crossed the North Sea. Once ashore in the Netherlands there was little to do apart from walk around the town or have a few drinks, then reassemble for the return trip. The combination of alcohol consumption and a rough sea crossing meant that most of our lot were either asleep or ill for the duration, while I enjoyed one of my rare exposures to the public eye, being give the chance to take to the turntables for an hour and play a selection of vintage soul records to those folk who took refuge in the bar or on the dancefloor. It was a strange experience – nice to be appreciated by those present (more international lorry drivers than captive soul fans), but the record decks took some getting used to! As you can imagine, it would be difficult playing records on a normal turntable during a sea voyage because of the motion of the boat, so the records were played on a turntable with a fixed arm, which became a sealed unit while the disc was playing.

After about a year at the Shooters Hill studio we moved to Crystal Palace – to the basement of a greengrocer's shop in Westow Hill (the main High Street). Technology had advanced to a point where the studio output was linked by microwave beam to the transmitter at a remote location, so that if the DTI tracked the signal they could confiscate the transmitter (costing around £100 to build, and easy to assemble) but would not get the rather more costly studio equipment (mixing desk, turntables, amplifiers and microphones, which were harder to replace and fundamental to continued operation). One unfortunate side-effect was the high incidence of pigeon fatalities: if they passed through the microwave beam they met a sudden end. As I recall, there was a fish and chip shop on the corner of Westow Hill, the roof of which was the site for so many pirate radio aerials that the area became known as Pirate Alley.

From Westow Hill we moved literally round the corner into a ground-floor flat in a huge Victorian terraced house in St Aubyn's Road, a turning off Westow Hill. Here JFM remained until the final and apocalyptic studio bust of September 1984 (in which the DTI took the equipment, the fan-mail and even the empty cups and mugs on the tables), by which time we had been on a twenty-four-hour, seven-day schedule in which I was presenting three shows a week – vintage soul on Wednesday evening, blues and R&B on Fridays and gospel on Sundays. JFM had also reached a point of brand awareness, quality of output and audience figures that meant a number of programmes were regularly listed in the daily broadcasting choice published in *Time Out*. I still have a cutting from their radio listings page giving yours truly a treasured accolade of 'Some of the best music programming around' when I was running through 'The A–Z of R&B' as a vintage soul theme.

Horizon

Horizon Radio also started life in 1981, broadcasting on Wednesday evenings and Sundays, with a small group of avid record collectors headed by Chris Stewart and including Andy Jackson (who had previously been on Radio Invicta), Richard Felstead, Jude James, Barry Tee, Bob Jones, Gary Lee, Nick Lawrence, C.J. Carlos, Gary Spence and Diane Hinds. It was on air in competition with JFM. I never listened to it, as I was too busy preparing and presenting my own shows and was happy listening to the output of JFM anyway.

In 1984 Horizon achieved what many thought to be impossible – broadcasting twenty-four hours a day, seven days a week for six consecutive months without being taken off air by the DTI. During that period the roster of DJs included Gary Kent, Graham Gold, 'Wing Commander' Patrick Meads, Sammy Jacob (aka Sammy J.), Tony Monson, Chris Best, Andy Bailey (ex-Radio Invicta), Mark McCarthy, Paul Buick, Andy Taylor, Gilles Peterson and Jez Nelson. Horizon became the most serious station of the time to challenge the appeal of Capital Radio. All of the live gigs promoted were filled to capacity, and it seemed that whichever High Street you walked down half the radios were tuned to Horizon. In short, the station had a massive reputation, but it all finished suddenly in October 1984 after a massive studio bust, though not before many of the DJs were household names in the London area.

The First Solar

I was to become very familiar with Horizon's DJs after a phone call from my old friend Tony Monson, a veteran of two decades of radio (from working in Bermuda in the early '60s through the days of the pirate ships), within days of JFM's demise. Tony planned to raise a phoenix from the combined ashes of JFM and Horizon –

and thus was born Solar Radio. Solar was an acronym of 'Sound Of London's Alternative Radio', and while the strains of 'London Town' by Light of the World would no longer herald the beginning and end of transmissions, Solar grasped JFM's mantle and built a DJ roster and twenty-four-hour programme schedule which would continue the crusade to promote soul and related music styles on the airwaves of Greater London. The station came on the air with an almost identical DJ line-up plus new names, such as Helen Mayhew, Louis St Clair and Tomek. The music format was similar to Horizon, except that more emphasis was placed on specialist music shows. I was offered, and accepted, a two-hour show on Sunday mornings in which I played a mixture of gospel, both traditional classic quartets and contemporary, vintage soul and mellow soul. The station was an instant success and, indeed, with its non-stop campaigning to be awarded a legal franchise it may well have paved the way for the eventual deregulation of the radio airwaves. JFM and Horizon had started this campaign and Solar continued it until 30 September 1985, when the station voluntarily went off the air in order to be allowed to submit a licence application.

Studio locations for the new station took me to parts of London I'd not visited before and haven't returned to since, with early morning drives before my Sunday 8am–10am slot to the conservatory of a terraced house in Leytonstone, a dingy first-floor room that always reeked of gas over a tiny shop in Stoke Newington and a flat on the seventh floor of a tower-block in Dalston. Things stabilised with a move to a room in an industrial estate unit in Tulse Hill, just a short distance from Pirate Alley. This was home to a number of presenters who practically became household names across Greater London, the likes of C.J. Carlos, Jude James, Paul Buick, Gary Kent, Garry Dennis, Chris Brown and Sammy Jay. The route to Solar's last studio as a pirate station was via an intricate maze of corridors, staircases and walkways to a tiny wooden door with a punch-pad combination lock, which opened to reveal a haven of technology. It was so far off the beaten track that you really did need written directions to get from the car park to the studio. In the (unlikely) event of a visit by the DTI, the escape route for the on-air DJ was through a small window which opened onto a murky corner of West Norwood cemetery!

When the time came for further deregulation of independent radio and the advertising of new FM licences, it was stipulated by the Radio Authority and the government that pirate broadcasters would be permitted to apply for a licence only if they ceased illegal transmissions by a given date in September 1985. In order to comply with this Solar went to great lengths to promote its last day on air, and organised a closing day schedule which included an evening special together with an outside broadcast link from a venue in north London by Nicky Lawrence. This turned into quite an occasion. There was a grand party at the studio, and rarely have so many radio DJs assembled in one room to take short turns in a farewell broadcast. Our application was not successful, and the grand finale heralded the end of this strand of pirate radio.

RTM

It was to RTM Radio in Thamesmead, south-east London, that I moved next. I joined the volunteer staff in 1988, when it was on a cable network which was built into the new town of Thamesmead in the late '60s when the concrete jungle architecture of tower blocks, elevated walkways and integral shopping precincts was in vogue. The dedicated broadcasting crew was working towards the target of a 'community of interest' FM franchise as announced by the Radio Authority. Following hints by the RA, the team put together a strong bid, with the informed assistance of Radio Development International (who also managed the subsequent successful Kiss application), and was granted an FM licence in March 1990. RTM began broadcasting on 103.8FM, and I was pleased to host a specialist soul show, though this was bounced around the schedule into various graveyard shifts, eventually gravitating to midnight on Sunday after a short run in the relatively peak slot of 10pm until midnight on Thursdays!

I enjoyed my air-time at Thamesmead/RTM. It gave me the opportunity to diversify into sports broadcasting when I teamed up with Charlton Athletic marketing executive Steve Sutherland to co-host *Charlton Chat*, initially on cable and subsequently holding down the 7pm–9pm slot on Sunday nights on FM, featuring a range of Charlton studio guests from players, directors, managerial and admin staff, and a red hot telecaster switchboard enabling us to take calls on air. This gave me valuable experience in the skills of 'tech op' (technical operator, effectively engineering the show by balancing microphone, record deck (later CD units) and phone lines, and production work – such as preparing logging sheets of records played, scheduling and playing the commercials. We carried on *Charlton Chat* winter and summer, though in the autumn of 1990 I dropped out of my music show in order to join the prestigious roster at Kiss.

Kiss

At the end of 1986, when it was apparent that the government plans for radio deregulation were to be postponed and that all the licence applications had been scrapped, Solar came on the air again, initially planning to broadcast twenty-four hours a day. By this time DJs such as Ralph Tee, Alan Sage, Steve Hobbs and Randall Lee Rose (aka Lee Randall) had been added to the roster. Unfortunately the venture was doomed, because of constant busts and frequent thefts of transmitters, links and so on; in addition Solar was at times deliberately jammed by rival pirates. The station struggled on valiantly for about eighteen months (weekends only at the end), before finally giving up the ghost thousands of pounds poorer.

With the advance of deregulation of independent radio into smaller 'community of interest' stations, various business groups formed to prepare applications for a licence advertised by the Radio Authority to serve Greater London, including competing groups based on the broadcasting and management teams of erstwhile soul pirate stations Kiss and Solar. Kiss had been launched in October 1985 by Gordon MacNamee (a former JFM DJ) and had introduced Paul 'Trouble' Anderson, Trevor 'Mad Hatter' Nelson, Coldcut, Bobby and Steve (Zoo Experience), Jazzie B, Norman

Jay and many others to the London airwaves. The station had started the massive 'rare groove' phenomenon, effectively record-collecting DJs giving airplay to and creating demand for soul dance 45s from the '70s, many of which had only been available as US imports when first released and were thus hard to find a decade later. The station also explored the alternative side of the emerging club/dance culture. Solar, under the business banner of Music Broadcasting Ltd, had a steering committee that included on-air staff Larry Coke, Andy Jackson and me, along with engineer Keith Renton, and with Liaison Manager Jackie Evans bringing such high-profile names as astrologer Russell Grant, sports agent Jon Smith and newspaper editor Eve Pollard (chairman) into the group. We (Music Broadcasting Ltd) presented a strong dossier to the Radio Authority, so much so that I, as nominated contact person, was pleased to get a phone call from RA Development Officer David Vick, and in the half-hour phone interview that followed I clarified the aims of our project.

The bad news was that our application was not successful. The good news was that Kiss FM was granted the licence in September 1990. It was blessed with the marketing man's dream of a broadcasting frequency of 100 megahertz – which was incorporated into the brand name, Kiss 100 FM. At least in its early days the station was able to give paid, legal employment to a large number of presenters and technicians who had spent the preceding decade flaunting the law to crusade for soul music as pirates.

As well as following a similar music policy, Kiss was led by a management team familiar to the Music Broadcasting crew, both as fellow DJs from pirate broadcasting days and, in my case, from management positions at other radio stations. My first involvement was a phone call from Programme Administrator Grant Goddard, who knew me from my involvement with RTM Radio. He offered me from launch a two-hour show on Sunday mornings from 6am to 8am, playing my usual mixture of vintage soul and R&B along with some gospel and soft soul. That was the good news! The only downside was the requirement for me to be at the studio an hour before going on air, so that 5am deadline meant getting up at 4am on Sunday morning for the half-hour drive from home in Grove Park, near Bromley in south-east London, to the studio in Holloway Road, through the Blackwall Tunnel, the Balls Pond Road, Dalston and Hackney, before sitting in Studio Two for the best part of an hour preparing the log-sheets.

I soon realised that my full name was a little clumsy for a radio handle, so I took to using just my initial (not really copying from renowned US DJ John 'R' Richbourg, from WLAC in Nashville, but happy to have some connection with that great broadcaster). I thus appeared on the published schedule as Clive R.

The on-air launch team at Kiss comprised pretty much everyone who was anyone in the world of London soul music radio and club DJ-ing, and a number of pre-launch presenter meetings served to build a team spirit, to cement together those who had been with Kiss in its pirate days and the relative outsiders who had come on board later, to give the station a comprehensive coverage of soul and related music styles. There were no playlists, so we had a free hand to play our own choice of records within the scope of the programmes, and were paid well for doing so. Thus began the first four happy months in the life of Kiss 100 FM.

Sadly, politics and world affairs got in the way, and the happy ship encountered troubled waters early in 1991 when the United States led the Coalition forces in the invasion of the Persian Gulf, to liberate Kuwait. The Gulf War lasted just over one month, from mid-January into late February, but during that time, with the need to take feed of regular news bulletins and to keep a close eye on the red telephone in the studio for urgent news, advertising revenue plummeted and the station was obliged to assess its financial situation. I received a phone call inviting me to attend a meeting with Gordon Mac one Monday morning, and travelled up to Kiss House by public transport for the first time.

As I signed in at reception I was a bit puzzled to be given a security pass, as I already had a presenter's staff pass. I made my way upstairs to Gordon's office, where the conversation was cordial but brief. In view of circumstances there had been a revision of requirements and they had to let me go. As I put my staff pass on the desk it became obvious why I'd been given a visitor's pass when signing in. That's when I learned that things tend to happen quickly in independent radio, and the niceties of notice periods belong to a different strand of business. My final pay cheque soon arrived, along with phone calls from six other presenters who had been similarly sacked as revenue dropped, and as the target audience changed from the general spectrum of Black music with various specialist elements to a more general dance music audience; from this were trimmed the luxuries of historic roots like classic soul, blues and gospel. There were brief discussions among the now ex-Kiss DJs about taking action or asking for compensation, but after taking some legal advice this was seen to be a waste of our time, effort and money. I put it down to experience and returned to the relative backwaters of RTM Radio, then in need of a Sunday midday presenter following the departure of Station Manager Bob Smith. By way of consolation, we later learned from friends still working for Kiss that presenter fees were cut by some 75 per cent. And was I really *that* disappointed at not having to get up at 4am on Sunday mornings?

Back to RTM

Fate has a habit of moving in mysterious ways. When I was dropped from Kiss I found that erstwhile RTM station manager Bob Smith had left Thamesmead, so I was able to volunteer myself to step into his vacated Sunday morning pop oldies show. I remained with the station until 2001, enjoying a good working relationship with long-time station manager Rodney Collins, and also fulfilling the role as the elected presenters' representative on the board of Independent Radio Thamesmead. *Charlton Chat*, though both popular and successful, was dropped somewhat perfunctorily from the schedule when a director of the Football Club decided that the club would pull the strings regarding the politics of the show and changed the approach from casual, easy-paced, friendly presentation to harder, tighter football journalism – with the introduction of Clubcall (the premium-rate telephone service which provided daily bulletins of news from football clubs) contributor Mark Mansfield as host of *The Beautiful Game*, as the show was retitled, after Pele's poetic description of football. Mark was an excellent match commentator, and RTM was to benefit (unofficially) from free feeds of his Clubcall commentaries for all Charlton Athletic away games. These were accessed by dialling into the Clubcall system from the studio, via a coded password. As well as assisting in studio on some Saturdays, I was frequently called in to drive special programmes that were built around midweek away games, talking through the pre-match build-up and bridging the half-time interval with music and comment. It helped being both a vintage music aficionado and an avid Charlton fan.

It was the Charlton fanbase which provided a large percentage of the (modest) audience for RTM. The TSA (Total Survey Area) for the station was assessed at a figure of 750,000, and the peak RAJAR rating audience figure was reported as 4 per cent, with similarly modest listening hours (the number of hours per week in which the average listener tuned in). Thus with the close of the decade approaching, a management decision was taken to rename the station and relaunch, publicising the fact that the original broadcasting frequency of 103.8 had moved along the dial to 106.8FM. Some approaches were made to potential buyers or station partners, including GWR and TKO, but as no deals were struck ownership remained with Thamesmead Town. The name was changed to Millennium Radio to cash in with the approaching year 2000 and the station's proximity to Greenwich and the projected Millennium Dome.

New name, same location, similar presenter roster, similar programming (alternate current hits and popular oldies, and the occasional option of a free play item), similar audience ratings. I remained on the schedule in the new 'strip-show' format, squeezing in more free plays than was intended, and covering several slots for absent presenters, culminating in programmes on Friday and Saturday nights. One Saturday I was just five minutes from going on air at 8pm when the duty presenter from the station's Asian service walked in and advised me that he was taking over at 8pm! An oversight in communication by the programme controller, apparently. I left the studio, wrote a bitter note to management describing my disappointment at the situation, and my involvement with RTM/Millennium Radio ceased at that point early in 2001, just weeks after I'd received desperation phone calls from station executive Sue Bell one Friday evening asking if I was available to provide emergency cover on air following the acrimonious departure of ... the Asian contingent!

The station was later bought by the Fusion Group and broadcast as Time FM until its closure in 2009.

Solar Reborn

The legal radio stations in the '90s may have started off with good intentions, but they are now totally led by market forces with few nods to the true soul music innovators (apart from a few specialist shows). Through the years there have, of course, been a handful of DJs on legal radio who have championed soul music. Many of them are mentioned above, but I should add Emperor Rosko and Andy Peebles, Peter Young and Tony Blackburn as having had a huge influence on the scene. Regionally pioneering DJs such as Dave Gregory (followed by John Leech) on Essex Radio and in the north Terry Lennane, Steve Agasild, Mike Shaft, Ray Rose and Louie Martin gained more airtime for soul on ILR. Unfortunately over the years, as radio stations have pushed for even larger audiences, many of these DJs have either been axed or marginalised, in favour of more so-called research-based programming.

By the late '90s it was obvious that, apart from the odd specialist show, soul radio was pretty much finished. Virtually all other music formats, whether pop, rock, indie, middle-of-the-road, classical, jazz, dance or country, were being covered in depth by other radio stations, but (just as in the early '80s) soul music was not being taken seriously as a format in itself. For this reason a team of people from the original soul pirate radio days got together to see if there was any chance of filling the gap. They were headed by Carl Webster from Starpoint FM, the pioneering station of the '80s that had also introduced one of the first soul based RSL (Restricted Service

Licence) broadcasts in the UK (at the Windsor Safari Park in 1991) and had latterly put on several successful RSLs at the Southport Weekenders in the early '90s. Carl joined forces with Tony Monson, who had worked on various stations including Kiss 100 since his involvement with Solar in the '80s.

Then in 1998 things began to move: an opportunity arose for the group to lease airtime from the classic rock satellite station EKR. On 1 October 1998 a new station was launched as Solar FM – broadcasting soul, funk and jazz across Europe from 10pm to 6am nightly on a sub-carrier of Challenge TV. By one of those better twists of fate, my precipitate departure from Millennium coincided with this phoenix-like return. The broadcasting base was a studio tucked away in the corridors of the BBC TV complex in Maidstone, Kent, but for ease and convenience most programmes were pre-recorded onto VHS videotape in a makeshift studio set up in a barren room on the first floor of a large Victorian house near Crystal Palace, where the only conveniences were a temperamental calor-gas heater and a somewhat primitive toilet. The trick was to ensure that your two hour slot was recorded onto the correct cassette, and that the recording had actually worked – that the pause button had released at the start of the session, as it wasn't always apparent from the LED display on the machine. The tapes were then taken to Maidstone for transmission, so you could sit and listen in comfort at the appointed time.

The response was very encouraging, and Solar built a significant audience and response during this frequency-share. We were able to sample this first hand on New Year's Eve of 1998, when several presenters made the journey to Maidstone, battled their way through the security and geography of the building and broadcast live for a few hours, also fielding listeners' phone calls from Britain and Europe. This built an added loyalty to the station, which proved to be an asset when circumstances forced Solar to take a significant risk with an upgrade to the Sky Digital platform.

Unfortunately EKR were having financial difficulties and in January 1999 were forced to discontinue broadcasting. Since we were sharing the same studio facilities and sub-carrier, Solar likewise had to go off the air. There was a determination to continue, and after a great deal of discussion and negotiation a deal was eventually secured with MTV. On 1 June 1999 we began broadcasting again, twenty-four hours a day on a sub-carrier of MTV, reverting to the original call-sign of Solar Radio.

In late May 1999 came some very sad news: Tony Johns – the soul pirate radio founder and leading light behind the original Radio Invicta in the '70s – had collapsed and died of a coronary. In recent years he had more or less retired from the music and radio scene, but Solar Radio chairman and founder Tony Monson had tracked him down and persuaded him to join the schedule of presenters on Solar while it was linked to EKR. The response to his shows had been really good. Tony was a man who truly loved the music and made a considerable contribution to the development of soul music radio.

To tie in with our radio launch on Tuesday 1 June we organised a party at a venue in the West End of London, with six DJs, and an excellent PA from Light Of The World (who had just released their first album for years). At 10pm we linked into Solar Radio's opening broadcast from Mike Shaft. The evening was a real success – and a portent for things to come.

The studio arrangements were easier than before, with a fairly convenient half-hour drive to a gloomy basement in Dulwich and the resumption of live airtime. The equipment was good quality, adequate for our needs, and now included a computer server on which were loaded not only a range of jingles, station idents and promotion announcements but also (sadly few) commercials and the beginnings of a recorded database of soul records, new and old, which has built up to become a library of close to 10,000 tracks, enabling remote programming to be compiled without the need to repeat any tracks, and serving to enable un-manned broadcasting through the night or at unsocial hours. The system is configured so that on the odd occasion when a live presenter is delayed the computer will kick in within a couple of seconds of dead air and ensure continuity of broadcasting. The studios have since moved to more salubrious premises, and the technology remains of prime broadcast quality.

With the advent of twenty-four-hour broadcasting new DJs came on board, including Lorna Hetherington, Mark Phillips, Paul Stenning, Mick Farrer and Steve Bennett (who together with Brian Hurst and his producer Alex James were to form internet-only station Soul 24-7 in May 2000). Some original Solar DJs also returned to the station, including Richard Felstead.

We started a series of weekend guest shows with many well-known soul and jazz DJs, including Jeff Young, Mark Webster and Ralph Tee, then expanded our service to reach a worldwide audience via internet audio streaming in August 1999. In February 2000 Solar returned to the FM airwaves in London for a twenty-five-day RSL transmission, which included the Soul of the Century Top 1000 chart, which had been originally broadcast when we entered the new millennium. This was a great success, bringing on board many new listeners and also those with fond memories of the station in the '80s.

The analogue satellite service continued until August 2000, and in September the next major milestone was reached with the switch to Sky Digital and the addition of DJs including Dez Parkes, Max Rees, Mike Stephens and Bigger. From its origins in the heady days of soul pirate radio in London to the new media opportunities of the digital age, Solar Radio has remained committed to bringing quality soul-related music to a wide audience, with every DJ having complete freedom of choice.

With the increasing diversity of broadcasting platforms, the main problem faced by Solar and a number of others variously established on Sky, DAB or as internet broadcasters is that of brand identity and an awareness beyond the captive specialist audience. Advertising agencies and similar bodies or organisations have become accustomed to the status quo of standard FM/AM/LW broadcasting, and because most stations are owned by major companies they can well afford the cost of various audience survey methods, the resultant figures tend to driving the allocation of advertising campaigns. Continental Surveys and RAJAR are the two best-known survey vehicles. As many stations on the DAB system tend to be either digital extensions of existing outlets, or broadcasting ventures of large combines, these can also be accommodated in the traditional manner. This leaves the problem of obtaining quantifiable audience figures for the new breed stations. Website hits can be counted, of course, but it can be difficult identifying unique hits among repeat visits from the same IP address, and the problem remains in counting any audience through Sky, who are keen to publish viewing figures for top football matches but are reluctant to divulge audience figures for any other of their myriad channels. Thus we are stuck, still seeking an identity beyond the specialist listenership, though now reaping some reward since the launch of our upgraded website in July 2010.

CHAPTER SIXTEEN

SHOUT! RECORDS

It started as a networking thing . . . Long-time friend and soul fan Dave McAleer had worked with Mark Stratford at Connoisseur Collection Records, where they had produced a multi-LP series entitled *The Classic Soul Years* – double LPs that were issued in 1989 and comprised hits and obscurities from the mid-'60s, some of which repertoire was sourced on a secondary licence deal from Charly Holdings. On completion of that project Mark was keen to make further use of the arrangement with Charly to generate a series of soul monographs, but Dave's diary as a freelance music consultant was so full that he referred Mark to me.

Mark left Connoisseur Collection in the early '90s to launch his own independent label, RPM Records, with the purpose of producing reissues of selected retro pop albums and compilations by often obscure but collectable singers – particularly girl singers (in his *Dreambabes* series) and groups, with the label strapline 'Compiled by collectors for collectors'. Though not encompassing soul at that stage, Mark was keenly aware of the demand for vintage soul music, and saw an opportunity to establish a quality reissue brand that might one day grow to match the reputation of Ace Records' soul reissue label Kent – ironically and coincidentally named after an R&B label from the US west coast empire of the Bihari brothers, Joe, Saul and Lester. During our first telephone conversation it was decided to name the new venture Shout! Records, after the magazine that I had been so closely involved with. The logo was derived from a mixture of the US Minit logo, Bert Berns' Shout and the UK Ember designs.

That first conversation with Mark concluded with me agreeing to write the booklet notes for a CD compilation of the complete SSS International recordings by Peggy Scott and Jo Jo Benson as the first soul release on Shout! Records. (Shout!'s first release was a blues album by John Lee Hooker, co-ordinated by Neil Slaven.) Mark had bought the SSS vinyl LP, liked what he heard and called for all the masters from Charly. I liked their hits 'Lover's Holiday' and 'Pickin' Wild Mountain Berries', had acquired the LP and was familiar with most of the sitar-soul-stompers in the catalogue, along with some excellent ballads, and so launched into a couple of thousand words for the booklet.

The CD looked and sounded good and, more to the point, sold steadily, prompting a further conversation with Mark. My first task was to search through the Charly Holdings licensing catalogue in search of ideas for the next batch of three releases. I chose compilations comprising the production work of Allen Toussaint from New Orleans (*The Toussaint Touch*), Bobby Robinson from New York (*The Fire and Fury of . . .*), and a compilation of duets entitled *It Takes Two* (but not including that particular title!). These were generally well received, and there was a reasonable quantity of memorabilia and photos with which to illustrate the booklet notes. Some of the Toussaint material had been available on Charly vinyl and some on more vintage Stateside LPs (namely the *Bell Cellar of Soul* series from around 1968). The duet tracks were selected via a trawl through the licensing catalogue. The Bobby Robinson project was more diverse in content, covering a range of musical eras and styles from blues and doo-wop to R&B and deep soul, mid-'50s to mid-'60s. It was a brave venture for the new label, which was targeting a more comfortable classic soul audience. Charly had issued some archive material from the various Robinson labels (Red Robin, Fire, Fury, Enjoy, Everlast, etc.) on a poorly distributed CD set, and I'd managed to acquire a three CD box set issue by Capricorn in the US in the mid-'90s, so I patched together a selection of greatest hits and great unknowns from Buster Brown, Wilbert Harrison and Lee Dorsey though the Rainbows, Charts and Bop-Chords to Elmore James, Bobby Marchan and Joe Hayward, borrowed some images from the Capricorn booklet and added some label-scans. The sequencing works quite well, given the diversity of the music, but we nearly ran into trouble when Bobby Robinson saw a copy of the CD. It seems his arrangement with Charly had expired before the tracks were licensed to us for use, but he was magnanimous enough just to comment on our transgression and take no further action!

Next came some single artist monographs as I cast my mind over a few decades of collecting and focused on key omissions from other reissue programmes. Again sourced from Charly, the Vee Jay singles of Jerry Butler, the Sound Stage 7 singles of Joe Simon – issued in the UK on Monument, which allowed me licence to pun with the *Monument of Soul* title. While Jerry Butler and Joe Simon had enjoyed prolific chart success in the USA with a succession of 45s breaking from the R&B chart into the Hot 100, neither had any reputation or success in the UK. Butler had a handful of singles from Vee Jay issued on Top Rank, Stateside and President, the latter two also risking the odd LP release, though Simon was better represented through the London catalogue, and also on Monument when Fred Foster's label gained its own UK identity. Both had gone on to achieve wider success during the next decade after Butler's move to Mercury (and subsequently to Motown and Philadelphia International) and Simon's to Raeford Gerrard's Spring Records coincided with the emergence and rise of the soul/dance music market. Thus both had a profile, not to mention a musical heritage of quality, to warrant a reissue of their formative back catalogue on Shout!.

As I recall, it was Mark Stratford's suggestion to take another listen to the Vee Jay tracks by Little Richard and, having not really given the soul side of Mr Penniman's early '60s output much of a listen before – other than the deep soul ballad gem 'I Don't Know What You've Got', issued on a UK Fontana single, I sat down and listened again to my Fontana and Joy/President LPs with a different ear. Having originally listened to Richard's rehashes of his Specialty classics with a feeling of disappointment, it was a comfort, if not a revelation, to place the material in a different perspective, still not good but acceptable, which description was also appropriate for the tracks cut for the soul market such as 'Dance What'cha Wanna' and 'You Better Stop'. In this context the bluesier tracks like 'Cherry Red' and 'Going Home Tomorrow' are oases in a desert of mediocrity – though it was diplomatic not to mention these shortcomings in the liner note! Another mistake was not to check the test pressing to ensure that the correct versions of 'I Don't Know What You've Got' were used. The assumption was made that the master version supplied would be the one on the UK Fontana 45, the hit single version, but in fact it was the LP alternate take. As a consequence the CD includes this twice and unfortunately omits the hit single version.

Next came two one-off projects involving Johnny Adams and Billy Preston. During my many visits to New Orleans in the '80s I had become friendly with Johnny Adams, partly thanks to my fan-worship of his voice and records, and partly because I had been closely involved with a reissue LP on Charly of his material from Shelby Singleton's SSS International label. Whether owing to the administration of royalties by Mr Singleton's people or by those at Charly, or a combination of the two, from Johnny's frequent comments to me it appears he didn't receive much money from sales of 'The Tan Nightingale' (which should have more correctly been titled 'The Tan Canary' from his nickname in New Orleans, but the avian connection was muddled by me in mid-Atlantic). Johnny tragically died of cancer in 1998, so with the turn of the century it seemed timely to compile a memorial album for Shout! release, again sourced from Charly licensed repertoire. This time it was extended to include tracks cut by Johnny under the production of Senator Jones and released on his various New Orleans labels, including primarily Hep'Me and JB. Thus came *Released . . . a memorial album* in 2001, using the front sleeve photo from the SSS LP *Heart & Soul* reversed for the booklet cover.

With Billy Preston, the original plan was to license *The Wildest Organ in Town* album from EMI/Capitol and combine it with club hit 'Billy's Bag', the best of his Vee Jay material and some tracks from his Derby LP, issued years back on UK Soul City entitled *Greazee Soul*, but the best laid plans of mice, men and Mark Stratford were scuppered on three fronts. First EMI declined permission to sub-license the Capitol LP as they intended to do an in-house reissue – which eventually appeared three years later with the most awful packaging (a line drawing of a keyboard). Then Mark found that ABKCO Records, representing Allen Klein, who owns the Sam Cooke music estate which includes Sar/Derby Records, were talking the proverbial telephone numbers for a licensing fee for a single track. On the third front it became quite a challenge to select enough good tracks from the soul and gospel material recorded by Billy on Vee Jay to mould into a respectable CD. In the end we opened with a few-seconds clip from Sam Cooke's 'Little Red Rooster' with Sam calling out 'play it, Billy', spliced together a couple of extracts from the *Greazee* LP as 'Soul Derby', picked out eleven tracks with a modicum of soul, with 'Billy's Bag' tucked neatly in the middle, used a six-minute live version of 'How Great Thou Art' to wind things up/down, and borrowed a few minutes of Billy's organ solo 'incidental music' from the soundtrack to *In the Heat of the Night*, credited as 'outro'. Thus we finally got an album, though silk purse might be a generous overstatement of the result from the proverbial pig's ear.

The next two releases came as a result of a networking friendship with Bob Fisher, whom I had known for many years as a contributor to *Shout* in the '60s and subsequently in his capacity as licensed repertoire manager for various labels, and whom Mark Stratford had worked with at Connoisseur Collection. Bob had left Connoisseur in 2002 just before the demise of that company, where he had been midway through a programme of reissuing all the LPs by Joe Tex on Dial Records in twofer packages (two vinyl LPs on one CD at single CD price). Bob had licensing clearance for the next two twofers in the intended series, and was happy that Shout! should inherit these. By good fortune I'm a big fan of Joe Tex, and had managed to collect most of his LPs (and numerous 45s) over the years, so was in a good position to provide LP sleeves for CD booklet covers and memorabilia for the artwork, as well as write the notes with a good knowledge of the product and the history of the artist. Thus came Joe Tex's *Live & Lively/Soul Country* and *Happy Soul/Buying a Book*. The connection with Bob, and more specifically some projects that had been in the Connoisseur Collection pipeline having been cleared for licensing by Universal Music, went on to provide Shout with three further releases: the Vibrations, Bobby Moore & the Rhythm Aces and the Knight Brothers, each of which had its own story to tell and a slightly different challenge for me.

I was comfortable with the Vibrations project, even if a two CD set (for single disc price) was something of a completist collection and a bit of an endurance to listen through at full length. I liked the group's style, which combined gritty, rocking doo-wop, smooth harmony ballads and some tracks which were on the cusp of the soul era. The research brought me into contact with Bobby Eli, the white Philadelphia-based session guitarist who had been an integral part of the mainly black MFSB studio band at Philadelphia International Records, and had also played in the Vibrations' road band in the early '60s when they were recording for OKeh. Bobby was a member of the Soulful Detroit Forum (an internet music chat-group which I had joined), and helped me with some information about their early years and the well-being of their personnel.

I had always written the booklet notes for the Shout! releases, and had provided some memorabilia to illustrate these, but with the Vibrations project (and onwards) I was given full responsibility for the contents of the booklet, including all the credits and so on. So began the hunt for photos, without wanting to pay huge sums to various libraries and other sources. Thus my collector's kleptomania bore fruit, after hours spent going through numerous storage boxes and magazines in order to supplement the various LP sleeves in my racks.

If I thought the Vibrations project was a challenge, the Bobby Moore was more so. I had acquired the *Searching For My Love* LP at some point, and had managed to accumulate a bunch of 45s by Bobby and the Rhythm Aces, but had never really listened to them. I found them pleasant, and had mentally consigned them to the OK category. Facing the task of researching and writing the notes as well as searching for photos, I had a bit of an uphill battle. The group has been mentioned in dispatches in a few books over the years, gaining some reputation from being the first major success to come from Rick Hall's Muscle Shoals productions, and they're still active on the cabaret circuit with a page on their agent's website. Thank goodness for the home scanner, with which I was able to furnish the booklet designer with a range of labels. I actually grew to like the material more while I was working on the CD, and was further gratified by the enthusiastic response to the finished CD.

The Knight Brothers was more a labour of love for which it was pleasing to receive reward. I had always liked the gospelly style of 'brothers' Richard Dunbar and James 'Jimmy' Diggs, and had collected a handful of Checker-label 45s over the years, while 'Temptation 'Bout To Get Me' has appeared on a couple of compilations, while a Mercury track was on one of Dave Godin's *Deep Soul Treasures* CDs. We actually managed to get some source-master CDs from Universal for this, so it was good to play through tracks I hadn't heard before while choosing the running order, and including the few tracks by the Carltons (who recorded for the same company albeit on the Argo label, and featured Jimmy Diggs at a time when the Knight Brothers' recording career was at a low ebb) for added value. Doing an internet search for the Knight Brothers yielded some useful contact information: Richard Dunbar is an active current member of the Original Drifters, and their website included an email address. I sent a brief message asking for any help, and by return received a phone number. Within an hour of sending the initial tentative email enquiry I was talking on the phone with Richard Dunbar! It was a short but helpful interview, from which I gained enough to make the booklet note more informative. After posting news of this contact on the Yahoo Southern Soul chat group I received a message from someone who was in touch with James Diggs, and after furnishing contact information (with approval of all parties) I understand that the Knight Brothers got back in touch with each other after decades of separation.

Jeffrey Kruger

Many of us have more than one hobby or interest away from the day job and domestic life, and it's not unusual for friends and acquaintances to be involved in more than one aspect of one's life. For example, I have tennis friends whom I also meet at football, and football friends who are also soul fans – and friends from both realms (and elsewhere) who are prepared to listen to my radio shows. It was the world of radio that served as the catalyst in generating the next three CDs in the Shout! catalogue. During my decade at RTM/Millennium Radio I worked with a number of station managers, for the longest time with Rodney Collins. Rod, a Londoner with a long pedigree in music journalism and promotion, came to Thamesmead from Scotland, where he had been managing Radio Clyde. He brought with him a wealth of experience in radio, an addiction to the music of Frank Sinatra and a gently persuasive management style, along with a lengthy list of industry contacts accumulated during his long career. One of these was Jeffrey Kruger, the originator of The Kruger Organisation (TKO), which had long been involved in many facets of the entertainment industry. When RTM was seeking a business partner around the time of the rebranding to Millennium, TKO was one of the suitors (though the potential partnership did not come to fruition). It was just a couple of years later, when Rod had left Thamesmead and relocated to Isles FM, at Stornoway in the Western Isles of Scotland, that this contact bore fruit in a different direction.

As well as the radio station on the island, Rod also ran a b&b with his wife Jackie and the help of daughter Sarah, where my wife, Barbara, and I went for a short holiday late in 2001. During an evening of music conversation and reminiscing, we mentioned Jeffrey Kruger as a mutual acquaintance. As I'd not been in touch with him for a number of years, Rod sent him an email mentioning my name and including my email address. Returning home a few days later, I was delighted to find an email from Jeffrey renewing our acquaintance. This prompted some conversations, both electronic and verbal, regarding the licensing of music from the Ember back catalogue for potential reissue on Shout!. A meeting was arranged with Jeffrey at his home in Hove, and the groundwork was prepared for some interesting projects involving material from King, LuPine and Herald/Ember. With the former two, specific tracks had been licensed by Ember Records in perpetuity, while Jeffrey's arrangement with the late Al Silver of Ember USA resulted in the whole catalogue being at our disposal, much of it from original 45s and unissued masters stored *chez* Kruger.

Always a pioneer in the realms of R&B and soul, Mr Kruger had released an early LP by James Brown and a couple of compilations from the LuPine catalogue featuring early tracks by Eddie Floyd and the Primettes (later the Supremes) among other less well-known soul artists, and from this repertoire I chose to reissue the James Brown and Eddie Floyd tracks in a *Soul Brothers* collection, gather around twenty tracks from the LuPine label into a *Roots of Motor Town* anthology, and package some fifty items from Herald and Ember, both vocal group 'doo-wop' gems and solo artist hits and obscurities into a double CD (at single disc price) entitled, in best punning tradition, *Heralding The Hits*.

More Catalogue Notes

Some four years later, in early 2005, a first LP/CD by Don Varner, a veteran of Southern Soul, was issued as a result of more networking. I posted a message on the Yahoo Southern Soul chat group announcing my intention to reissue material from the Quinvy/South Camp labels, and received an email from label owner David Johnson warning me that our licensor, Charly Holdings, no longer had rights to the material. The next message I received was from Mrs Francine Varner, Don's widow, advising me that she had acquired rights to all of Don's recordings. A quick bit of lateral thinking gave me an alternative idea: if the Quinvy catalogue was not available to license, then why not revise my plan to focus just on Don Varner? I suggested this alternative to Francine, who was receptive, and to Mark Stratford, who also liked the idea given the market for Don's material and its scarcity. Then I put Mark in touch with Francine to handle the legal complexities, and the seed of an idea sown in January 2005 bore fruit in June, helped by the fact the music magazine *Mojo* published a special feature on Southern Soul that month, and included a track by Don from our project on their sampler CD. This reaped dual reward: wider exposure for the Shout! CD and extra royalties from the use of 'Mojo Hannah' on the *Mojo* disc.

While all of this was going on we had a request in with Universal Music for permission to reissue two LPs by Don Covay from the mid-'70s – *Superdude* and *Hot Blood*. This was granted, and resulted in their appearance in the Shout catalogue in the autumn of 2005. The promotion campaign for this batch of releases became known as 'The Three Dons', and I'm pleased to report that they all achieved very respectable sales in the first months of their release, sufficient to gain high positions in the distributor's chart.

Projects followed on McKinley Mitchell and the Five Du-Tones, early '60s Chicago soul licensed from LicenseMusic.com, an extension of Charly, and Joe Hinton and Anna King, both courtesy of Universal Music Group. Dame Fortune also smiled when Sony granted permission for a compilation of Ted Taylor's singles from OKeh and also a Roy Hamilton collection. It had been my intention to collate the more R&B-styled tracks from Roy's numerous LPs on Epic, but the permission granted limited my choice to the pick of a list of forty tracks, some of which were more easy listening than I would have liked but had to be included in the final selection in order to provide a worthwhile running time. Unfortunately it's not easy to convey such parameters to reviewers, other than by discreet phrasing in the booklet notes, and as a consequence some reviews reasonably questioned the inclusion of some lush ballads in what was promoted as an R&B-based selection.

Early in 2006 I had some communication with Jim Lancaster in Florida, who purchased the Playground Recording Studio in Valparaiso, once owned by Finley Curry in partnership with Shelby Singleton, and had found numerous boxes of unissued master tapes. Jim made mention of this on the Yahoo Southern Soul group, and I expressed interest in licensing a compilation of Playground Soul. While that project didn't come to fruition, Jim put me in contact

Shout! Records

with veteran music producer Bob McRee, who had been involved with Peggy Scott & Jo Jo Benson recordings with Singleton's SSS International label, and had also produced some solo material for Peggy Scott during the late '70s which had remained unissued. Bob dusted off the master tapes, signed a contract and licensed these to Shout for an album which I gave the title *She's Got It All*. David Cole at *In The Basement* magazine kindly gave me access to the transcript of his interview with Peggy, and I was also able to make contact with her by telephone and email at her funeral parlour business in California to confirm details for the booklet notes.

Contact with another Bob, Mr Grady in Macon, Georgia, also came via the Southern Soul list, with list-member David Porter, who runs the Vivid Sound Mail Order CD business in Nayland, Essex, sending me samples of two recent releases on Bob Grady's BGR label. One marked the return to disc of '60s legend Oscar Toney Jr, and the other brought my first direct contact with Wilson Meadows, whose roots are with the Zircons in the doo-wop era and the Meadows Brothers at Muscle Shoals in 1981, before a solo CD on BGR. A deal was struck with Bob which resulted in CDs by both Oscar and Wilson in the Shout! catalogue.

Subsequent releases have featured New Orleans singer Marva Wright, with a blues-styled CD from Blue Sky Records adapted into a strong soul-blues set on Shout!, and an interesting project which brought Memphis-based club singer Barbara Blue to a global audience, adding half a dozen bonus tracks to an existing album to provide a strong vehicle to promote her, backed by Taj Mahal's Phantom Blues Band, and gaining good response and airplay in the UK.

2007 also brought the welcome reissue of Liberty material by the Rivingtons, including not only their novelty R&B smash 'Papa Oom Mow Mow' but also some great soul ballads, followed by a double CD of hard-to-find tracks by Johnny Adams and reissues of a blues CD by T-Bone Walker and ballads by the Dells in conjunction with Universal, plus the highly collectable Columbia LP by the Spellbinders, early protégés of writer/producer Van McCoy, and including their non-album 45s from Columbia and Date as bonus tracks, making it a quintessential purchase for many fans of Northern Soul.

More networking with friends and acquaintances from years ago led to two projects of London-recorded tracks by major Southern Soul stars to start 2008. My vinyl collection includes albums released on Contempo Records in the late '70s by Oscar Toney Jr and Doris Duke. I hadn't played the Oscar LP for some thirty years before I tracked through it while researching the booklet notes for the album licensed from Bob Grady, and I was struck by the quality. It would have been close on thirty years since I had last had any contact with John Abbey, who owned Contempo and thus the rights to these albums, but I have been in (slightly) more frequent contact with David Nathan, who worked for John in those days and is now co-owner of www.soulmusic.com, a useful and valuable source of quality soul releases, and also a presenter on Solar Radio. David provided me with an email address for John, contact was made, a deal was struck, and both Contempo albums now grace the Shout! catalogue.

We were then offered the chance to re-package the 1969 Little Milton Chess LP *If Walls Could Talk* by Universal Music, who generously agreed to let me add bonus tracks in the form of both sides of three Chess 45s, and approval was granted by EMI for me to combine a collection of Lloyd Price's hits for ABC Records with the best selected cuts from a rare LP in my collection, *Lloyd Price Sings the Million Sellers. Mr Personality* was the result.

One of the challenges of licensing records for reissue is that of finding the correct current ownership of tracks cut several decades ago. Some have reverted to the artist or owner of the original label, some have been bought by more recently formed companies for reissue on their own custom labels, and some have floated around within existing major companies, surviving mergers and takeovers. I had long treasured copies of three 45s cut by Roy Hamilton for AGP Records in Memphis shortly before his death in 1969, one of which ('Dark End of the Street'/'One Hundred Years' had been issued in the UK on Dave Godin's Deep Soul label. The other two had been given to me as review samples by Trevor Churchill in his role as Bell Records label manager in 1969.

Shout! Records

As a fan of Roy Hamilton I had also bought several of his 45s on RCA, and now, by the magic of major mergers, BMG, the current corporate face of RCA and combined with Sony, also controlled the rights to the Bell catalogue – so there was a possibility of a project that combined Roy's RCA and AGP material. To our pleasant surprise approval was given by Sony/BMG, and the 'Tore Up' project was born, eventually coming to fruition on Shout! 44, with the kind assistance and co-operation of Roy's surviving family, Roy Jr and his wife Maria, who had also given generous help and a supply of personal photographs for our earlier *Don't Let Go* CD from the Epic vaults.

Having found that the time lapse between requesting permission to license material and gaining approval can often be a year or two, we reviewed our schedule early in 2008 and saw that we had a potentially fallow summer. We turned our attention to the realms of Public Domain – music recorded more than fifty years ago, and thus out of copyright in Europe and the UK as British law stands. I took a considered look at what was – or more accurately what wasn't – available already, for which I had clean source vinyl in my collection, and the result was albums by Linda Hopkins (from Savoy, Federal, Atco and some small independent labels), *Rock and Roll Blues* (Shout! 45), Solomon Burke (his first recordings for Bess Berman's Apollo label), *This Is It* (Shout! 46) and Linda Hayes (mainly from Hollywood Records plus a couple of tracks from Antler and early items with the Platters from Federal), *Atomic Baby* (Shout! 49).

Meanwhile, by another twist of fate, Cherry Red Records, who distribute the Shout label, had done a deal with Nashville-based publishers Tree Music to represent the catalogue in the UK. Tree Music to me means Joe Tex, and I jumped at the chance to reissue the first dozen singles that Joe recorded for the Dial label, predating the big hit with 'Hold What You've Got', and many of which were included on an obscure LP issued on London in the 1960s and entitled *The Best of Joe Tex*, which wasn't strictly accurate! With the help of Jack Jackson in the Sony Nashville office, who located and supplied a couple of rare source masters, and UK collectors Craig

Butler, John Marriott and John Ridley (who have also helped by supplying MP3 files of rare 45s for other reissue projects), we were able to complete First On the Dial (Shout 47) to add to the range of Joe Tex albums available in the Shout! catalogue.

When browsing through my racks of vinyl, mainly in search of old favourites which have not been reissued (to my knowledge) on CD, once in a while I come across an album by an artist who is not a household name, nor even regularly mentioned on specialist internet forums, and think 'I wonder . . .'. Such was the case with a Sandra Feva LP on Venture, bought upon release in 1980 and probably not played more than once since then. Wonderful things, computers. A search for Venture Records linked me to the website of Tony Camillo, who owned the label and had produced the album, and a speculative email to the contact address brought a helpful reply. Yes, the album was available to license – what sort of deal could we offer? Working on the principle of if you don't ask, you don't get, I made an offer along normal Shout! financial lines. The reply asked me what I expected for that sort of money, so I asked for all the tracks from the *Savoir Faire* LP plus four or five bonus tracks. Tony's answer was in the affirmative, the deal was struck, masters were sent and the advance was paid, all within a few weeks. *Savoir Faire Plus* hit the streets in January 2009 (Shout! 51), drawing rave reviews in print and on air and bringing Sandra to a whole new audience. By helpful coincidence David Cole had recently found Sandra and an interview had been published in *In The Basement*, and with David's help and a pleasant transatlantic phone conversation the project was completed with the co-operation of the lady herself.

It isn't always thus, however. I made approaches to the owner of a small West Coast label to license some '70s tracks by Sugar Pie DeSanto, but the asking price of $1,000 *per track* was an insurmountable obstacle. Later, following a very pleasant phone conversation with Jesse James (veteran of albums on 20th Century in the '60s and hit 45s on Zea in the early '80s), suggesting a comprehensive package of his music, a similar financial scenario arose. Sometimes the proverbial telephone number advances get in the way of economic reality, as people overlook the fact that 10 per cent of something is worth more than 100 per cent of nothing.

The debut LP by Willie Hutch from RCA, Soul Portrait (Shout! 52), was a February 2009 release, followed by the last album by Philippe Wynne, on Sugar Hill (Shout! 53) and a twofer package combining LPs by Randy Brown from Parachute and Chocolate City (Shout! 54).

Late 2009 saw the release of an anthology of mainly unissued tracks by New York-based singers who had worked with the late Jimmy Radcliffe. Jimmy's son Chris put together a compilation called *Super Baby Cakes* to present some fine tracks by Pat Lundy, Barbara Jean English and Vivien Reed amongst others, and Shout also reissued an album recorded for United Artists by Sam & Dave in 1974, produced by Steve Cropper. Having sold the initial pressing of 1,000 units, we were advised that Mrs (Sam) Moore was unhappy with our new cover artwork, some booklet note quotes from a 1971 interview by Sam with *Blues & Soul* editor John Abbey and the production credit to Steve Cropper. Several months were spent changing the offending elements of the package, only for permission to re-press to be denied in November 2010 – so if you have a copy of the CD, look after it! By the time you read this I expect the Shout catalogue will also include George and Gwen McCrae, the Tymes, the Four Tops and Erma Franklin, together with Brenda & the Tabulations, the Dixie Hummingbirds and a King Curtis album first issued in 1961. Now I'm off to search through my racks for some other LPs which have been overlooked for reissue these past three decades!

CHAPTER SEVENTEEN

INTO THE NEW CENTURY

Now almost everything can be done with the click of a mouse. Even an ageing soul fan such as me, past the landmark of sixty years on the planet, spends an hour or so ('and the rest' says my wife) each day peering into the computer monitor screen, clicking the mouse at frequent intervals, to buy CDs and books, to search for biographies and discographies of singers, to scan through lists of releases on record labels of half a century ago, to listen to music, either from web-based radio stations or stored on the PC, to listen to samples of new releases, and to cherish video clips from past decades via You-Tube.

Gone is the era of poring over browser boxes of cardboard LP sleeves, buying music magazines at the newsagents and looking through the soul racks in the High Street record shop, or even tuning regularly to an FM radio station in the London area to listen to a comfortable range of classic soul or R&B.

Each time I venture into a branch of any remaining High Street CD dealer to search for specialist music, I vow to myself that it will be the last time, but the lure of a potential bargain, either in sale stock or modestly priced reissue, draws me back inside either in my south-east London home territory or in the West End. The trend of racking soul material among the general rock and pop sections, which I first encountered in New York and New Orleans at the turn of the new century, has now reached across the Atlantic, making it even more laborious to find anything interesting by browsing, though sometimes one can strike lucky and find a few Motown and Atlantic gems alongside the latest product in the urban section – that's if you can fend off the intrusion of in-store music played at deafening volume. I had the temerity to complain once in a Virgin megastore, mentioning that the noise had been annoying enough to prevent me making a purchase of £50 or so, only to be told that 'Sir Richard insists that we play in-store music loudly'. Oh well . . . I'll sit at home and order from Amazon or Play, with some quiet blues or jazz on in the background in my own living room – and get more for my money, *and* get it post-free! The pleasures of browsing have been eroded significantly, and even when you find an interesting CD in the rack the print on the inlay card is either too small to read or rendered invisible by using a green font on a red background.

Live shows? The last concert I saw in London was the Lamont Dozier showcase at the Royal Festival Hall in September 2001, where he topped a bill comprising new local black music acts including Roachford and Mis-Teeq, and the limitations of these two and others were only too evident after the first few bars had been sung by Mr Dozier. Since then, I've not bothered overmuch. The trek to the Jazz Café in Camden Town, where a number of soul and jazz-funk stars have played in recent years, isn't arduous in itself, but as the star act generally doesn't go on stage until around 10pm, the thought of battling back from the top end of Camden High Street to south-east London after midnight doesn't appeal to me, and the few shows I've seen there were less than comfortable. I did my share of standing for an hour in a hot and crowded venue decades ago. The journey to Hammersmith Apollo (as the Odeon was rebranded several years ago) is similarly awkward, though was more bearable after seeing Aretha Franklin, Bobby Bland or Jimmy Reed and the American Folk Blues Festival in past decades.

In the past few years I've also been discouraged by ticket prices to see concerts by artists who are past their peak. £75 to see James Brown, aged about seventy, at the Tower of London? £60 for 'An Evening With Dionne Warwick' at the Shaw Theatre – even if this price did include a programme and glass of champagne? I didn't bother to find out if her stage show still comprises extended versions of two or three hits and medleys of a dozen or more others. New Year 2006 brought a soul extravaganza to town, when US impresario David Gest gathered together Peabo Bryson, original Stylistics lead singer Russell Thompkins Jr and the New Stylistics, Martha Reeves and the Vandellas, Candi Staton, Deniece Williams, Billy Paul, Freda Payne, Carl Carlton, Dorothy Moore and William Bell, plus British pop singer Bonnie Tyler. He presented this illustrious cast for three nights at the prestigious Cadogan Hall in Victoria, SW1, and by all reports it was an excellent concert – though I was again discouraged by ticket prices ranging from £49 to £99 for the first two nights, and an outlandish £125 and £150 for the Sunday show, which was New Year's Eve. Say no more!

Record Collecting

As I've mentioned, the whole science has changed. The record store has largely been replaced by internet-based merchants, able to discount retail prices by placing bulk orders and servicing them from huge central warehouses rather than paying rent and overheads on shops. We have access to a vast range of CDs and an increasing number of DVDs, containing vintage film and TV footage from the past fifty years.

Mention of fifty years brings me neatly to Public Domain, and the fact that recorded music is protected by copyright law for fifty years from the end of its year of origin in the UK – as mentioned briefly above. After that time it can be reissued without payment of any royalty to the performer. The consequence of this is that the music of the mid-'40s to mid-'50s, which was the formative period of rhythm and blues leading into the golden years of rock 'n' roll, has become available to release at modest cost. This rich vein has been tapped by some companies through specific PD-focused labels, including Indigo and Proper, and it has become commonplace to buy multi-CD compilations of such vintage material for budget prices. Indigo, for example, have released a series of CDs entitled *The R&B*

Years, which began with a single CD of twenty-two tracks for 1946 and gradually expanded to double and multiple CDs in subsequent years, so that the releases for 1955 and 1956 comprised three CDs, each containing twenty-eight tracks and retailing at under £10! While Indigo tend to concentrate on various artists compilations, Joker have featured a number of single artist releases from the early '50s, as have Rev-Ola, and the respective catalogues are growing with names like Big Joe Turner, Chuck Willis, Fats Domino, Ruth Brown, Anisteen Allen and the Clovers, along with a wealth of other major names from the roots of R&B. An added bonus is that the CD packages include not only the hits but also archive material, making them into a collector's paradise.

The downside is that the artists or dependents receive no royalties on PD releases, having often been paid only modest amounts (if anything) on sales of the original recording all those years ago. There are, however, some reissue companies (notably Ace Records) who don't take advantage of recordings being out of copyright and pay royalties on their large catalogue of vintage music.

The other side of the collecting coin is lists of records for sale and/or auction. The era of Hugh McCullum's quarter-inch thick sheaf of paper entitled *Records for sale/auction* is long gone, replaced in recent years by the doubtful pleasures of eBay. The theory of an online auction is fine, especially with the option of 'buy it now', but in practice the availability of software to control your bidding remotely has made it a frustrating lottery for the occasional bidder. In addition a good percentage of cut-outs, overstocks and the like, which used to be routed into the sale bins of high street stores, now tends to find its way primarily to eBay dealers.

Radio

Forty years ago soul fans were heralding the launch of Radio 1 as a new dawn, and the inclusion of a specialist show on the schedule seemed to confirm that the authorities acknowledged that there was an audience for Black music. I have already recounted the Kiss saga, and now it's worth talking about Jazz FM.

Jazz FM launched in 1992 with (like Kiss) an impressive schedule of specialist programmes. Kiss covered a full range of soul and dance styles, modern and ancient, and Jazz gave airplay to everything from be-bop to big band via the blues. Again like Kiss, Jazz FM found it necessary to shuffle not only their schedule but their broadcasting identity, having found that playing Dixieland jazz doesn't pay many bills. Over the years they changed to JFM (not to be confused with the '80s soul pirate station), back to Jazz FM, then in November 2004 to Smooth FM. Not content with 'ironing out the jazz spots' (to paraphrase Don Covay's soul song title), owners Guardian Media Group requested a further change, and a December 2006 meeting of radio regulatory body OfCom approved a change of name and format, to Smooth Radio, and dropping jazz and soul content to focus on music for the over-fifties – this following GMG's acquisition of the Saga Radio brand, which had been broadcasting a gentle blend of music from the '40s, '50s and '60s to their niche mature audience on regional FM (Midlands and Scotland) and the national DAB (Digital Audio Broadcasting) satellite multiplex platform.

Thus Smooth Radio was born in March 2007, with a bland playlist of music from five decades, following an identikit format similar to those of London's other easy-listening pop stations Magic and Heart, and effectively setting back the cause of soul radio by some forty years. There is now a choice of stations but little variation in playlists and format. Rock fans have XFM and Virgin, I hardly dare tune to Radio 1 or Capital, and Radio 2 seems to think that its daytime mature audience turns into heavy metal rockers between 10pm and 2am!

Solar Radio has grown from strength to strength in reputation, audience size and brand awareness since joining the Sky platform in 1998, advancing to Sky Digital in 2000 and maintaining live internet streaming from the beginning. We continue to fly the flag, and with any luck we bring the pleasures of R&B and soul music to a wider audience.

Soul Radio in London? Following a pedigree which includes David Simmons, Robbie Vincent and Greg Edwards, there comes

Peter Young. Peter is a veteran of some twenty years on the London airwaves, many of those spent presenting *The Soul Cellar* on Capital until he joined Jazz FM upon their launch in 1990. PY, as he is generally known, took the show title with him and continued to hold regular prime-time slots for eleven years until his sudden resignation on May 2001. He moved briefly to BBC London before answering a plea from the jazz station to return to their schedule in 2003. Peter then held a regular Sunday afternoon slot until a schedule shuffle moved him to Saturday evening early in 2006. He also survived the rebranding to Smooth FM and metamorphosis into Smooth Radio, and in various forum postings relating the dilution of musical output on the station he has often been referred to as 'a beacon of quality broadcasting in a sea of dross'.

DAB radio is a recent alternative in the broadcasting spectrum, with the downsides of requiring special receiving equipment and a very limited amount of soul or R&B being broadcast (there's only a ghetto slot on BBC 6 in the London area). There are also geographic limitations to the number of stations that can be heard in any given location, and even then reception can vary each time you tune in. Hardly testimony to a reliable source of listening!

Thank goodness (again) for the internet. There are numerous web-based radio stations playing continuous soul, R&B and blues, though copyright issues arose during 2006 which served to reduce the number of operators able to comply with payment of the required fees in order to retain their licences. Some had overlooked the fact that public performance of recorded music triggers a copyright payment to the songwriter via his or her publisher. It's great having the freedom to play your own choice of music to a voracious audience, but let's not forget to pay the necessary dues.

The Internet

It occurs to me that the internet has now become such an integral part of my life that it needs a separate section as I come to the end of this memoir. What kind of impact has it had on the spread of news and information, and how vital it is as a means of communication?

Sadly it is now the bearer of more bad news than good, as in recent times the musical heroes of my younger years have more frequently been the subject of obituary notices than of record reviews, and the various forums and specialist collectives have become a ready source for bringing us sad tidings, either from local newspaper columns or from direct contact with those who knew them. But at least this is more immediate than reading a column in a monthly magazine.

Nipping off briefly at a tangent, it's a further sign of the times that the deaths of major names from the soul world such as James Brown, Isaac Hayes and Norman Whitfield were deemed to be of sufficient note for inclusion in the headlines of BBC and independent radio news, whereas they used to be consigned to a footnote in the broadsheet press.

Internet sources are now invaluable as a research tool, which has a direct and positive effect on me when preparing booklet notes for CD projects as well as in doing background notes for my radio show. I have a loft full of boxes of specialist magazines dating back to the early '60s (one of the benefits of remaining unmarried for so many years was that there was never any domestic pressure for household space!), and my hoarding tendencies have proved useful in proving a rich source of magazines and illustrations to use in Shout! booklets, along with label scans from vinyl LPs and 45s stored in steel racking in the shed and spare bedroom. However, while in past years my desk and floor would be strewn with magazines and books that I was referring to, so much of this information is now available online that it's now far easier to click between windows on the PC monitor – though I'm not sure this is beneficial to my eyesight!

As well as research, networking is another key benefit of the internet era – not so much networks of computers as linking up with fellow fans, and in many cases resuming acquaintances and friendships that originated in the days of the printed word. Membership of various web-based discussion groups keeps me up to date with news and opinion, and also provides valuable insight into which records are available (or otherwise), and thus gives me clues for reissue projects. Fellow collectors are also willing and useful sources of missing tracks for certain projects. This is especially helpful when a major licensor cannot locate a master for a track, and the magic of email and MP3 solves a problem.

The contacts within these specialist forums is not restricted to fans, however, as the computer age has embraced people from all aspects of the industry, with Spyder Turner and Al 'Caesar' Berry (of the Tymes) active contributors to Soulful Detroit, and Jerry 'Swamp Dogg' Williams Jr and George Soule in the Yahoo Southern Soul community. Some forums can be more cliquey than others, and tend to post comments for a narrower spectrum of readership, but the information and views shared are helpful to those in need.

Major networking sites such as MySpace and Facebook also provide a ready shop window for artists ancient and modern to display and sell their music – in my case doubly helpful in allowing me to hear material for radio air-play or for potential licensing. The Solar Radio MySpace site receives numerous friend requests from singers and musicians, and as computer awareness spreads to older generations I am also finding that soul and blues singers from regions of the USA that are still off the beaten track are tapping into this new medium. Not only am I able to hear audio clips of their records on their social network site or their website, but the supply of a mailing address can reap rich reward. Artists who may have been restricted to hometown gigs for years are now able to enjoy global airplay, which hopefully leads to sales, money and greater recognition.

A negative aspect of the internet, at least to an oldie like me, is the increasing trend for major labels to reissue back catalogue product in download-only format. EMI Records seem to be a leader in this market, and a recent glance at the Stateside Records website revealed a number of very appealing reissues and compilations unavailable in physical format with an illustrated booklet and informative notes. The concern, certainly among older buyers, is that we will be driven to listening to more music on iPods and similar devices, and while it is good that the music is available there's surely more comfort in putting a CD in the player and sitting down to read about the music as it's playing. Sure, you can save the download to your computer (a number of presenters on Solar Radio build their programmes by sorting music files into the required sequence on their laptop computer and playing it through the mixing desk via a USB cable), but this would seem to put collecting into a whole different perspective. But then, I suppose music on CDs is a world different from putting a stylus onto the run-in groove of a piece of vinyl!

APPENDIX

WHERE ARE THEY NOW?

One of the reassuring aspects of having followed soul and R&B music over the past four decades is that of the loyalty of the fans.

Researching this book has not presented many major difficulties, partly because I'm a hoarder – my ever-patient wife Barbara will testify to a loft full of magazines, newspaper cuttings, discographical files, photographs and concert programmes which have accumulated since the mid-'60s, while the vinyl record collection goes without saying – and partly because I have remained in contact with quite a lot of the people I first met all those years ago, most of whom have remained loyal fans of the music.

John Abbey
Originator of *Home of the Blues/Blues & Soul*, then Contempo Music. Moved to the USA in the '80s and ran Ichiban Records, signing numerous soul and blues artists to record new LPs. Went out of business late '90s. John is still living in Atlanta, Georgia, and remains active in the music business, most recently handling international management of the Three Degrees.

John Broven
Originally involved with *Blues Unlimited* magazine and subsequently with Juke Blues. Writer of authoritative books on the music

of New Orleans, South Louisiana and US independent R&B record companies. Consultant to Ace Records, John now lives in the USA.

Trevor Churchill
I first encountered Trevor's name in the list of winners of the *Record Mirror* Soul Quiz of 1967, then met him as a friendly face as label manager for licensed product at EMI, handling first the Bell label then Tamla Motown. He went on to join Ace Records, where he has held an executive position for a number of years.

Stuart Colman
London pub rock 'n' roll DJ who found the limelight when he headed a crusade to get a rock 'n' roll show on Radio 1. Stuart became a regular presenter on Radio 1, then on Radio London, also playing bass in a rock group and producing records. He moved to the USA in 1995 and still resides there – having overcome serious illness.

Tony Cummings
The man without whom a percentage of this book would never have come about. He took me into the fold of fanzine editorship with *Soul Music/Shout*, then gave me the reins and left me to it! Tony was editor of *Black Music* magazine in the '70s, then took the path of religion and became a devout Christian. He joined Crossrhythms, then a Christian music magazine, and is now an executive at www.crossrhythms.co.uk.

Alan Curtis
Ran the first UK fan club for James Brown. I lost contact with Alan about forty years ago, but this was restored courtesy of Jacques Perin of French soul magazine *Soul Bag* when Alan's obituary of and tribute to James Brown was published therein in February 2007. He is still living in south London and is still a keen James Brown fan.

Sharon Davis
Following in the footsteps of Dave Godin, Sharon ran the Motown Ad Astra fan club in the '70s, then went on to PR work with Motown and Fantasy Records. Author of *Motown The History* and monographs on various Motown artists including Stevie Wonder and Marvin Gaye. Long-time columnist for *Blues & Soul* magazine, she is also a commissioning editor for Bank House Books. Without her encouragement and guiding hand this book would have remained an unpublished manuscript.

Greg Edwards
CBS promotion man turned Capital Radio soul DJ. Until recently he presented the Saturday evening soul show on Capital Gold.

Bob Fisher
His first contribution to *Shout* was a Lowell Fulson interview as a member of the Leicester Blues Society. Moved to London and ventured further into journalism with *Let It Rock* and *Record Mirror*. Bob worked for EMI on the Fantasy and Motown labels in the late '70s, then with Charly in the '80s and Connoisseur Collection in the late '90s, before launching his own independent company and subsequently the Acrobat reissue label. Now a music consultant.

Charlie Gillett
Graduated from Columbia University, New York, having written a music thesis entitled *Sound of The City*. This was serialised in *Shout*, then published in hardback format by Souvenir Press. Charlie wrote for *Record Mirror* and *Let It Rock*, and later established himself as a firm favourite with his *Honky Tonk* R&B-based show on BBC Radio London. An acknowledged authority on world music, he broadcast weekly on Radio London until his death in March 2010.

Dave Godin
Remained active, always crusading for the soul world and its performers, latterly as consultant for Ace Records until his death in October 2004.

Dave McAleer
An early fan of the music from Muscle Shoals, Alabama, Dave ran the Fame-Goldwax Followers fan club and fanzine before joining the *Soul Music* editorial team. He went on to enjoy the inside of the record industry as product/label manager at RCA and Pye, compiling several great soul LPs before becoming an independent music consultant. Compiler of several major reference books of chart hits, he now acts as co-ordinator for numerous soul and blues reissue projects for Universal Music Group.

Gloria Marcantonio
Was an active member of the Tamla Motown Appreciation Society and also secretary of the Shirelles/Dionne Warwick/Scepter-Wand fan club. I didn't keep in touch with Gloria, who died in 2000.

Bill Millar
An original contributor to Tony Cummings's soul magazines from the beginning into the era of *Soul Music/Shout*. The first of 'our' strata of specialist journalists to write a book, Bill's authoritative works on the Drifters and the Coasters remain landmarks in the field. A regular columnist for *Record Mirror* in the '70s, Bill's love for and knowledge of rockabilly music brought him numerous commissions to compile and annotate LPs during the '70s boom in that music, and he's since been a regular contributor to various specialist music magazines. Author of *Let The Good Times Rock* in the Music Mentor catalogue.

David Nathan
An early and enthusiastic member of the Tamla Motown Society, also secretary of the Nina Simone fan club. A close friend of Dave Godin, he went into partnership (along with Rob Blackmore, whom I never knew nor met) to open Soul City record shop. Became regular contributor to *Blues & Soul*, moving to New York in the '70s as their US correspondent, then on to Los Angeles in the '80s. Author of a couple of books on US female soul singers, David now runs a very successful website, www.soulmusic.com, selling soul

CDs to the world market, until recently had a regular weekly show on Solar Radio, and now produces reissue CDs on the Soulmusic. com label.

Jon Philibert
An avid fan of jazz and soul organ music, he ran the Organisation fan club and fanzine in the early '60s before joining the editorial team at *Soul Music/Shout*. Without the Philibert family duplicating machine, and the patience and generous of Jon's mum and dad in allowing us free use of the machine in Jon's bedroom, *Shout* wouldn't have happened. Jon became a songwriter, with the good fortune to have one of his songs on the B-side of a major US country hit single – which reaped a deserved reward. He remains an avid fan of country and soul music in the company of his brother Anthony, who is also a jazz fan.

Mike Raven
After serving in the armed forces during the Second World War, Mike had career spells as ballet dancer, conjuror and TV executive. He was involved in producing *Woman's Hour* on BBC radio, then became a pirate radio presenter on King and Radio 390 before presenting an R&B show when Radio 1 was launched in 1967. After his radio career he became a movie actor, featuring in several low-budget horror films, then moved to Cornwall and became established as a sculptor before his death in 1997.

Roger St Pierre
Contributor *to Soul Music Monthly* magazine, then to *Blues & Soul*. An avid cycling fan and regular journalist in that subject, Roger ran his own PR agency in the '70s, working for Jeffrey Kruger on tours with Marvin Gaye and Gladys Knight. Was involved with Beacon Records, including the Showstoppers chart hit 'Ain't Nothing But A Houseparty'. Presented a late night soul and blues show on Solar Radio for some years. Now a full-time travel writer and media consultant.

David Simmons
DJ on Radio 1, then Radio London and on to BBC World Service radio. Now living in North London but no longer involved in radio.

Ray Topping
With a voracious appetite for discographical information and a massive collection of vinyl records, Ray was a bastion of discographical contributions to *Shout* throughout the years of publication. He was a consultant with Ace Records for many years before ill-health prevented him from continuing. Ray sadly died in January 2009.

Robbie Vincent
Radio talk-show host and sometime soul music presenter. Still working in radio on an irregular basis, including an occasional guest show on Solar Radio.

Alan Warner
Friendly and helpful to small circulation fanzines, Alan provided review copies of ABC and Modern LP compilations from his EMI office, then sent me the first ever promo sample of Patti Austin's incredible 'Family Tree' debut 45 on United Artists. Having compiled the *Many Sides of Rock 'n' Roll* double LP series on UA, he kindly pointed World Record Club in my direction to provide notes for their similar six LP boxed set, adding no little prestige to my journalistic pedigree! Alan is also a world-renowned expert on movie music (having been responsible for issuing the Laurel & Hardy hit 45 'On the Trail of the Lonesome Pine', and is the author of reference books on the subject. He moved to Los Angeles in the '80s, produced a four CD boxed set entitled *The Sue Records Story* in the '90s, and still works in the industry on the west coast of the USA.

Lightning Source UK Ltd.
Milton Keynes UK

177871UK00005B/33/P